中泰缅大学生英语拒绝策略探索

ZHONGTAIMIAN DAXUESHENG
YINGYU JUJUE CELÜE TANSUO

» 许岚 著

四川大学出版社
SICHUAN UNIVERSITY PRESS

项目策划：梁　平　杨　果
责任编辑：刘　畅
责任校对：于　俊
封面设计：璞信文化
责任印制：王　炜

图书在版编目（CIP）数据

中泰缅大学生英语拒绝策略探索 / 许岚著. — 成都：四川大学出版社，2021.8
ISBN 978-7-5690-3356-4

Ⅰ．①中… Ⅱ．①许… Ⅲ．①英语－语言学习－研究 Ⅳ．① H319.3

中国版本图书馆 CIP 数据核字（2020）第 011129 号

书　名	中泰缅大学生英语拒绝策略探索
著　者	许　岚
出　版	四川大学出版社
地　址	成都市一环路南一段 24 号（610065）
发　行	四川大学出版社
书　号	ISBN 978-7-5690-3356-4
印前制作	四川胜翔数码印务设计有限公司
印　刷	四川盛图彩色印刷有限公司
成品尺寸	170mm×240mm
印　张	12.75
字　数	278 千字
版　次	2021 年 8 月第 1 版
印　次	2021 年 8 月第 1 次印刷
定　价	58.00 元

◆ 版权所有 ◆ 侵权必究

◆ 读者邮购本书，请与本社发行科联系。
　电话：(028)85408408/(028)85401670/
　(028)86408023　邮政编码：610065
◆ 本社图书如有印装质量问题，请寄回出版社调换。
◆ 网址：http://press.scu.edu.cn

四川大学出版社
微信公众号

前　言

拒绝言语行为是跨文化交际中常见的言语行为之一。本书主要探讨中泰缅大学生英语拒绝言语行为策略使用异同情况，不同性别的中泰缅大学生英语拒绝言语行为策略使用异同情况，不同英语水平的中泰缅大学生英语拒绝言语行为策略使用异同情况，以及中泰缅大学生英语拒绝言语行为策略使用是否受到情景因素的影响。

本书的研究对象为280名大学生，分别来自中国的贵州大学、泰国的苏兰拉里理工大学，以及缅甸的曼德勒大学。抽样方式采用方便原则和随机抽样原则相结合。数据收集方法为书面表达语篇补全对话（Written Discourse Completion Tasks，WDCT）和半结构化访谈（Semi-structured Interview）。WDCT共含校园生活的12个拒绝言语行为交际场景，覆盖拒绝邀请、拒绝请求、拒绝给予和拒绝建议，用以了解中泰缅大学生的拒绝策略使用情况。

本书的数据分析方法包括定量数据分析和定性数据分析。定量数据分析主要采用描述性统计分析法和单因素方差分析法，定性数据分析采用内容分析法。描述性统计分析法用以了解中泰缅大学生的拒绝策略使用频率。单因素方差分析法用以了解中泰缅大学生在拒绝策略使用频率上是否存在国籍、性别、语言水平的差异，以及是否受到情景因素的影响。内容分析法主要用于分析半结构化访谈数据，用以了解影响学生的拒绝策略使用的因素。

结果显示，从总体上看，中泰缅大学生拒绝策略使用频率不高，且参与调查的学生在拒绝策略使用上存在国籍、性别、语言水平的差异，并受到情景因素的影响。本书还讨论了产生以上拒绝策略使用差异的原因。

本书以国籍、性别和英语水平为变量研究了中泰缅大学生的拒绝策略使用异同，丰富了跨文化交际言语行为研究文献。此外，本书还从不同的情景因素的角度，分析了中泰缅大学生的拒绝策略使用情况。笔者希望本书的研究成果能为中泰缅跨文化交际提供参考，提升三国间的跨文化交际效果。

目　　录

第一章　概　论 …………………………………………………（1）
　　第一节　研究背景 ………………………………………………（1）
　　第二节　问题陈述 ………………………………………………（2）
　　第三节　研究动机 ………………………………………………（4）
　　第四节　研究目标和研究问题 …………………………………（6）
　　第五节　研究意义 ………………………………………………（7）
　　第六节　研究术语 ………………………………………………（9）
　　第七节　研究范围和研究局限 …………………………………（11）
　　第八节　本书结构 ………………………………………………（12）
　　本章小结 …………………………………………………………（13）

第二章　文献综述 ………………………………………………（14）
　　第一节　语用学及其研究范畴 …………………………………（14）
　　第二节　Grice 的合作原则 ……………………………………（17）
　　第三节　言语行为 ………………………………………………（19）
　　第四节　礼貌原则 ………………………………………………（26）
　　第五节　语用学和交际能力的关系 ……………………………（32）
　　第六节　语用失误和跨文化交际的关系 ………………………（35）
　　第七节　拒绝言语行为实施策略的特点和分类 ………………（37）
　　第八节　拒绝言语行为数据收集方法 …………………………（39）
　　第九节　拒绝言语行为研究综述 ………………………………（43）
　　本章小结 …………………………………………………………（61）

第三章　研究方法 ………………………………………………（62）
　　第一节　研究设计 ………………………………………………（62）
　　第二节　预研究 …………………………………………………（72）
　　本章小结 …………………………………………………………（74）

第四章 研究结果······（76）
第一节 不同国籍的中泰缅大学生英语拒绝策略比较······（76）
第二节 不同性别的中泰缅大学生英语拒绝策略比较······（94）
第三节 不同英语水平的中泰缅大学生英语拒绝策略比较······（109）
第四节 中泰缅大学生英语拒绝策略总体使用情况······（125）
第五节 不同情境因素下中泰缅大学生英语拒绝策略使用情况······（130）
本章小结······（138）

第五章 讨 论······（139）
第一节 不同国籍的中泰缅大学生英语拒绝策略使用异同讨论······（139）
第二节 不同性别的中泰缅大学生英语拒绝策略使用异同讨论······（147）
第三节 不同英语水平的中泰缅大学生英语拒绝策略使用异同讨论······（155）
第四节 不同情景因素下中泰缅大学生英语拒绝策略使用异同讨论······（160）

第六章 结 论······（166）
第一节 研究结果小结······（166）
第二节 教学启示······（167）
第三节 本研究的研究局限······（169）
第四节 对将来研究的建议······（171）
本章小结······（172）

参考文献······（173）

附 录······（185）
附录一 Self-assessment of Spoken English Proficiency······（185）
附录二 Discourse Completion Task Questionnaire······（187）
附录三 半结构化访谈问题······（194）
附录四 Classifications of Refusal Strategies For Assessing the Performances of Written DCT······（195）

第一章 概 论

本书着眼于比较中泰缅三国大学生英语中介语拒绝策略使用情况,所有场景均设计为校园生活场景。本章介绍本书的研究背景、问题陈述、研究动机、研究目的、研究问题、研究意义,并解释了本书的术语,阐释了研究范围和研究局限。最后,本章描述了本书结构。

第一节 研究背景

学者们认为成功的英语学习者需要具有接近于英语母语使用者的语言能力(McKay,2003)。Kuchuk(2012)指出,可以将目标语的示例作为外语学习者或二语学习者的学习目标。同样,Yano(2006)认为,很多英语教师将教学的重点放在了引导学生理解英语本族语者的世界观和价值观。但英语教学更重要的是要教会学生如何进行跨文化交际。对于英语二语学习者或外语学习者而言,英语学习成功与否的判断标准则是和英语母语使用者的语言使用加以比较得出的结论(Cook,1999)。

英语学习者的语用能力是语言学家的研究兴趣之一(Sairhun,1999;Kwon,2003;Wannaruk,2005,2008)。学者们常常将英语二语或外语学习者和英语母语者的某种言语行为表现进行比较研究(Kasper,Schmidt,1996)。结果显示,尽管英语母语使用者和非母语使用者在言语行为表现上存在一定的相似性,但他们仍然存在言语行为表达话语上的差异(Pearson,2010)。换言之,非英语母语使用者在进行言语行为表达时,会不时出现表达不合理的情况,这种情况通常是母语迁移所致(McKay,2002;Pearson,2010;Allami,Naeimi,2011)。母语迁移现象不但能体现出跨文化交际障碍,还表现出英语非母语使用者想达到和母语使用者同样语言能力的期望,这也恰好说明了非母语使用者的语言水平很难达到母语使用者的水平（Kuchuk，2012）。近年来，随着经济文化的发展和国际交流的日益频繁，英语使用者也逐渐增多，英语已成为一门世界语言（Liu，2004；Sasaki，Suzuki，Yoneda，2006）。Mckay（2002）认为英语作为世界语言，被英语母语使用者、二语学习者，以及英语和其他语言的双语使用者广泛用于跨文化交际。McKay（2002）还进一步指出由于交际目的不同，不同的英语使用者在交际中也表现出不同的英语交际水平。

随着英语学习者的不断增加，英语非母语使用者的数量已经超过了英语母语使用者（Clyne，Sharifian，2008；Misso，Maadad，2011），这一现象让人们重新对英语所有者的概念发生了改变。Wildner-Bassert（1994）提出英语所有者不但属于英语母语使用者，还属于英语二语或外语使用者。不同的英语使用者所使用的英语对英语母语使用者的语言使用习惯的改变都应该被接受（Kuchuk，2012）。也就是说，英语非母语使用者对英语使用规则的改变都可被接受。正如Seidlhofer（2003：9）所说："In the use of EIL (English as an international language) conditions, it is held that when a language is obviously associated with its place of origin or its native, whether it is spoken by the native speakers or by the people who have learnt it as a second or foreign language: different expectations and attitudes should prevail, and different norms should apply."

由此可见，EIL不同于英语母语使用者的语言，EIL可体现在语用能力方面（Kuchuk，2012）。McKay（2003）提出，作为一门国际语言，英语属于它的使用者。因此，对于在不同语境下如何适当地使用英语，英语使用者们有不同的认识。英语二语或外语学习者在使用英语的过程中，在一定程度上会受到母语文化和本国价值观念的影响（Kwon，2003；Han，2006；Guo，2012；Boonkongsaen，2013；Shishavan，Sharifian，2013）。

第二节 问题陈述

英语是一门通用语言（lingua franca）。Kachru（1992）将英语的使用分为以下几个范畴：美国、英国、加拿大、澳大利亚、新西兰等国将英语作为母语，这几个国家的使用者称为"inner circle"；马来西亚、新加坡、印度、加纳、肯尼亚等国曾经是英国或美国殖民地，这几国的英语使用者称为"outer circle"；中国、日本、希腊、波兰等国英语使用者称为"expanding circle"，这些国家将英语作为二语或外语。将英语作为二语或外语的英语使用者就是本研究关注的焦点。

虽然英语是一门通用语言（ELF），人们通常将英式英语及其发音作为教学的标准。同样，英语母语使用者的语用知识也被作为英语教学目标和标准。英语母语使用者指的是来自美国、英国、加拿大、澳大利亚、新西兰的英语使用者，然而，越来越多的学者致力于研究英语通用语使用者使用英语进行的跨文化交际（Knapp，2011）。当中泰缅学生用英语进行交际时，他们会用其母语的合理度（degree of appropriateness）标准判断交际对方的语用合理度。值得一提的是，这些学者提倡接受带有其母语色彩的 ELF 的语用标准（Schneider，2011）。

尽管英语作为通用语言这一观点已被越来越多的学者接受，然而，在用英语进行跨文化交际时，各个国家的英语使用者都会受到其母语文化和母语语言习惯的干扰。作为英语二语或外语使用者，无论其英语水平处于何种程度，也只能无限接近英语母语使用者，很难达到母语使用者的水平。因此，对于英语二语或外语使用者而言，其使用的英语也成为英语中介语。再者，英语母语使用者由于其也来自不同的国家，其语言使用上也会受到其本国文化的影响，母语使用者之间的语言使用习惯也存在一定的差异。中泰缅三国的英语学习者都属于英语二语或外语使用者，也就是英语中介语使用者。中泰缅三国都有自己语言的语用习惯，三个国家也各有自己的文化特色。三个国家的英语学习者在学习该语言的过程中都以英语母语使用者的语言使用习惯和语法习惯为标准，但同时也会受到其本国本土文化的影响，这些文化的影响无时无刻不渗透在其英语使用中。因此，对中泰缅三国的英语使用者进行英语言语行为比较研究，可以发现其英语中介语语言使用上的共性和差异，并在此基础上分析其母语语言习惯和母语文化对其英语使用的语言迁移情况，以缓解三国间的跨文化交际障碍，发现其交际障碍产生的根源，促进不同语言文化背景下的英语使用者跨文化交际效果。

尽管英语二语学习者的跨文化交际已经备受关注，但截至目前，笔者还没发现将中泰缅三国英语学习者的言语行为策略进行比较的研究。比较不同国家英语学习者的交际策略，是促进国与国之间友谊，增强其跨文化交流效果的必然；研究中泰缅三国英语使用者言语行为策略，有助于了解其英语使用习惯和差异，减少其跨文化交际障碍，促进跨文化沟通和合作。

第三节 研究动机

为了加强中泰缅三国的跨文化交流，有必要开展中泰缅三国英语通用语跨文化交际研究，并以性别、英语语言能力以及情景因素，如亲密度（degree of intimacy）、地位差距（relative power）、强加级别（ranking of imposition）为变量。

本研究着眼于了解中泰缅三国大学生的英语拒绝言语行为。拒绝言语行为属于面子威胁言语行为（Eslami, 2010），在实施该言语行为时，交际一方都希望另一方在交际中顾及自己的面子（Locastro, 2003），对拒绝言语行为的不当表现会构成面子威胁，并引起冲突和矛盾（Al-Shboul, Maros, Yasin, 2012），或留下不好的印象（Wannaruk, 2005），甚至会影响社会关系（Prachanant, 2006）。文化知识的掌握对于合理实施拒绝言语行为具有重要作用（Gass, Houck, 1999）。拒绝，对于很多非英语母语使用者来说，是一项实施过程中具有难度的言语行为（Al-Kahtani, 2005），也是一项使用频率较高的言语行为。和文化内（intercultural）交际相比，在跨文化（intercultural）交际中，实施如拒绝言语行为时，出现令人不满意的社会交流的频率会更高，这样的社交有可能导致矛盾和冲突。在跨文化交际中，如果交际双方能够意识到如何适当的表达自己的不悦，就能避免很多潜在的矛盾和冲突。因此，了解交际双方对拒绝言语行为的表达习惯，有助于中泰缅三国学生更好地用英语进行跨文化交际（Korsko, 2004）。

在交际中，中国学生为了实现和谐的人际关系，会采取委婉的表达方式（Liu, Xie, 2014）。因此，为了避免直接拒绝可能造成的冲突，中国人在交际中会用"yes"而不是"no"，以让对方满意。但这样的回答，可能会使其他文化背景的人理解为对邀请、请求等的完全接受。此外，Liu 和 Xie（2014）指出中国人的拒绝分为实质性的拒绝（substantial refusals）和礼节性的拒绝（ritual refusals）。实质性的拒绝是指明明心里想拒绝，却表达"答应"的意思。礼节性的拒绝是指尽管交际一方出于礼貌，对别人的给予或邀请说了"no"，但实际上却打算接受。中国人礼节性的拒绝常常在跨文化交际中产生误解。

泰国学生受到其文化的影响，在交际中多考虑交际对方的感受

(Knutson，1994)。因此，他们很少拒绝别人，尤其是在别人需要帮助的时候(Chaidaroon，2003)。因此，为了不伤害别人的感情，避免矛盾，泰国学生通常会较为婉转，即使不愿做的事也会回答"yes"(Chuenpraphannusorn，2002)。此外，当和比自己年长的人发生意见不一致的情况时，泰国人通常只是保持沉默(Kubota，1994)。在泰国文化影响下，间接拒绝更容易被泰国人接受。然而，泰国人的拒绝方式可能会被其他文化背景的交际对象认为不恰当甚至引起误解(Wannaruk，2005)。

缅甸人的宗教信仰对缅甸文化影响极深，缅甸人的文化教育、语言文字、文学艺术等，都受到佛教文化的影响。缅甸学生在实施拒绝言语行为时，通常较为委婉。考虑到直接拒绝可能给交际对象造成的心里不适，并以不伤害交际对象的面子为前提，他们常常采用较为间接的拒绝策略。

尽管中泰缅三国的文化对社会和谐都具有重要影响，三国学生在拒绝言语行为表达中都遵循了礼貌原则，但拒绝言语行为的实施会受到本国文化和价值观的影响。因此，本研究的开展可以帮助了解中泰缅学生在跨文化交际中的拒绝言语行为策略异同，并了解来自不同国家的学生在拒绝言语行为策略是用方面是否会造成误解或面子威胁。

本研究将交际场景设计为校园生活场景。随着国际交流的日益频繁，越来越多的学生走出国门，去各国求学，英语则成为其日常生活学习所使用的主要语言。在校园生活场景中，学生需要和同学、老师以及学校工作人员进行大量的跨文化交际。尽管拒绝是交际中的常用言语行为，但人们却很少规范地使用拒绝言语行为。此外，近年来，虽然拒绝言语行为越来越受到人们的关注，但有关它的研究仍有以下不足。

第一，有关语言能力和语用迁移关系的研究缺乏一致性。例如，Takahashi (1987) 认为语用负迁移对语言能力高的学习者影响大过语言能力低的学习者。同样，Azarmi 和 Behnam (2012) 研究发现在跨文化交际中，语用迁移在高水平的英语学习者中的体现强于中等水平的英语学习者。相反，Trosborg (1995) 研究表明在使用语用策略方面，语用正迁移对语言水平高的学习者影响大于语言水平低的语言学习者。Galleher (2011) 也发现语言水平高的学生对缓和策略的掌控能力高于语言水平中等的学生。因此，开展更多的语言能力和语用迁移关系的研究是很有必要的。

第二，有关性别和语用策略的研究还不充分。学者们的研究结果也各执一词。Gidden (1981) 和 Li, Zheng, Yang (2006) 发现性别对言语行为策略使用的影响不大。相反，Kraft 和 Geluykens (2002) 发现不同性别的言语行为表现不同，这些不同不体现在直接程度和礼貌原则上。Gallaher（2011）研究表明俄语二语女性学习者对拒绝策略的表现较男性更为显性。因此，对于性别和语用策略使用关系的研究还有待丰富。

第三，社会距离对语用策略使用影响的研究还颇具争议。Wolfson（1983）认为和谐的对话总是在中等社会距离的人群中发生，比如朋友、熟人等。不同的是，Boxer（1993）声称，陌生人间对话表现的社会距离和朋友间相近。他同时认为陌生人或亲密无间的人在交际中最容易实现和谐。鉴于不同的学者对社会距离和交际策略的使用还存在分歧，因此，在这一方面还有待进一步研究。

第四，在学者们的前期研究中，多数学者用DCT作为数据收集工具，研究的拒绝言语行为使用场景主要包括工作场景、餐厅或朋友家等。少有学者研究校园生活场景的拒绝言语行为使用策略，如Geyang（2007）、Farnia和Wu（2012）。到目前为止，笔者还没有发现研究本科生在校园生活场景下进行英语拒绝言语行为的文献，因此，开展这方面的相关研究是很有必要的。

第五，前人对拒绝言语行为的研究多集中在比较英语母语使用者和非母语使用者的拒绝策略使用上，如Beebe，Takahashi和Uliss－Weltz（1990），Wannaruk（2005，2008），Allami和Naeimi（2011）。只有少数的学者对不同母语使用者的拒绝言语行为进行比较研究，如Farnia和Abdul Sattar（2010），Farnia和Wu（2012），Al－Shboul等（2012）。然而，到目前为止，笔者还没有发现比较中泰缅三国英语使用者拒绝言语行为的研究。因此，本研究立足于探讨中泰缅三国的二语或外语学习者英语拒绝言语行为实现情况。

第四节　研究目标和研究问题

本研究旨在探讨中泰缅大学生实施英语拒绝言语行为的策略使用情况，以跨文化语用学、英语通用语跨文化语用学及中介语语用学为研究框架，拟定了以下研究目标：

（1）探讨中泰缅大学生英语拒绝言语行为策略使用异同情况；

（2）探讨不同性别的中泰缅大学生英语拒绝言语行为策略使用异同情况；

（3）探讨不同英语水平的中泰缅大学生英语拒绝言语行为策略使用异同情况；

(4) 在不同的情景因素场景下，中泰缅大学生在英语拒绝言语行为策略使用上有何异同。

基于以上研究目标，本研究拟回答以下研究问题：

(1) 中泰缅大学生在英语拒绝言语行为策略使用上有何异同？

(2) 不同性别的中泰缅大学生在英语拒绝言语行为策略使用上有何异同？

(3) 不同英语水平的中泰缅大学生在英语拒绝言语行为策略使用上有何异同？

(4) 在不同的情景因素场景下，中泰缅大学生在英语拒绝言语行为策略使用上有何异同？

为了回答以上研究问题，本研究将结合定量和定性的研究方法，对中泰缅三国大学生英语拒绝语言语行为语料进行分析。此外，本研究还将说话者的国籍、性别、英语语言水平及情景因素（社会距离、地位差距和强加程度）考虑在内。定量研究方法主要用来收集和分析中泰缅三国大学生在不同交际场景中用英语实施拒绝言语行为时的策略使用情况数据，采用单因素方差分析比较不同变量下的中泰缅大学生英语拒绝策略使用频率的异同。定性研究方法则用于对收集到的中泰缅大学生拒绝策略使用情况语料和访谈数据进行内容分析，以更深入了解中泰缅大学生英语中介语拒绝策略使用情况以及在策略使用背后的根源。

第五节　研究意义

本研究立足于比较中泰缅三国大学生英语拒绝言语行为的策略使用情况，并将国籍、性别、英语语言水平，社会距离、地位差距，以及强加程度3个情景因素纳入分析。本研究不仅可为跨文化交际领域的研究提供文献补充，还能为英语语用能力教学提供参考。

在跨文化交际中，面临的挑战之一是如何理解跨文化言语行为的能力（Fahey，2005）。特定文化背景下的语言使用者需要了解该文化背景下言语行为知识，以便在该文化背景下实现成功和有效的交际（Farnia，Wu，2012）。本研究将为比较不同文化背景下和不同语言背景下的英语学习者拒绝语策略使用情况提供参考依据和文献补充。本研究的研究成果将为不同文化背景下的语言学习者在实施跨文化交际中的面子威胁言语行为时增进相互了解，削弱因文化差异导致的交际障碍，减少交际失败发生的频率。不同国家的外语学习者在跨文化交际中增进了解后，才会更开放地接受彼此，也会在交际中更注意对方的文化习惯，适当选择交际策略，尊重交际对象母语文化，防止面子威胁的发生，最终实现成功交际（Wannaruk，2005）。

  本研究还将进一步研究由于性别差异所致的英语二语或外语学习者的拒绝语策略使用异同情况。性别是语言教学研究中备受学者们青睐的变量之一，不同性别的外语学习者在礼貌程度和策略使用上都存在区别。研究不同性别英语二语或外语学习者的拒绝语语用策略使用的异同，有助于加强交际双方的相互理解，并有针对性地提高跨文化交际效果。本研究将对拒绝言语行为进行研究，比较不同性别的中泰缅大学生用英语实施英语拒绝言语行为的策略使用情况。拒绝言语行为属于面子威胁行为，在实施该言语行为时，容易对交际对象的面子造成威胁，比较不同性别的语言学习者拒绝策略的使用情况，可以了解其策略使用异同，以及影响其策略使用的因素，并在此基础上制订教学计划和教学方案，帮助不同性别的英语学习者合理使用拒绝言语行为等面子威胁言语行为策略，增强跨文化交流效果。

  本研究还将英语语言水平纳入变量，比较研究不同英语水平的学习者实施拒绝言语行为时的策略使用特点。一些学者认为，语言能力对语用能力产生较为直接的影响，因为语用能力是语言水平的重要组成部分，言语行为则包含在语用能力范畴内。研究不同语言水平的英语二语或外语学习者拒绝语策略使用情况，可以进一步了解语言能力和语用能力的关系，发现语言能力强的学生和语言能力弱的学生语用策略的使用特点，以便在教学中针对不同语言能力的学习者进行目的语语用规则和语用习惯的培养，最终提高跨文化交际的语用理解能力。

  情景因素也在本研究的研究范畴内，有学者表示，在不同情景的交际场景下，语言使用者言语行为实施策略也会有所不同。语言使用者的言语行为策略使用受到如社会距离、地位差距以及强加程度的影响。本研究将探讨在社会距离近和社会距离远、地位平等和地位"高－低"、强加程度强和强加程度弱的交际场景中，中泰缅大学生用英语实施拒绝言语行为时，在策略使用方面都有哪些特点；并在此基础上深入探讨在不同情境因素下，学生策略使用特点产生的文化根源，以进一步了解中泰缅三国的文化差异，增进彼此了解，加强跨文化交际效果。

  本研究结果将为中泰缅等国的英语跨文化交际策略教学提出建议。为了不受英语母语文化影响，专注于研究英语非母语使用者的英语通用语跨文化语言使用（McKay，2003；Kuchuk，2012），McKay（2003）提出通过提高跨文化交际频率的策略，增强语言学习者对不同文化背景语用规则的认知能力。言语行为是语用学的重要组成部分（Safont，2003），将言语行为溶于英语教学，可以帮助学生理解在不同文化背景下如何合理使用英语；在教学中帮助学生了解不同国家的英语二语或外语学习者的语用策略使用特点，可以更好地实现英语作为世界通用语的交际功能，提高语言使用者在交际过程中对交际对象语言使用的容忍度，提高其沟通能力和跨文化能力，最终实现成功交际。

第六节 研究术语

本研究从英语通用语跨文化语用的视角，比较中泰缅三国英语学习者实施拒绝言语行为时的策略使用情况。基于跨文化语用学的框架，探索不同国籍、不同性别和不同英语语言能力的学习者的母语语用迁移情况，并将情景因素纳入考虑，探讨在不同的社会距离、地位差距、强加程度情景因素下，中泰缅大学生的拒绝策略使用异同情况。本研究有如下核心术语：

（1）英语通用语（English as a lingua franca）。

英语通用语指不同母语的英语二语或外语使用者将英语作为交际的常用语言（Seidlhofer，2005）。本研究的英语通用语是指中泰缅大学生将英语作为二语或外语，并将其使用在校园生活场景中的跨文化交际语言。

（2）英语通用语跨文化语用学（ELF intercultural pragmatics）。

跨文化语用学指不同文化背景的语言使用者如何实施或接受目标语言语行为的学问（Gallaher，2011）。英语通用语跨文化语用学研究不同母语背景的英语学习者如何使用英语通用语实施言语行为（Seidlhofer，2005）。在本研究中，主要比较中泰缅英语学习者如何实施英语拒绝言语行为。

（3）中介语语用学（Interlanguage pragmatics）。

中介语语用学是指非英语母语使用者如何综合、产出和习得英语目标语言语行为，以及如何提高目标语语用能力的学问（Kasper，Rose，2002）。本研究的中介语语用学着眼于研究中泰缅英语学习者是否在实施拒绝言语行为时受到其母语迁移的影响，以及性别、英语语言能力和情景因素是否对其实施英语拒绝言语行为的策略使用构成影响。

（4）语用迁移（Pragmatic transfer）。

Kasper（1992：207）将语用迁移定义为"The influence exerted by language learners' pragmatic knowledge of languages and cultures instead of L2 on their comprehension, production and learning of their L2 pragmatic information"。在本研究中，语用迁移指的是中泰缅英语学习者进行拒绝言语行为时受其母语影响的情况。母语语用迁移可体现为母语语用正迁移，也可体现为母语语用负迁移。语用正迁移对学生使用目标语时实施言语行为产生积极影响，语用负迁移则会对学生使用目标语实施言语行为时产生消极影响。

（5）拒绝策略（Refusal strategies）。

在本研究中，拒绝策略是指基于 Beebe 等（1990）对拒绝策略分类，对中泰缅英语学习者在校园生活场景中在拒绝邀请、请求、要求和建议时使用的策略。Beebe 等（1990）将拒绝策略主要分为直接策略、间接策略和附加语策略三个大类，每个大类中含有若干具体策略。本研究共设计了 12 个要求实施拒绝言语行为的交际场景，并将对每个场景中每位学生使用的拒绝策略进行统计。

（6）校园生活情景（Campus life）。

在本研究中，校园生活情景可定义为中泰缅大学生在有关学习、校园活动、学术会议、学术论文等一切和教学和校园日常生活相关的讨论中和老师、同学、室友、系主任、院长等对邀请、给予、请求和建议的拒绝场景。本研究中的校园生活场景均体现为书面表达语篇补全对话形式，场景设计来源于学生的日常生活。选择学生熟悉的交际场景，目的在于获取中泰缅大学生在日常生活中可能使用的贴近于真实生活的语料。

（7）社会距离（Social distance）。

社会距离是指说话者和听话者之间的亲密度或熟悉度（LoCastro，2003）。在本研究中，笔者将交际场景分为熟悉和不熟悉两类。说话者为在校本科生，其和老师、朋友、室友间的社会距离被认为是熟悉（+），和部门领导、院长、新朋友或硕博士生的社会距离则被认为是不熟悉（−）。根据以上对交际场景社会距离的划分，不能研究共设计了 6 个说话者和交际对象熟悉的拒绝场景和 6 个说话者和交际对象不熟悉的拒绝场景。

（8）地位差距（Relative power）。

地位差距是指在校园生活场景中说话者和听话者的权威性差距（Brown，Levinson，1987）。在本研究中，笔者将交际策略分为"高−低"（+）［即"high−low"（+）］和"平等"（−），即"equal"（−）两类。其中，部门领导、院长、老师和学生之间地位差距被认为是"高−低"（+），而同学、新朋友、室友和学生的社会差距被认为是"平等"（-）。本研究共设计了6个说话者和交际对象地位差距为"高-低"的拒绝场景和6个和说话者和交际对象地位差距为"平等"的拒绝场景。

（9）强加程度（Rank of imposition）。

本研究中的强加程度是指对交际对象在校园生活情景中进行邀请、给予、请求或建议时，为了让交际对象接受而施加的压力。在本研究中，笔者将交际策略分为强加程度强和强加程度弱两类。部门领导、院长、老师对学生的邀请、请求、给予、建议被认为是强加程度强（+），而同学、新朋友、室友对学生的邀请、请求、给予、建议被认为是强加程度弱（-）。本研究共设计了6个说话者和交际对象强加程度强的拒绝场景和6个和说话者和交际对象强加程度弱的拒绝场景。

第七节 研究范围和研究局限

本研究着眼于探索在校园生活场景中，中泰缅大学生的实施拒绝言语行为时的策略使用情况，并以国籍、性别、语言能力和情景因素为变量，比较大学生的拒绝策略使用异同。尽管笔者精心设计了本研究的研究场景、数据收集工具、数据收集方法、数据分析方法，并根据实际研究需要和实际情况选取了研究对象，但仍然存在以下研究局限：

第一，本研究对中泰缅的文化特点不能进行充分和完全的阐释。本研究对三国文化的了解主要基于对周围中泰缅留学生或教师的访谈，以及文献资料记载。由于研究时间和条件的限制，笔者虽在泰国常住达4年之久，对泰国文化有一定的切身体会，但对缅甸文化的了解相对有限。因此，本研究中所诠释的文化背景差异对中泰缅大学生拒绝策略使用的影响只能起到抛砖引玉的作用。中泰缅三国文化都有深远的历史根源，并体现在语言文字和日常生活的方方面面。本研究着眼于对中泰缅三国大学生拒绝言语行为的策略使用研究，也只能从局部反映各国特有文化。

第二，本研究探讨了校园生活情境下中泰缅大学生的英语拒绝言语行为实施情况，共有180名学生参与了本次研究，其中中泰缅大学生各60名。本研究的研究对象比较有限，所有学生均在大学本科学习层次，且每个国家仅选取一所大学的学生，其学习英语的时间也参差不齐，英语水平差异较大。尽管本研究选取了不同专业的学生作为研究对象，但本研究的研究成果不能代表所有中泰缅英语学习者的拒绝言语行为实施情况。

第三，本研究的数据收集手段采用的是语篇补全对话（discourse completion task）。虽然Beebe和Cummings（1996）认为通过语篇补全对话的形式收集到的数据在形式和语义套语方面和在自然环境下产生的数据是接近的，但也有学者认为语篇补全对话（DCT）的数据收集方式和自然环境下产生的数据有所区别（Wannaruk，2008；Al－Shboul，Maros，Yasin，2012）。本研究主要采取书面语篇补全对话的数据收集方法，是因为该数据收集方法可以控制每个情景的场景因素，还可以在短时间内收集大量数据（Barron，2003）。除了书面DCT以外，本研究还采用了采访的数据收集方式收集数据，以便更深入了解中泰缅三国大学生在拒绝中使用各种拒绝策略的原因。

第四，在本研究中，学生语言水平的评估依靠自我评估（self-assessment）的方式进行。在这种评估方式下，学生可能对每一等级的英语水平评定标准产生各自的理解。此外，如果学生对自己的英语语言能力没有较为客观的了解和评价，则会影响本研究中根据学生英语语言水平对学生的分组。这些因素都有可能导致本研究对英语语言能力这一变量的研究结果的客观性。

第五，本研究的效度主要依靠对拒绝言语行为的回顾性语料。回顾性数据是社会科学研究中常用的数据收集手段。本研究假设学生在完成书面表达DCT时提供的语料具有较高信度。如果学生在完成书面表达DCT时没有真实反映其在现实生活中的拒绝言语行为实施情况，则本研究的研究结果不能完全体现真实性，也必然会影响笔者对中泰缅三国大学生英语拒绝策略使用的判断。

第八节 本书结构

本书共有六章。

第一章为概论。本章对本书内容进行了整体的介绍，包括研究背景、问题陈述、研究动机、研究目标和研究问题、研究意义、研究术语、研究范围和研究局限。

第二章为文献综述。本章首先对相关概念进行了回顾，如合作原则、言语行为、礼貌原则以及拒绝言语行为；其次讨论了语用学和交际能力的关系，以及语用失败和跨文化交际的关系；最后介绍了跨文化交际中拒绝言语行为策略使用的前期研究成果。

第三章为研究方法。本章分三个部分介绍了本研究的研究方法：首先是DCT设计；其次介绍了数据收集和数据分析方法；最后介绍了预研究过程和结果，预研究的目的在于保证DCT的信度和效度，并根据预研究结果调整访谈问题。

第四章为研究结果。本章首先比较了不同国籍的中泰缅大学生英语拒绝言语行为策略使用情况，其次分别比较了不同性别和不同英语语言水平的大学生英语拒绝言语行为策略使用情况，再次从总体上分析了中泰缅大学生的拒绝策略使用情况，最后分析了情景因素对中泰缅大学生英语拒绝语策略使用的影响。

第五章为讨论。本章对第四章的研究结果进行逐一讨论。首先讨论了不同国籍的中泰缅学生英语拒绝语策略使用的异同，其次讨论了不同性别大学生英语拒绝策略使用的异同，再次对不同英语语言水平大学生的英语拒绝策略使用异同进行讨论，最后讨论了情景因素对中泰缅大学生英语拒绝语策略使用的影响。

第六章为结论。本章首先对研究结果进行了总结，其次根据研究结果提出了本研究对教学的启示，最后指出了本研究的不足之处和对将来研究的建议。

本章小结

本研究探讨了中泰缅大学生在校园生活情境下的英语拒绝策略使用情况。本研究的开展基于英语通用语已作为中泰缅大学生校园生活情境下进行跨文化交际的主要语言的前提。英语拒绝言语行为是一种面子威胁行为，如使用不当，则会影响交际效果。尽管随着经济文化的发展，各国间的跨文化交际行为日益频繁，但有关中泰缅英语学习者拒绝策略的比较研究还寥寥无几。本章明确了研究目标和研究问题，并对本研究的核心术语进行了阐释。下一章为文献综述部分，笔者将对相关概念和相关前期研究进行回顾。

第二章 文献综述

本章对本研究的相关理论进行了阐释，回顾了有关英语拒绝言语行为的前期研究。本章共分为九节：语用学及其研究范畴、Grice 的合作原则、言语行为、礼貌原则、语用学和交际能力的关系、语用失败和跨文化交际的关系、拒绝言语行为实施策略的特点和分类、拒绝言语行为数据收集方法、拒绝言语行为研究综述。

第一节 语用学及其研究范畴

Blum-Kulka 和 Olshtain（1984）认为，学者们对语用学领域的研究兴趣都围绕着"the need to account for the rules that govern the use of language in context"展开。简单地说，语用学研究说话者如何使用语言在某种交际场景中实现交际目的；也就是说，语用学研究在特定语境下说话者为实现某种交际目的所进行的语言选择（Gallaher, 2011）。例如，在不同的文化背景下，属于面子威胁行为的请求言语行为可以通过祈使句或疑问句实现。语用学研究说话者在特定语境下的语言使用，以及语言形式和语言使用的关系。正如 Cap 和 Nijakowska（2007：viii）所说，"using language conveys cognitive process, which takes place with a variety of cultural constraints in a social world"。这一叙述暗示了语用学家在进行语用学研究时，和语言学家一样，在研究过程中需要进行如心理学、社会学、人类学等多学科知识的融合，多学科知识贯穿于语用学的各个分支中。下面将介绍社会语用学（sociopragmatics）、语用语言学（pragmalinguistics）、跨文化语用学（cross-cultural pragmatics）、中介语语用学（interlanguage pragmatics）的基本理论。

一、社会语用学和语用语言学

语用能力是合理使用语言的能力。在交际中，当人们不能合理使用语言时，就会出现语用失败（pragmatic failure）的现象。根据导致语用失败的原因，Leech（1983）将语用能力分为社会语用能力（sociopragmatic competence）和语用语言能力（pragmalinguistic competence）两个方面。社会语用能力指在不同的文化背景或语言使用群体、不同的社会阶层等范围内，人们对合作原则和礼貌原则的不同理解，并在此基础上产出的语用行为；而语用语言能力指"the particular resources which a given language provides for conveying particular illocution"（Leech，1983：10）。在实际交际中，社会语用能力和语用语言能力共同形成了交际双方的交际语言，构成其交际行为，并对其交际效果产生直接的影响。

以上对社会语用能力和语用语言能力的定义表明，社会语用能力聚焦于社会规则和文化观念，研究在一定社会文化背景或跨文化背景下如何合理使用语言进行交际（Brown，Levinson，1987；Gallaher，2011）；语用语言能力则强调说话者在交际时语言策略的使用，如直接策略、间接策略、语言形式等。总而言之，社会语用能力以文化背景为前提进行研究，而语用语言能力则以语言使用为前提展开研究。无论是文化背景或是语言使用，不同国家的英语使用者都会受到其本国文化和本国语言使用习惯的影响。因此，当英语二语或外语使用者用英语进行交际时，也会在一定程度上显现其本国文化或本国语言使用的特点，这也为跨文化交际中言语行为研究提供了可能。

社会语用能力和语用语言能力概念和 Quirk（1978）提出的"act of referring"和"manner of referring"不谋而合。前者在判断是否合理实施言语行为时将情景因素，如社会距离、地位差距以及强加程度纳入考虑。而后者则将话语选择作为对说话者是否合理实施言外行为的判断依据。例如，实施"道歉"这一面子威胁行为可以通过拒绝他人"邀请吃饭"等言语进行。在该言语行为中，说话者有可能通过"道歉"言语行为表示对自己不能应邀一起吃饭的歉意，以缓解对拒绝交际对象邀请的面子威胁程度。

Chang（2011）研究了在二语学习者语用能力发展过程中，社会语用能力和语用语言能力的关系。她的研究结果显示社会地位对说话者的面子威胁程度、策略选择、直接程度以及强硬程度都会产生影响。同时，Chang（2011）还发现社会语用能力和语用语言能力都和说话者的语言能力呈相关关系。此外，感知数据和产出数据都可以帮助理解社会语用能力和语用语言能力的关系。也就是说，根据Chang（2011）的研究发现，说话者语用能力的两个构成要素，即社会语用能力和语用语言能力，都会对说话者的语言输入和产出产生影响，进而影响交际效果。

社会语用能力（act of referring）和语用语言能力（manner of referring）共同成为语用能力的构成要素（Leech，1983）。Bachman（1990）认为语用能力由语言策略知识和社会文化知识组成。这一观点使社会语用能力和语用语言能力的界限模糊化，也使社会语用能力和与用语言能力成为语用能力不可分割的重要构成要素。换句话说，任何语言策略的使用都需要以社会语用能力和语用语言能力为基础。

二、跨文化语用学和中介语语用学

跨文化语用学是语用学领域交叉研究的一个分支，其研究焦点是言语行为在全球范围内的实施情况。跨文化语用学研究在不同语言和文化背景下，人们如何实施言语行为。在某种文化背景下，人们实施言语行为的策略不一定就符合在另一种文化背景下的礼貌原则或其他交际规则（Blum-Kulka，House，Kasper，1989）。本研究开展的是跨文化的研究，所涉及的跨文化语用研究包括中国文化、泰国文化以及缅甸文化和英语国家文化的交叉文化。

在跨文化语用研究中，Blum-Kulka和Olshtain（1984）的跨文化言语行为实现形式项目（Cross-cultural Speech Act Realization Patterns Project）在言语行为研究中扮演了极为重要的角色。在该项目中，他们认为言语行为研究应当基于不同文化背景的各种交际场景下进行，从而对相同或相似场景下的言语行为实施途径加以比较。本研究接受了Blum-Kulka和Olshtain（1984）的这一观点，立足于比较不同国家文化背景下的非英语母语使用者英语拒绝言语行为策略使用情况，因此，本研究也属于跨文化语用研究。

中介语语用学属于二语习得研究范畴。中介语语用学研究非母语使用者如何用目标语综合、产出以及习得言语行为，以及非母语使用者如何在二语学习过程中提高目标语语用能力（Kasper，Rose，2002）。二语或外语学习者在学习过程中容易将其母语或已经习得的其他语言中的元素迁移到中介语系统中（Odlin，1989）。这种说话者将其母语知识应用于目标语交际的现象，就是母语迁移。母语迁移可以被视为问题解决策略（DeCapua，1989）。中介语语用学根据二语或外语学习者在中介语言语行为实施和目标语规则的融合或差异来判断其对母语进行了正迁移或是负迁移。当二语或外语学习者的语用规则相近时，语言学习者则可能进行母语正迁移，当其语用规则不同，或语言学习者的目标语水平较低时，语言学习者则有可能进行母语负迁移。然而，根据 Sapir－Whorf 猜想，在用非母语进行交际时，说话者的思维方式可能会发生变化，那么中介语语用行为则在跨文化交际中处于母语和目标语不合作状态。

第二节　Grice 的合作原则

本研究是有关语用能力的研究，也就是关于某种语言在特定语境下如何使用的研究（Chapman，2000；Cutting，2002；Mihalicek，Wilson，2011）。合作原则（cooperative principle）是语用能力研究的重要理论。该理论由语言哲学家 H. P. Grice 基于说话者和听话者在语言互动交际中的合作假设下提出。在该假设下，说话者有意表达某种意图，听话者也能意识到说话者的交际意图（Yule，1996；Chapman，2000）。Grice（2008：28）提出合作原则表达了以下基本概念："Make your conversational contribution such as is required, at the stage at which it occurs, by the accepted purpose or direction of the talk exchange in which you are engaged."

合作原则包含了会话双方的 4 个合作方面的内容，分别是数量准则（maxim of quantity）、质量准则（maxim of quality）、关系准则（maxim of relation）和方式准则（maxim of manner）（Chapman，2000）。以下是对这 4 个准则内容的简要概括（Grice，2008：28-29）。

　　Maxim of Quantity: The quantity of information to be provided.
　　(1) Make your contribution as informative as is required (for the current purposes of the exchange).
　　(2) Do not make your contribution more informative than is required.
　　Maxim of Quality: Try to make your contribution one that is true.
　　(1) Do not say what you believe to be false.
　　(2) Do not say that for which you lack adequate evidence.
　　Maxim of Relation: Be relevant.
　　Maxim of Manner: Be perspicuous.
　　(1) Avoid obscurity of expression.
　　(2) Avoid ambiguity.

(3) Be brief (Avoid unnecessary prolixity.)
(4) Be orderly.

  在遵循合作原则的前提下，交际须遵守以上 4 个准则（Yule，1996）。换言之，以上准则要求在对话中，说话者所传递的信息具有准确性、相关性和真实性的特点。合作原则在交际中的作用可以通过 Yule（1996）的例子加以说明：一位女士问她的朋友午饭时吃的汉堡怎样？她的朋友答道："汉堡就是汉堡。"Yule（1996）解释道，这个回答看上去似乎没有意义，毫无疑问"汉堡就是汉堡"。然而，根据合作原则，这位女士假定她的朋友在对话中是合作的，她朋友想要表达的意思超出其话语中的字面意思。在交际中的这种现象叫作隐含含义（implicature）。Yule（1996）进一步解释道，听话者对隐含含义的理解基于其已有知识。因此，在本例中，Yule（1996）认为这位女士可以将"汉堡就是汉堡"理解为她的朋友对汉堡不做评价，或者也可以根据其语境理解为别的含义，如"这仅是一个汉堡而已，谈不上有多美味"，或"汉堡当然好吃啦"等。

  在对话中的隐含含义叫作会话隐含含义（conversational implicatures）。会话隐含含义分为两类：总体会话隐含含义（generalized conversational implicatures）和部分会话隐含含义（particularized conversational implicatures）（Chapman，2000）。总体会话隐含含义指"the use of a particular word/words and based on the hearer's knowledge of the literal meaning of this word/words together with his/her assumption that the speaker is behaving co-operatively"（Chapman，2000：134）。部分会话隐含含义指听话者在特定语境下从会话话语中推断出特有的隐含含义（Peccei，1999）。交际中的隐含含义，需要说话双方具有一定的共有背景知识，并在特定的交际场景下才有可能得以实现。正是因为如此，在跨文化交际中，由于交际双方的共有知识和文化背景有限，则很容易由于对交际对象隐含含义无法理解，导致交际障碍甚至交际失败。在语用学领域，除了合作原则以外，言语行为也是重要的基本概念之一，下一节将对其进行介绍。

第三节 言语行为

在社会交际中，言语行为（speech acts）无处不在（Kuriscak，2010）。有学者将言语行为称为语言行为（language acts or linguistic acts）（Searle，2008）。言语行为的概念最早由 Austin（1962）提出，Austin 于 1955—1962 年期间在哈佛大学开展的系列讲座中提出了"言语行为"这一概念。于是，他开始思考话语如何影响社会行为，以及当话语没有清楚的表达交际意图时，如何推断说话者的真实交际目的。尽管言语行为不是语用学的全部内容，但也作为语用学的中心概念备受学者们关注（Martinez-Flor，Uso-Juan，2010）。言语行为的研究可以大致被分为以下三个方面（Gass，Houck，1999）：①使用某种语言实施言语行为；②跨语言实施言语行为；③非母语使用者产出和认识言语行为。本节主要介绍言语行为的概念和言语行为理论。

一、言语行为定义

不同的学者给言语行为下了不同的定义。Sadock（2006）认为，言语行为是说话过程中实施的行为。在该定义中，言语行为指所有在说话过程中发生的行为，"from aspirating a consonant, to forming a sentence, and to insulting a guest"（Sadock，2006）。Searle（2008）和 Cruse（2000）对言语行为的定义更为具体，他们强调了话语的言外之意（illocutionary force）或说话者的交际意图（communicative intention）。Searle（2008：8）认识到当人们说出一个话语时，不同的行为便产生了。然而，只有可以被理解为做出陈述、提出问题或发出命令的话语才具有言外之意。

> In a typical speech situation involving a speaker, a hearer, and an utterance by the speaker, there are many kinds of acts associated with the speaker's utterance. The speaker will characteristically have moved his jaw and his tongue and made noises. In addition, he will characteristically have performed some acts within the class which includes informing or irritating or boring his hearers; he will further characteristically have performed acts within the class which includes referring to Kennedy or Khrushchev or the North Pole; he will also

have performed acts within the class which includes commands, giving reports, greeting, and warning. The members of this last class are what Austin called illocutionary acts...

值得一提的是，有些学者将言语行为称作言外行为（illocutionary acts）。Yule（1996）指出无论是言语行为还是言外行为，都指话语的言外之意。Searle（2008）和Cruse（2000）也认为当人们通过语言进行交际时，他们说出的话语一定带有言外之意。通过发出的话语，人们实施各种特别的行为，如陈述、许诺、警告、威胁等。这些行为就是言语行为。在本研究中，笔者借用了Searle（2008）和Cruse（2000）对言语行为的定义。

二、言语行为理论

哲学家Austin一直被认为是言语行为之父（Martínez-Flor, Usó-Juan, 2010）。言语行为理论最基本的概念来源于Austin在哈佛大学做的题为"How to Do Things with Words"的讲座（LoCastro, 2003; Sadock, 2006）。在讲座中，Austin（1962）认为我们越将陈述（statement）看作行为（act），而不是将其看作句子（sentence）或命题（proposition），则整个话语就更能表示行为。总的来说，根据Austin的观点，在交际中"an utterance which people produce should be seen more as a form of an action, rather than as a form of a statement"（LoCastro, 2003）。

话语就是行为，为了更好地说明这点，Austin将话语（utterance）分为做行话语（performative utterances）和叙境话语（constative utterances）两类（Verschueren, 1999）。Sadock（2006）认为做行话语是用来做事的，而叙境话语则主要用来讲事情。和叙境话语不同，做行话语不能用来判断话语是否具有真实性，只能用来了解是否能让交际双方愉悦（Verschueren, 1999）。换言之，在特定语境中，做行话语不能以正确或错误去评判它，而只能以合理或不合理去评判。合理的做行话语则更容易让交际双方愉悦，而不合理的做行话语则有可能导致交际双方产生不愉悦的情绪。

Austin（1962）认为，当人们发出话语时，人们可以通过能清楚表达行为的做行动词（performative verbs）实施行为（LoCastro, 2003）。此外，这些行为是在合理的环境（felicity circumstances）下产生，并能如预期般实现（Yule, 1996）。所谓合理环境，指的是交际的语境和交际中各种角色能被交际各方认识，交际行为得以完全实施，交际参与者在交际中有正确的并能被交际对象理解的交际意图（Cutting，2002）。

然而，在此之后，Austin又对他关于话语能实施行为的说法进行了补充。他发现不仅是做行话语可以实施行为（Martínez-Flor, Usó-Juan，2010），所有的话语都含有描述和影响两种功能，也就是说，它们同时既是陈述也是行为（Verschueren，1999；Sadock，2006）。因此，在分析言语或者话语时，需要考虑两个方面，即信息和行为（Chapman，2000）。言语既有传递信息的功能，也具有实施行为的作用。

Austin（1962）指出，对言语行为的分析，可从三个层次进行：言内行为（locutionary acts）、言外行为（illocutionary acts）、言后行为（perlocutionary acts）。言内行为是指使用特定语言形成发音和单词，以创造有意义的话语的行为，这里的意义指话语的字面意义（Peccei，1999）。言外行为和说话者产出话语的意图有关，言外行为也被称为"言外之力"（illocutionary force）（Chapman，2000），也就是说，言外行为指说话者通过话语可以表达道歉、抱怨、赞扬、邀请、承诺、要求之义（Yule，1996）。言后行为，是指说话者的话语对听话者或听话者对相关话语的反应产生的影响（Cutting，2002）。

Peccei（1999）观察到言语行为三个层次的关系并不是单向的。由于语境的不同，同样的言内行为会产生不同的言外之力和言后影响；同样的言后之力可以通过不同的言内行为获得，并产生不同的言后影响；同样的言后影响可以通过不同的言内行为和言外之力获得。例如，言内行为"I have an important appointment on this Sunday"的字面含义为说话者星期天有个重要的约会。言外之力则可能是拒绝听话者的邀请，言后行为则可能时说话者星期天不能到场。同样，该言内行为的言内之力也可能是向听话者宣布某一计划得到了重要进展，言后行为则可能是计划可以继续进行。但对言后行为和言外之力的判断需要依靠交际行为的具体语境。很多时候言内行为和言外之力很难清楚地分辨，只有当话语中出现做行动词（performative verbs）时，如apologize，admit，promise，thank，warn和order等时，话语才能清楚地表达言语行为。

Austin（1962）进一步将话语分为施为句（performatives）和叙事句（constatives）两类。施为句不单单是表达"断言"（assertion）这一言语行为，同时也能描述某一言语行为；在施为句中，说话者使用的动词需要描述一个在控制范围内的行为，如许诺、请求、感激、道歉、拒绝、建议等。然而，叙事句可能与施为句描述同一言语行为，但在叙事句中，不含有做行动词。

对于这三个层面的行为，Austin研究最多的是言外行为（Martínez-Flor, Usó-Juan，2010）。Austin根据做行动词的种类将言外行为分为五类

（Peccei，1999）。Sadock（2006）对每类言外行为进行了描述：

（1）Verdictives, acts of delivering a finding (e. g. , acquitting, and reading something as)；

（2）exercitives, acts of making a decision for or against a course of action (e. g. , appointing and ordering)；

（3）commissives, acts of committing the speaker to a course of action (e. g. , contracting and giving one's word)；

（4）behabitives, acts of expressing attitudes towards others' actions, fortunes, or attitudes (e. g. , apologizing and welcoming)；

（5）explosives, acts of presenting views, making arguments, and clarifying (e. g. , denying and informing).

Searle（1976：3）评论了 Austin 对言外行为的分类：its confusing performative verbs with illocutionary verbs and even types of illocutionary forces，lack of a clear or consistent principle or set of principles to construct the taxonomy，a great deal of overlap from one category to another and heterogeneity within some of the categories。

为了弥补 Austin 对言外行为分类的不足，Searle（1976）将做行动词分为 3 个大类（illocutionary point，sincerity condition，direction of fit）和 9 个小类［① illocutionary force；② interest of the speaker and the hearer；③relative status of speaker and hearer；④ relations to the rest of the discourse；⑤ propositional contents determined by illocutionary force-indicating devices (IFIDs)；⑥acts being speech acts or those that can be，but need not be performed as speech acts；⑦ acts requiring extra-linguistic institutions for the performance or not；⑧ acts where the corresponding illocutionary verb has a performative use or not；⑨the style of performing the illocutionary act］。

在此基础上，Searle 根据做行动词将言语行为重新分为五大类（Peccei，1999）。Searle 主要依据功能特点对做行动词进行了分类（Yule，1996；Martínez-Flor，Usó-Juan，2010）。Cutting（2002）对 Searle 言语行为的分类进行了描述：

(1) declarations, utterances that can change the world (e. g., "I declare" and "I resign");

(2) representatives, utterances that state what is believed to be the case (e. g., describing and predicting);

(3) expressives, utterances that are used to express feelings (e. g., apologizing and congratulating);

(4) directives, utterances that are used to make the hearer do something (e. g., requesting and commanding);

(5) commissives, utterances that commit the speaker to do something in the future (threatening and volunteering).

根据以上分类，本研究所关注的拒绝言语行为属于第五类，即 commissives。然而，Leech（1983）认为 declarations 不属于交际言语行为，而仅仅是更大的范畴"习惯用法"中的语言组成部分。此外，Leech（1983）指出 Searle 的分类主要考虑了语言行为和说话者意图，但却忽略了言语行为的言后影响。因此，他提出在言语行为分类中增加 rogatives，以表达请求之意。这一考虑是基于使听话者能够理解说话者之意。笔者将以上 3 位学者的言语行为分类进行了总结（表 2.1）。

表 2.1 Taxonomy of illocutionary verbs and acts

	Austin（1962）	Searle（1975）	Leech（1983）
Coverage	performative verbs	illocutionary acts	illocutionary acts perlocutionary effects
Category	verdictives exercitives commissives expositives behabitives	representatives directives commissives expressives declarations	representatives directives commissives expressives rogatives

为了实现预期的言后影响，言外之意需要在合理交际的前提下才能实现。继 Austin 之后，Searle（1969）提出言外之意要实现言后影响需具备以下 3 个条件：①准备条件，即说话者或听话者对特定言语行为的背景知识；②命题内容条件，即说话者或听话者对语句意思的理解；③忠诚条件，即说话者的真实交际意图；④本质条件，即话语的分量。

同样，Olshtain 和 Weinbach（1993：108）也提出了实现合理交际的 4 个

条件：①the hearer performs a socially unacceptable act (SUA) contrary to a social code of behavioral norms which is shared by both the speaker and the hearer; ②the speaker perceives the SUA as having unfavorable consequences for him/herself or the general public; ③ The speaker's verbal expression relates post facto indirectly or directly to the SUA, thus having the illocutionary force of censure; ④the speaker perceives the SUA as i) freeing him/herself (at least partially) from the implicit understanding of a socially cooperative relationship with the hearer; and ii) giving the speaker the legitimate right to require repairing aims at undoing the SUA, either for his/her benefit or for the public benefit。

Searle 根据言语行为的语言结构和功能，将言语行为分为直接言语行为 (direct speech acts) 和间接言语行为 (indirect speech acts) 两类 (Peccei, 1999)。Searle 认为直接言语行为在说话者意图表达话语的字面意思前提下产生，也就是说话语形式就是话语功能。例如，宣告 (declarative) 言语行为与声明 (assertion) 对应，命令 (imperative) 言语行为与请求 (request) 对应，询问 (interrogative) 言语行为与问题对应 (question) (Yaghoobi, 2002)。然而，间接言语行为体现了话语形式和话语意图的间接关系，单词的字面意思不能准确表达说话者的初衷 (Yule, 1996)。例如，"Can you help me to call a taxi?" 是一个询问话语，既可以表示直接言语行为，也可以表示间接言语行为。当说话者意图询问听话者是否有能力帮忙叫出租车时，该话语则表达了直接言语行为；当说话者要表达请求之意时，该话语表达了间接言语行为 (Verschueren, 1999)。

Gallaher (2011) 认为直接言语行为指符合交际意图的语言结构，间接言语行为则指表面不符合交际意图的语言结构。DeCapua (1989) 指出，直接言语行为和间接言语行为的区别在于，直接言语行为关注话语表达的面子威胁程度，而间接言语行为则需要考虑母语使用者习惯性接受的超出话语字面意思的含义。DeCapua (1989) 指出的直接言语行为和间接言语行为的区别表明，"直接"如同存在于层次连续体中，从隐藏的使人不悦的表达到构成威胁。例如，在表达对邀请的拒绝言语行为时，采用"If I join in the club, my mum will kill me"的表达比"I couldn't join in the club"直接，"I couldn't join in the club"的表达又比"I really want to join the club, but I am afraid I can't"直接，"I may join in the club if my mum agrees"则可以被看作间接言语行为。总的来说，Gallaher (2011) 所指的"直接"着眼于语言结构和言外之力的契合,而 DeCapua(1989)所指的"直接"则强调言外之力的面子威胁程度。在英语中,为了遵循礼貌原则,间接言语行为比直接言语行为更具有主导作用(Yule,1996)。

言语行为理论也存在一定的局限性。言语行为理论属于交际能力的范畴,其影响已经辐射到哲学、语言学、人类学、民族学,以及语言教学和应用语言学领域(Hymes,1972;Canale,1983)。多数研究都关注于非母语使用者如何实现中介语言语行为。然而,Searle(1969)提到并不是所有的言语行为都可以清楚地识别和定义,因为当说话者发出话语时,他/她要表达的意思可能是多方面的。Brown 和 Levinson(1987)也提出他们对言语行为理论持保留意见。他们认为言语行为理论"forces a sentence-based and speaker-oriented mode in analysis, and requires attribution of speech act categories in which the thesis requires that utterances are equivocal in force"。同样,DeCapua(1989)认为定义言语行为是基于说话者意图和信念基础上的,而没有完全考虑交际双方复杂的交际行为。此外,DeCapua(1989)注意到 Searle 在对言语行为的分类中,强调了言语行为随着一系列或一连串的话语产生。DeCapua(1989)认为这样的分类法过于机械化、简单化。LoCastro(1996:169-170)也指出了言语行为理论的四个局限性:①difficulty in recognizing the illocutionary force of non-conventionally indirect speech acts; ② incapability of understanding how a conversation proceeds without the consideration of the adjacent sociolinguistic context; ③ lack of explanation to the multi-function illocutionary acts; ④ limitation in analyzing surface level of linguistic forms without considering the psycholinguistic reality。

为了弥补言语行为理论的不足之处,Hymes(1972)提出了评价说话者交际能力的框架,该框架指出社会、文化、语法因素在交际中具有相互作用,并提出言语行为各要素的层次关系。Hymes(1972)认为在交际能力中,言语情景(speech situation)位于最上层,位于中间的是言语事件(speech event),位于底层的是言语行为(speech act)(表2.2)。

表 2.2 Hymes' interaction hierarchy

Hierarchy	Definition	Example
speech situation	circumstances where activities happen	meals, auctions, parties, conferences, etc.

续表2.2

Hierarchy	Definition	Example
speech event	activities or aspects of activities governed directly by language rules	party conversations, lectures, advertising, etc. It is analyzed with its constitutive components: participants, setting, ends (purpose), key, act sequence, instrument, norms, and genre
speech act	the basic unit which constitutes act sequence	greetings, apologies, etc.

例如,"I really have no time to play this weekend. If you need someone to play football with you, you'd better invite some others"。在该交际场景中,不难推断,说话者周末不能和听话者一起踢足球。根据 Hymes(1972)的交际能力框架进行分析,可以从话语分析中得出说话者和听话者是熟人关系,说话者正在实施拒绝言语行为。说话者已知会使听话者感到不悦,因此提出了补救措施。在该言语行为实施过程中,Hymes 提出的言语事件出现了和某个说话者语义套语不合作的情况。Fraser(1981)将言语事件称为复合言语行为(compound speech act),Van Dijk(1977)将它称为宏观结构(macrostructure),Ferrara(1985)将其称为宏观言语行为(macro speech acts),Blum-Kulka 和 Olshtain(1984)称其为言语行为组(speech act set)。总的来说,无论学者们如何命名这一概念,他们都旨在表示说话者可能发出的语义套语。

第四节 礼貌原则

礼貌原则的概念可以追溯到 Lakoff(1975)提出的礼貌规则:①不强加于人;②给予选择机会;③让听话者心情愉快。他认为礼貌是在社会交往中使人们减少摩擦的方法和手段。

一、礼貌原则特征

礼貌原则(politeness)是语用学的重要概念之一,礼貌原则是实现成功和谐交际的重要元素。Cutting(2002:45)将礼貌原则描述为"the choices which are made in language use, and the linguistic expressions which give people space and show a friendly attitude to them, if they want to save face or be appreciated in return". Yule (1996) 提出礼貌原则不仅仅指交际行为的合理性或在交际中体现特定文化背景下的礼节,还指听话者对超出话语字面含义理解的影响,以及由说话者和听话者关系决定的对话语是否粗鲁或考虑不周的评判。因此,为了避免交际冲突,增进人际关系,人们在交际中需要遵循合理原则和礼貌原则 (Mihalicek, Wilson, 2011),并使用间接话语表达隐含意义 (Peccei, 1999)。在跨文化交际中,不同国家文化背景的交际对象对礼貌的理解和要求不同,因此,了解交际对象的文化特点对于成功交际也尤为重要。

礼貌原则是许多语言学家、社会学家以及语言哲学家在语用学领域关注的焦点 (Prachanant, 2006)。学者们也在语用学框架下提出了礼貌原则理论。本研究关注礼貌原则中的面子保留 (face-saving),因为拒绝言语行为属于面子威胁行为。在实施该言语行为时很难避免对交际对象造成面子威胁,不同拒绝策略的使用会在拒绝过程中强化或缓解面子威胁的程度。面子保留是说话者在交际过程中需要考虑的重要方面。面子保留理论由 Brown 和 Levinson (1987) 提出,也是至今为止广为接受和有影响的礼貌原则理论。本研究将 Brown 和 Levinson (1987) 的礼貌原则理论作为研究的理论基础。

二、Brown 和 Levinson (1987) 的礼貌原则理论

Brown 和 Levinson (1987) 提出的礼貌原则理论假设说话者和听话者都是意图使用最为有效的策略实现交际目的的理性个体 (Barron, 2003)。礼貌现象在社会交往中普遍存在,这种现象的存在不受交际双方关系亲疏远近的影响 (Gumperz, 1987)。但是,礼貌原则的概念在不同的语言和文化背景下可以有所区别。换而言之,在某种文化背景下的礼貌行为在另一种文化背景下未必礼貌 (Wannaruk, 2005; Mihalicek, Wilson, 2011)。正因如此,不同国家的说话者和听话者在进行跨文化交际中,就需要增进对彼此文化背景和风俗习惯的了解,促进交流的顺利开展。

在此基础上,Watts (1992) 将"合理性"这一概念引入礼貌原则,"合理性"是指在特定社会背景下得以接受的交际行为。Watts (1992) 认为礼貌行为指在任何社会交往中的一切合理的社会文化语言行为。Blum-Kulka (1992: 275) 也提出 "appraisals of politeness should be motivated by cultural determinants of face wants and variable degrees of linguistic conventionalization",但礼貌原则同时也受到文化背景的影响。同样,Eelen (2001) 认为交际中的礼貌等同于交际中的合理,也等同于说话者的交际行为符合听话者的心理预期。

要实现较集中的合理,就需要实现交际双方的文化认同和礼貌认同。

总的来说,以上关于礼貌原则的论述包含了几个组成部分:合作(cooperation)、理性(rationality)、面子(face)以及合理性(appropriateness)。面子是其中的一个核心概念。

从本质上讲,面子指人的名声、社会地位、个人成就以及道德。从心理学的角度讲,面子是一个极为抽象的概念。Goffman(1967:5)将面子定义为"the positive social value one person effectively claims for him/herself by the line others assume he/she has taken in a particular contact"。Zhang(2006)将面子描述为在特定社会标准下,对社会行为表示尊重或羞辱的体现。Brown 和 Levinson(1987)指出面子是在公众面前的自我形象,并且交际双方都希望对方可以认识到其自我形象。Yule(1996)认为礼貌原则指在交际中理解交际对象的面子,并在交际中保留交际对象的面子(Barron,2003)。Brown 和 Levinson(1987)提出面子可分为两种类型:积极的面子(positive face)和消极的面子(negative face)。积极的面子指得到交际对象喜爱的愿望、被交际对象看到积极的方面或被接纳为团队中的一员;消极的面子指在交际中具有独立的愿望或不受他人影响的愿望(Yule,1996;Peccei,1999;Cutting,2002;LoCastro,2003)。

礼貌原则的第二个核心概念和言语行为有关。Brown 和 Levinson(1987)提到有些言语行为实质上属于面子威胁行为(FTAs),本研究所关注的拒绝言语行为则属于此类。这些言语行为的实施对说话一方或双方所期待的公众自我形象或积极的或消极的面子构成了威胁(Yule,1996;Barron,2003)。在社会交际中,一些属于面子威胁的言语行为会不可避免地发生,Brown 和 Levinson(1987)根据说话者或听话者的面子是否受到威胁将面子威胁行为进行了如下分类(表2.3)。

表 2.3 面子威胁行为分类（Brown，Levinson，1987：65－68）

Category	Definition	Examples
Hearer's negative face is at stake	Those acts that predicate some future act of the hearer, and in so doing put some pressure on the hearer to do (or refrain from doing) the act	orders and requests, suggestions, advice, reminding, threats, warnings, and dares
	Those acts that predicate some positive future act of the speaker toward the hearer, and in so doing put some pressure on the hearer to accept or reject them, and possibly to incur a debt	offers and promise
	Those acts that predicate some desire of the speaker toward the hearer or hearer's goods, giving the hearer reason to think that he may have to take action to protect the object of the speaker's desire, or give it to the speaker	compliments, and expressions of strong (negative) emotions toward the hearer
Hearer's positive face is at stake	Those that show that the speaker has a negative evaluation of some aspect of the hearer's positive face	expressions of disapproval, criticism, contempt or ridicule, complaints and reprimands, accusations, insults, contradictions, or challenges, disagreements
	Those that show that the speaker does not care about (or is indifferent to) hearer's positive face	expressions of violent (out-of-control) emotions, irreverence, mention of taboo topics, bringing of bad news about the hearer, or good news about the speaker, raising of dangerously emotional or divisive topics, blatant non-cooperation in an activity, and use of address terms and otherstatus-marked identifications in initial encounters

续表2.3

Category	Definition	Examples
Speaker's negative face is at stake	Those that put some pressure on the speaker to fulfil some future act for the hearer	(1) expressing thanks; (2) acceptance of the hearer's thanks or the hearer's apology; (3) excuses; (4) acceptance of offers; (5) responses to the hearer's faux pas; (6) unwilling promises and offers
	Those that show the speaker is not worth being liked	(1) apologies; (2) acceptance of a compliment; (3) breakdown of physical control of body, bodily leakage, stumbling or falling down, etc.; (4) self-humiliation, shuffling or cowering, acting stupid, self-contradicting; (5) confessions, admissions of guilt or responsibility; (6) emotion leakage, non-control of laughter or tears

根据以上对面子威胁行为的分类，不难发现，一些面子威胁行为同时威胁了说话者和听话者的消极面子或积极面子，如拒绝、抱怨、威胁等。当说话者不得不实施面子威胁行为时，需要注意交际中的礼貌原则，以缓解对面子的威胁。在跨文化社会交际中，如何成功地实施面子威胁行为非常重要。在实施言语行为时，任何偏离母语使用者的语言规则之处都有可能不合理地威胁到交际双方的面子，导致交际失败（Gallerher，2011）。

因此，为了建立和谐的交际关系，人们在交际行为中总是会使用一些缓解面子威胁行为的话语（Yule，1996）。在缓解面子威胁程度时，说话者需将以下几个方面的需求纳入考虑：①交流面子威胁行为内容的需求；②有效或紧急交际的需求；③给听话者保留面子的需求（Brown，Levinson，1987）。在此基础上，Brown 和 Levinson（1987）提出了五种可以缓解面子威胁的策略，其中第二种和第三种是礼貌策略的核心概念。Brown 和 Levinson（1987）对这五种策略都进行了较为详细的解释：

(1) Doing the FTA without redressive action, baldly: The FTA is performed in the most direct and clearest manner. In other words, the communicative intention of the speaker is unambiguously conveyed to the hearer (e. g., "Do X!").

(2) Doing the FTA with redressive action (positive politeness): The FTA is performed with the speaker's attempt to notice the hearer's face. Its performance is aimed at showing recognition of the hearer's positive face for the super-strategy and positive politeness.

(3) Doing the FTA with redressive action (negative politeness): The FTA is performed with the speaker's attempt to acknowledge the hearer's face, but this super-strategy is oriented towards the hearer's negative face.

(4) Doing the FTA off the record: The FTA is performed unambiguously to express more than one communicative intention for the purpose of not committing the speaker to the future action.

(5) Don't do the FTA: In some situations, the FTA is performed not by the speaker's words, but by his/her gestures.

Brown 和 Levinson（1987）认为，面子威胁行为的实施受到三种社会因素的影响：①社会距离（social distance）；②地位差距（relative power）；③强加级别（absolute ranking）。社会距离和地位差距体现了交际双方的关系（Yule，1996）。社会距离可以分为熟悉或不熟悉两类（Barron，2003）。社会距离还受到年龄、性别、角色、教育程度、阶层和种族的影响（O'Keeffe et al.，2011）。地位差距可以用 superiority 和 inferiority 进行描述。强加级别表现为在特定文化背景下，FTA 对面子威胁的程度（O'Keeffe，Clancy，Adolphs，2011）。例如，向别人提出借支笔的请求比向别人借车的请求强加程度就小得多。

根据听话者受到面子威胁的类型，即积极面子或消极面子，Brown 和 Levinson（1987）将礼貌分为两类，即积极礼貌（positive politeness）和消极礼貌（negative politeness）。积极礼貌的出发点在于保护听话者的积极面子或积极的自我形象。也就是说，积极礼貌着眼于维护听话者在群体、朋友等心目中的得到认可或喜欢的性格特征。消极礼貌的出发点是避免损坏面子。也就是说，消极礼貌着眼于满足听话者的消极面子和保持其基本的自主权利。

了解积极礼貌和消极礼貌的区别有助于进行跨语言研究，帮助理解不同的文化，也可以区分积极礼貌文化和消极礼貌文化。积极礼貌文化，也称植根于礼貌文化的积极面子，积极礼貌文化更多表现在"matter-of-factness, directness, friendly back-slapping, and the like"方面（Olshtain, Cohen, 1989：59）。与之不同的是，消极礼貌文化，也称为植根于礼貌文化的消极面子，消极礼貌文化更多表现在"maintenance of social distance and face-saving"方面（Olshtain, Cohen, 1989：59—60）。

Brown 和 Levinson（1987）提出的礼貌原则理论和本研究所关注的拒绝言语行为密切相关，拒绝言语行为从本质上讲属于面子威胁行为。在本研究中，笔者在设计研究工具时考虑了以上所有社会因素。下一节将进行对语用学和交际能力的关系进行阐释。

第五节 语用学和交际能力的关系

语用学是语言分析的重要学科领域，是语言学家有关语言形式和语言结构研究的兴趣所在。语用学是研究在实际对话中语言使用的学科（Martínez-Flor, Usó-Juan, 2010）。简单地说，语用学是研究在真实场景中语言使用的学科。语用学概念是交际能力（communicative competence）概念形成的基础。交际能力指在特定交际场景中为了特定的交际目的说话者合理使用语言知识（包括句法结构、语义、语素、音素、词汇）的能力（Niezgoda, Röver, 2001）。基于对交际能力的理解，语言学家们提出了不同的交际能力模型。

一、Hymes 的模型

Hymes（1972）认为在真实交际环境中，交际能力应包含语言运用（linguistic performance）能力和语言使用（language use）能力。Hymes（1972：221）提出交际能力是"knowledge of rules for understanding and producing either the social or referential meaning of a language"。Hymes（1972）认为，交际能力是关于"何时说，何时不说，和谁说，说什么，在哪说，怎么说"的能力。Hymes（1972）率先提出了交际能力（communicative competence）概念，并从交际功能（communicative function）的角度进行语言研究，引入了社会因素对交际效果影响的研究。

二、Canale 和 Swain 的模型

Canale 和 Swain（1980）提出交际能力有四个组成成分：①语法能力（grammatical competence），即对语言代码（包括有声的和无声的）和语言规则（包括词汇、拼写、单词和句子构成）知识的了解；②社会语言能力（sociolinguistic competence），即对社会文化规则和篇章规则知识的了解；③篇章能力（discourse competence），即有关在不同语体中将语法形式和意义联系的知识；④策略能力（strategic knowledge），即为了补偿交际障碍或提高交际效果而采用的有声或无声策略的知识。Canale 和 Swain（1980）还提出社会语言能力（sociolinguistic competence）是社会文化知识（sociocultural knowledge）在语篇中的反映。通过社会文化知识，可以将话语的字面意义和说话者意图联系起来，使听话者理解说话者真实意图。Canale 和 Swain（1980）的交际能力模型较 Hymes（1972）的模型更加完整。

三、Bachman 的模型

Bachman（1990），Bachman 和 Palmer（1996）对 Canale 和 Swain（1980）的交际能力模型进行了进一步发展。Bachman（1990）将该模型称为交际语言能力（communicative language ability）模型。他将交际语言能力分为三个组成部分：①语言表达能力（language competence），包含组织能力（organizational competence），即语法能力（grammatical competence）、文本能力（textual competence），以及语用能力（pragmatic competence）［即言外能力（illocutionary competence）和社会语言能力（sociolinguistic competence）］；②策略能力（strategic competence），即合理运用语言能力进行交际的心智能力；③心理生理机制（psycho-physiological mechanism），即和语言使用相关的神经心理过程。Bachman（1990）指出策略能力和语言能力、语境及语言使用者的世界知识（knowledge of the world）紧密联系。Bachman 和 Palmer（1993）认为策略能力包含元认知策略。此外，语言的使用还需要主题知识（topical knowledge）、情感要素（affective schemata），以及其他知识。实际上，Bachman（1990）的交际能力模型更加复杂，该模型和之前其他学者提出的交际能力模型最根本的区别在于 Bachman（1990）突出了策略能力在交际中的中心地位，而不是补充成分。

四、Wen 的模型

Wen（2000）对交际能力模型进行了系统的研究，并在已有交际能力模型的基础上提出了跨文化交际能力（cross-cultural communicative competence）模型。她指出，跨文化交际能力包含交际能力（communicative competence）和跨文化能力（cross-cultural competence）两个部分。其中，交际能力由语言能力（linguistic competence）、语用能力（pragmatic competence）和策略能力（strategic competence）构成。跨文化能力包含敏感性（sensitivity）、忍受度（tolerance）和灵活性（flexibility）三个要素。20世纪末，学者们对交际能力的研究进行了跨学科的尝试。Wen（2000）在研究中将Bachman（1990）提出的语用能力融入了交际能力中。

五、Celce-Murcia 等的模型

Celce-Murcia，Dörnyei 和 Thurrell（1995）也提出了交际能力模型。Celce-Murcia 等（1995）认为交际能力包含四个方面：①篇章能力（discourse competence），即选择、排序和将单词、结构、句子及话语进行书面或口头整理的能力；②社会文化能力（socio-cultural competence），即在特定社会文化背景下，在真实交际场景中，合理使用语言的能力；③语言能力（linguistic competence），即关于句法、语素、词汇、音素和拼写的知识；④行动能力（actional competence），即涵盖和理解交际意图的能力。Celce-Murcia 等（1995）对其交际能力模型个元素的描述更为生动。该模型强调了语言使用者的实际语言运用能力和文化背景知识。Celce-Murcia 等（1995）将 Canale 和 Swain（1980）模型中的社会语言能力（socio-linguistic competence）发展成为行动能力（actional competence）与社会文化能力（socio-cultural competence）。Celce-Murcia 等（1995）的交际能力模型见图 2.1。

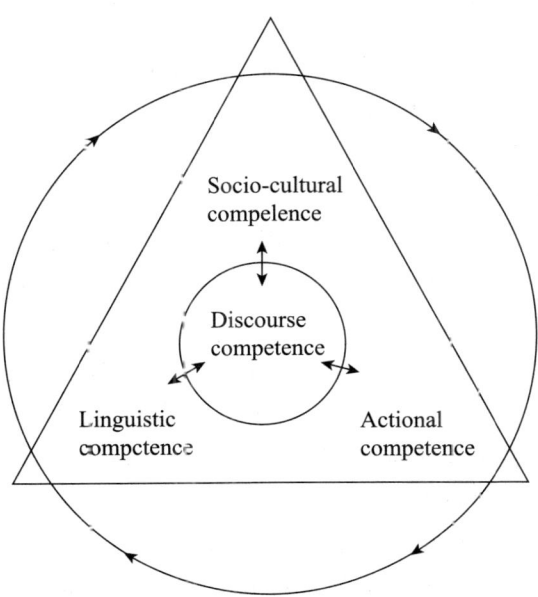

图 2.1 交际能力模型（Celce-Murcia，Dörnyei，Thurrell，1995：10）

从以上交际能力模型可见，语用学知识在交际能力中扮演着重要角色，它在 Canale 和 Swain 的模型（1980）中体现为社会语言能力，在 Bachman（1990）和 Wen（2000）的模型中体现为语用能力，在 Celce-Murcia 等（1995）的模型中体现为社会文化能力和行动能力。语用学知识不仅要求语言使用者能够在特定语境下合理使用语言，还要求其在交际中能够涵盖和理解交际意图。如果在交际中，尤其是在跨文化交际情景下，交际双方不能有效地使用语用学知识，则会导致交际失败。

第六节 语用失误和跨文化交际的关系

Thomas（2006：22）指出，语用失误是造成跨文化交际误解和障碍的重要原因，语用失误指"the inability to understand what is meant by what is said"。也就是说，说话者发出话语的目的被听话者误解或曲解。Thomas（2006）将语用失误分为以下几种情况：

(1) The hearer interprets the force of the speaker's utterance stronger or

weaker than the speaker intends;

(2) The hearer interprets the speaker's utterance as an order whereas the speaker intends to deliver a request;

(3) The hearer interprets the speaker's utterance as ambivalent whereas the speaker intends no ambivalence;

(4) The hearer is expected by the speaker to be able to infer the force of his/her utterance based on the knowledge or beliefs which they do not share.

Thomas（2006）认为，尽管跨文化语用失误通常发生在母语使用者和非母语使用者的交际行为中。但实际上，由于不同社会文化下的语用规则各有不同，语用失误可以发生在任何不同社会文化背景交际双方的交际行为中。也就是说，语用失误既可以发生在母语使用者和非母语使用者之间，也可以发生在不同母语背景的非母语使用者之间。然而，值得一提的是，跨文化语用失误正是母语使用者或非母语使用者间或非母语使用者间的交际特点（Barron，2003），也是语用学家研究的焦点之一。

Thomas（2006）将语用失误分为两大类：语用语言失误（pragmalinguistic failure）和社会语用失误（sociopragmatic failure）。她提出，在语用语言失误中，说话者表达施加在话语中的语用用意（pragmatic force）和接近于母语使用者的说话者表达的语用用意存在根本不同，因此让交际双方造成了理解上的严重差异，达不到成功交际的目的。Thomas（2006）还提到这类语用失误是由于教学误导或语用语言迁移导致的。例如，说话者不合理地使用了直接策略（directness）或缓和策略（modification），听话者就可能将"命令"理解为"请求"（Barron，2003）。社会语用失误，是由于交际双方对强加程度、社会距离、地位差距、权力、义务、得失等影响交际效果的社会因素的不同理解导致的（Thomas，2006）。例如，说话者可能对其交际对象的地位评判低于交际对象本身的地位，就会认为交际对象的交际行为不够礼貌（Barron，2003），从而达不到交际目的。由此可见，语用失误会导致跨文化交际障碍。语用失误也会发生在言语行为中，拒绝言语行为也不例外，下一节将介绍拒绝言语行为。

第七节 拒绝言语行为实施策略的特点和分类

一、拒绝言语行为特点

拒绝言语行为一直以来都受到语言学家的关注（Gass，Houck；1990），拒绝言语行为是跨文化交际中许多非母语使用者的症结所在（Beebe，Takabashi，Uliss-Weltz，1990）。拒绝言语行为有以下特征：①拒绝言语行为是使用相对较少的言语行为之一，该言语行为可作为其他言语行为的回答，如请求、邀请、给予、建议等（Gass，Houck，1999）。②拒绝言语行为要求交际另一方做出及时回答，因此，对于拒绝一方来说，在实际交际中没有足够的时间进行该言语行为的计划和实施（Gass，Houck，1999）。③因拒绝言语行为和说话者的预期相悖，该行为属于面子威胁言语行为。因此，拒绝言语行为也被称为不受欢迎的言语行为（Eslami，2010）。换句话说，实施拒绝言语行为就是说一些让交际对方不悦的话语。说话者通常需要附加一些理由以避免听话者感到尴尬（Beebe，Takabashi，Uliss-Weltz，1990）。④拒绝言语行为的实施可采取直接策略或间接策略。为了缓解直接拒绝在交际中的消极效果，有时会采取间接策略。例如采用副词"unfortunately"等对面子威胁程度进行缓和，或使用表示心理状态的表达方式如"I don't think..."，提供选择的表达方式如"Why don't we..."等来缓解面子威胁的程度（Félix-Brasdefer，2008）。此外，拒绝言语行为的实施还可采纳协商的方式进行（Beebe，Takabashi，Uliss-Weltz，1990；Gass，Houck，1999）。⑤拒绝言语行为的形式和内容可以随着拒绝的内容（如请求，邀请，给予，建议）和其他社会因素（如说话者的社会地位）而改变（Beebe，Takabashi，Uliss-Weltz，1990）。⑥为了合理地实施拒绝言语行为，拒绝的一方需较好地掌握语用知识和交际双方的文化背景知识（Gass，Houck，1990；Eslami，2010）。

二、拒绝言语行为的分类

学者们对拒绝言语行为的研究兴趣不仅在于关注不同文化背景下如何实施该言语行为，同时关注如何将拒绝回答进行分类。最早对拒绝言语行为进行分类的学者是 Rubin（1983，引自 Eslami，2010）。Rubin（1983）首先指出了非英语母语使用者在拒绝时需要运用三类知识："a form-function relation, the social parameter of delivering *no*, and the underlying values for non-native speakers to send or receive the message of *no*." Rubin (1983: 12–13) 将跨文化拒绝言语行为分为以下 9 类：

(1) Be silent, hesitate, show a lack of enthusiasm;
(2) Offer an alternative;
(3) Postponement;
(4) Put the blame on a third party or something over which you have no control;
(5) Avoidance;
(6) General acceptance of an offer but giving no details;
(7) Divert and distract the addressee;
(8) General acceptance with excuses;
(9) Say what is offered is inappropriate.

然而，Gass 和 Houck（1999）以及 Sinthukiow 和 Modehiran（2013）都认为 Beebe 等（1990: 72–73）对拒绝言语行为的分类更加合理。Beebe 等（1990: 72–73）将拒绝回答以语义套语（semantic formulas）的方式进行划分。语义套语既包含表达拒绝的话语，也包含其他要素（adjuncts），如不能独立用来表达拒绝，但却可以和语义成分同时使用的话语（Gass, Houck, 1999; Eslami, 2010）。语义成分可以进一步分为两类：直接拒绝和间接拒绝。具体划分请参见附录四。

多数学者对拒绝回答的分类研究都基于语义成分（Beebe, Takahashi, Uliss-Weltz, 1990）。如 Amarien（1997），Wannaruk（2008），Nguyen（2006），Geyang（2007），Farnia 和 Abdul Sattar（2010），Abdul Sattar、Che Lah 和 Raja Suleiman（2011），Farnia 和 Wu（2012）以及 Guo（2012）。在本研究中，也将采纳 Beebe 等（1990）对拒绝回答的分类方法对中泰缅大学生的拒绝言语行为进行分类研究。下一节将介绍学者们对拒绝言语行为研究的数据收集方法。

第八节 拒绝言语行为数据收集方法

英语非母语使用者的言语行为是学者们关注的焦点（Gass，Houck，1999），本研究也不例外。学者们为收集言语行为数据，采用了多种数据收集方法。总的来说，可以将这些数据收集方法分为人种志的数据收集方法（ethnographic data collection）和启发式的步骤（elicitation procedures）（如启发式对话、角色扮演、产出性问卷等）（Barron，2003）。

一、人种志的数据收集方法（Ethnographic data collection）

人种志的数据收集方法主张通过实地观察收集数据，因此获得的数据更加高质（Nurani，2009）。人种志的数据来源于自然对话场景（Hinkel，1997），所以更加真实并接近生活（Yuan，2001）。人种志数据收集方法不仅可以收集言语行为中的话语数据，还可以收集笑声、眼神、语气和动作等数据，可以使语料更加丰富，并能更加客观准确地反映交际双方的策略使用情况（Golato，2003）。尽管人种志的数据收集方法有很多优点，同时也存在一些不足之处。例如，在观察说话者在真实语境下的对话时，观察者不对其对话内容进行法律和道德的限制，这就给说话者很大的自由空间（Hinkel，1997）。此外，在真实交际中，无法对诸如社会关系、权力、地位差距、性别、年龄等进行限制（Yuan，2001）。这就使收集到的数据不够全面，很难从不从的角度反映不同情境下下人们交际任务的完成情况。人种志数据收集的弊端在于研究者很难进行跨文化交际的比较研究（Prachanant，2006）。由于自然获得的数据具有局限性，所以学者们对一些启发式的数据收集方法进行了尝试，如角色扮演（role play）、产出性问卷（production questionnaires）、语篇补全对话（discourse completion tasks，DCT）等。在这些启发式数据收集方法中，语篇补全对话最受学者们青睐（Martínez-Flor，Usó-Juan，2011）。

二、角色扮演（Role-play）

Mackey 和 Gass（2005）认为角色扮演可以分为两类：封闭式的和开放式的。封闭式的角色扮演指参与者在规定场景下，根据交际需求，模仿示例或规定句型，进行单向口头回答。开放式角色扮演指研究者向参与者指定交际场景、交际目的和人物关系，交际具体内容则是开放性的。角色扮演者可根据情景需求，按照自己的想法设计交际内容（Schauer，2009）。通过角色扮演的数据收集方法，研究者不仅可以观察到社会语用数据，还可以收集到口头表达的双向数据，并观察到交际双方的协商过程。角色扮演的数据收集法可收集到实际交际中较为自然的数据，因此受到学者们的关注和青睐（Golato，2003；Martínez-Flor，Usó-Juan，2011）。

一些学者将角色扮演数据收集方法作为拒绝言语行为主要数据收集方法。例如，Félix-Brasdefer（2004）采用角色扮演的数据收集方法探讨了美国西班牙语使用者的礼貌策略使用情况。在他的研究中，他设计了10个角色扮演场景：含6个拒绝场景和4个道歉或抱怨场景。6个拒绝场景含正式场景和非正式场景。正式场景和非正式场景都包含拒绝邀请、拒绝建议和拒绝请求。此外，Félix-Brasdefer（2004）还采用了访谈的数据收集方法。在访谈中，Félix-Brasdefer（2004）对西班牙语母语使用者和二语使用者都采用了西班牙语为访谈语言，同时对英语母语使用者采用了英语作为访谈语言。

Félix-Brasdefer（2008）对美国男性西班牙语二语学习者进行了西班牙语拒绝言语行为研究。该研究的研究对象均为高年级西班牙语学习者，研究内容为拒绝邀请，数据收集工具为开放式角色扮演。邀请的场景包括：邀请朋友参加生日聚会（正式邀请），邀请同事参加上司的欢送会（非正式邀请）。在角色扮演中，每一位西班牙语二语学习者在拒绝生日聚会邀请场景中和一名西班牙文学大学教授对话，在拒绝上司欢送会邀请场景中与一名西班牙大学生对话。

一些学者也将角色扮演的数据收集方法用于拒绝言语行为教学干预效果的研究。例如，Bacelar Da Silva（2003）在教学干预前测、后测中分别设计了不同的拒绝言语行为角色扮演场景，以研究教学干预对学生拒绝策略使用的影响。在场景设计中，说话双方的社会地位相同，亲密度中等。

尽管角色扮演数据收集方法有很多优势，但也存在一些不足。角色扮演数据收集方法的不足之处主要表现在对角色扮演者实施不合理语言行为（如粗鲁）的后果无法体现。然而，在真实交际中，不合理的语言行为将会在很大程度上影响交际效果和人际关系（Golato，2003）。此外，角色扮演数据收集和整理也非常耗时（Prachanant，2006），还需要使用录音录像设备，并不适合大规模的数据收集。

三、语篇补全对话（Discourse completion tasks，DCT）

语篇补全对话的数据收集方法具有较为明显的优势。它能在短时间内收集大量数据（Tanck，2004），该数据收集方法也易于掌握。Blum-Kulka（1982）率先将 DCT 用于言语行为研究。Kasper 和 Dahl（1991）将 DCT 定义为一种问卷形式的言语行为数据收集方法。在完成问卷时，研究者首先会向研究对象描述一个场景，该场景将引出某种言语行为，参与研究的研究对象将根据引出的言语行为完成书面对话。Nurani（2009）指出 DCT 大致可以分为以下五类：

(1) *The classic DCT*：In this DCT format, a rejoinder is presented at the end of the situation and/or an interlocutor's utterance is presented at the beginning.

(2) *The dialogue construction*：In this DCT format, the dialogue may be initiated by an interlocutor's utterance; however, different from the previous format, the rejoinder is not provided.

(3) *The open item verbal response*：The participants' responses are not restricted by an interlocutor's initiation or the rejoinder. They are free to respond to the given situation verbally.

(4) *The open item free response construction*：The participants can give either a verbal response, or a non-verbal response, or even no response at all to a given situation.

(5) *The content-enriched DCT* developed by Billmyer and Varghese (2000)：This DCT format is a modification of the open item verbal response. The differences between them are that the content-enriched DCT provides detailed contextual information about a situation, especially place and time (Félix-Brasdefer, 2010), and the participants are required to write down their responses.

DCT 被广泛运用于言语行为研究数据收集，其中也包括拒绝言语行为。例如，Duan（2008）在 Wannaruk（2004，2005，2008）研究的基础上采用 DCT 收集英语中介语拒绝言语行为教学干预前后的数据。Duan（2008）设计了 12 个交际场景，包含拒绝邀请、拒绝给予、拒绝建议和拒绝请求场景各三个，每类拒绝场景分别涵盖一个不同的地位差距（高-低、平等、低-高）场景，她还将社会距离也纳入考虑因素。

语篇补全对话包含口头语篇补全对话（Oral discourse completion tasks，ODCT）、书面语篇补全对话（Written discourse completion tasks，WDCT）、多项选择语篇补全对话（Multiple-choice discourse completion tasks，MDCT）三种形式。

口头语篇补全对话要求学生先听一段场景描述的录音，然后根据听到的场景大声说出在该场景下要说的话。通常情况下，数据收集需要借用一些录音录像设备，但也有学者会采用现场评分的方式。口头语篇补全对话的言语行为数据收集方法有很多优点，如可以引出较为真实的数据，并且在收集口语内容表达数据的同时，还可以收集到动作、手势、口头禅等其他数据。此外，口头语篇补全对话的数据收集方法可以在短时间内掌握。但是，口头语篇补全对话也有一些不足。例如，对口头语篇补全对话评分较难。在评分过程中，要对评分员进行培训，评分前还要对对口头数据进行书面转换，该过程需耗费大量的人力物力财力。

WDCT 由于其操作性较强（Golato，2003；Billmyer，Varghese，2000）、变量容易控制（Golato，2003；Schauer，Adolphs，2006）、在短时间内可以收集大量数据（Billmyer，Varghese，2000；Tanck，2004）、在进行数据分析时不需要转录（Duan，2008）等特点，成为言语行为研究领域最常用的数据收集方法（Kasper，Dahl，1991；Félix-Brasdefer，2010）。尽管 WDCT 有诸多优点，但也存在一些不足之处。例如，Tanck（2004）提出，使用 WDCT 在收集数据时，不能收集到真实场景的数据。因在书面语表达中，对话参与者可以改变其回答，但在真实交际场景中，说话者是不能改变其回答的。不过，也有学者认为通过 WDCT 收集的数据在主要形式和表达用语上接近于真实场景下流露的话语（Beebe，Cummings，1996）。

MDCT 要求学生首先阅读场景描述，然后根据事先提供的选项选择最适合该场景的一项。一些学者认为多项选择语篇补全对话是一种综合考查语言学习者言语行为的数据收集方法（Rover，2006；Nemati，Rezaee，Mahdi，2014；Tabatabaei，Farnia，2015）。MDCT 的数据收集方法有很多的优点。例如，MDCT 可以在短时间内收集到大量数据；MDCT 收集到的数据易于统计。此外，MDCT 收集数据时仅需要纸和笔，工具容易准备。但是，MDCT 数据收集工具也有一些不足之处。例如，MDCT 收集不到文字描述性数据，因此收集到的数据不能准确反映语言学习者的真实想法，语料缺乏充分性；MDCT

不能收集到口头数据,因此对学习者的口语表达能力无法进行评判。

本研究将采用 WDCT 作为数据收集方法,笔者基于以下几点考虑:首先,本研究的研究对象样本较大,共有 180 名学生,而且学生分布地域较广,分布在三个国家,采用角色扮演或口头表达语篇补全对话的数据收集方法需要对每名语言学习者进行录音或录像,还需要对不同国家的数据收集人员进行前期培训,且笔者不能随时提供现场指导,其可行性较小。而 MDCT 虽然操作方便,但不能收集到文字表达数据,学生自由发挥度小,在数据收集过程中会出现语料不充分的问题,不利于深刻分析中泰缅三国学生的拒绝言语行为策略使用情况。而尽管 WDCT 也不能收集到学生的口头表达数据,但已经综合了其他言语行为研究常用数据收集方法的优点,如操作简便、可在短时间内收集大量数据、可收集文字表达数据等,该数据收集方法更适合应用于本研究。

第九节 拒绝言语行为研究综述

Beebe 等(1990)探究了英语二语学习者拒绝言语行为的语用迁移。在他们的研究中,共邀请了 60 名英语二语学习者参与。其中日语母语说日语的参与者 20 名,日语母语说英语的参与者 20 名,以及美国英语母语说英语者 20 名。数据收集采用 DCT 进行,DCT 共含 12 个场景,包含拒绝请求、拒绝邀请、拒绝给予、拒绝建议各 3 个场景。每一类场景都包含对地位高、地位平等和地位低的交际对象各 1 个。Beebe 等(1990)将 DCT 收集到的拒绝言语行为数据通过语义套语进行分析,数据编码通过拒绝策略分类进行。结果显示,日语母语的英语说英语学习者在拒绝策略使用上主要有 3 类母语负迁移情况:语义套语顺序、语义套语使用频率、语义套语内容。值得注意的是,用日语参与的日语母语者和用英语参与的日语母语者间在拒绝地位比自己高或地位比自己低的交际对象时采用了不同的拒绝策略,而美国英语母语参与者在拒绝地位和自己相同的交际对象和比自己地位高的交际对象时采用了不同的拒绝策略。

Sairhun(1999)研究了泰国英语学习者拒绝言语行为中语用迁移情况。在他的研究中,研究对象包括 50 名美国大学生和 50 名泰国大学生。美国大学生用英语实施拒绝言语行为,泰国大学生用泰语和英语两门语言实施拒绝言语行为。数据收集采用 DCT 的形式,DCT 一个设计了 12 个场景,其中 6 个为请求场景,6 个为建议场景。研究结果发现,美国学生用英语表达和泰国学生用泰语表达时,都存在拒绝策略的选择和话语内容表达上的不同。确切地说,泰国学生在拒绝时多用间接策略,而美国学生则喜欢使用直接策略。同时,本研究还发现当泰国学生使用英语进行拒绝时,在以下几方面受到了母语负迁移的影响:①对加强策略(intensifiers)的使用,如采用"very"或"really"等词,来表达遗憾或感激;②采用"Yes, but..."的结构以表达积极态度;③采用回避策略(hedging),如使用"I am afraid..."的表达形式;④以家庭成员为由进行解释;⑤采用"警告"(admonishment)的表达方式。此外,不论用泰语还是英语进行拒绝时,交际对象的社会地位对泰国学生的策略使用影响更大。

Kwon(2003)研究了韩国英语外语学习者的拒绝言语行为语用迁移情况。在该研究中,共有118名研究对象参与,其中韩语母语使用者40名,美国英语使用者37名,韩语为母语的英语使用者111名。Kwon(2003)根据其英语语言水平的不同,将111名韩语为母语的英语使用者分为初学者、中等水平学习者和高水平学习者三组。数据编码根据Beebe等(1990)的拒绝策略分类进行,数据分析结合了定性数据分析方法和定量数据分析方法。结果显示,高水平的英语学习者由于其语言水平较高,受到语用迁移的影响最大。换句话说,高水平的英语学习者更能将韩语母语拒绝策略正迁移到英语使用中。例如,他们可以将"Pause fillers""Postponement""Hedging""Statement of solidarity""Statement of alternative""Statement of acknowledgment"等拒绝策略进行语用正迁移。同时,英语水平高的韩语母语使用者还能较好地迁移拒绝策略使用的语调。和英语水平低和水平中等的英语学习者相比,英语语言水平高的学习者使用直接策略的频率更高;他们更能脱离韩语规则的束缚,采纳如"Gratitude""Positive feeling"等英语目标语拒绝策略。此外,英语语言水平高的学习者在拒绝时比韩语母语使用者和英语母语使用者更加啰嗦和委婉,对韩语拒绝策略和英语拒绝策略都存在过度使用现象。

Tanck(2004)比较了12名英语母语使用者和13名英语外语学习者的拒绝言语行为和抱怨言语行为实施情况。13名英语外语学习者包括以中文、海地克里奥尔语、韩语、波兰语、俄语、塞尔维亚语、西班牙语和泰语为母语的学习者。Tanck(2004)将交际场景设计均为大学学习生活场景。交际双方的地位包含平等和不平等关系。结果显示,英语母语使用者和英语外语学习者在拒绝邀请时都普遍使用了以下交际策略:"Excuse""Expression of regret""Offer of alternative"。但是,相比之下,在拒绝教授的邀请时,英语外语学习者比英语母语使用者较少使用"Excuse"或"Offer of alternative"策略;

当拒绝同学的邀请时，英语外语学习者比英语母语使用者较少使用"Expression of regret"或"Offer of alternative"策略。英语母语使用者在拒绝教授邀请时常使用"Excuse"策略，这和英语外语学习者拒绝同学的邀请时采用的策略一样。

Al-Kahtani（2005）比较了英语母语使用者和英语外语学习者的拒绝策略。该研究的研究对象为3组不同语言文化背景的英语使用者，分别为10名美国英语母语使用者、10名阿拉伯英语学习者，以及10名日本英语学习者。数据收集采用了Beebe等（1990）设计的拒绝言语行为DCT，数据分析依据Beebe等（1990）总结的拒绝策略分类。研究发现，3组参与者在以下3个方面表现不同：①语义套语的顺序；②语义套语的使用频率；③语义套语的内容。但以上区别并不是在每个场景中都有所体现。阿拉伯英语学习者和日本英语学习者在表达"Excuse"时不如美国英语母语使用者清晰。日本英语学习者使用"Statement of principle"和"Statement of philosophy"策略的频率高于其他两组研究对象。此外，阿拉伯英语学习者和日本英语学习者在交际中比美国英语母语使用者更倾向于使用正式的表达方式。

Wannaruk（2005，2008）研究了泰国学生用英语进行拒绝时的语用迁移情况。该研究共有120名研究对象，其中40名泰国学生用泰语进行拒绝，40名泰国学生用英语进行拒绝，还有40名美国学生用英语实施拒绝言语行为。数据收集采用DCT和采访相结合的方式进行。DCT共有12个交际场景，包含4个方面的内容：3个请求场景，3个建议场景，3个邀请场景以及3个提供帮助场景。每类场景都包含社会地位高、平等或低的交际对象各一个，每类场景中还含有熟悉和不熟悉社会距离的交际对象。所有场景根据大学生的学习生活进行设计。Wannaruk（2005，2008）的研究结果发现，泰国学生使用英语实施拒绝言语行为时，在以下3个方面受到了其母语或母语文化的影响：①拒绝策略选择；②拒绝策略表达话语长度；③拒绝策略内容。在该研究中，3组学生的策略选择都受到了交际对象社会地位和拒绝话语引出行为的影响。同时，对于用英语表达拒绝的泰国学生来说，其英语语言水平还会影响其"Explanation"策略的内容。换句话说，英语语言水平高的泰国学生能够更加清楚完整地说明拒绝的原因，而英语水平低的泰国学生在进行解释时则更像是逐字逐句翻译母语。

Nguyen（2006）也研究了英语母语使用者和非母语使用者实施拒绝言语行为时的异同。该研究的研究对象为40名澳大利亚英语母语使用者和40名越南英语外语学习者。场景全部为拒绝请求。数据收集方法为DCT。DCT包含

19个日常生活交际场景，交际场景覆盖不同的社会距离，即密友、熟人和陌生人，以及两种性别关系，即同性和异性。研究结果发现，澳大利亚英语母语使用者和越南英语外语学习者在拒绝策略使用上既有相似之处，也有所不同。越南英语学习者在交际中使用"Regrets""Statement of empathy""Explanation""Addressing term"策略的频率明显高于澳大利亚英语母语使用者。同时，澳大利亚英语母语使用者在拒绝时更加直接，他们采用"Statement of principle""No"和"Unwillingness/doubt"策略的频率明显高于越南英语外语学习者。两组英语使用者拒绝策略使用的差异是其不同的文化背景导致的。越南英语学习者在策略选择时更易受到社会距离和地位差距的影响。此外，在交际双方为异性时，两组英语使用者都较多采用"Regrets"策略。在拒绝同性时，越南英语学习者更倾向于使用"No"和"Statement of principle"策略，澳大利亚英语母语使用者则在拒绝异性时采用这两种策略的频率较高。

Han（2006）研究了中国英语学习者的社会文化迁移现象，并探讨了影响其社会文化迁移的因素。共有100名学生参加了该研究，含50名中国英语学习者和50名英国英语母语使用者。数据收集方法为DCT和半结构化访谈。Han（2006）设计了16个和大学生学习生活密切相关的交际场景。DCT以语义套语为单位，根据Liao和Bresnahen（1994）设计的拒绝策略分类进行编码分析。研究结果发现，中国学生在选用语义套语时，受到母语社会文化迁移的影响，这种影响体现在：①反问句的使用；②对他人帮助的回报；③接受矛盾状况，即接受解释和负面后果。Han（2006）还发现影响中国学生社会文化迁移的因素包括传统的社会心理观念、社会体制、政治因素，以及经济因素。

Geyang（2007）调查了来自3个不同文化背景的英语学习者拒绝策略使用情况。研究对象包括26名日本英语学习者、31名中国英语学习者，以及5名美国英语母语使用者。数据收集采用DCT工具。DCT的设计包含两个学术场景：①教师对报告的建议；②好朋友给予的参加口语班的建议。研究结果发现，在对以上学术场景进行拒绝时，所有参与者都采用了"External reasons"及"Disagreement"进行拒绝。然而，与日本英语学习者和中国英语学习者相比，美国的英语母语使用者更习惯直接表示拒绝。日本英语学习者比其他两组英语使用者使用了更多语义套语，他们通常在第一个场景，即拒绝教师对报告的建议时，使用了"Positive evaluation""Gratitude""Explanation""Request""Mind"策略；在场景二，即拒绝好朋友给予的参加口语班的建议时，采用了"Positive evaluation"策略。中国英语学习者在使用

"Disagreement"方面和日本英语学习者相似,在使用"Mind"和"Gratitude"策略时和美国英语母语使用者接近。从拒绝话语结构来看,日本英语学习者使用"yes-but sequence"结构较多,中国英语学习者采用"(because-) so sequence"结构较多,然而美国英语母语使用者实施的拒绝话语顺序和以上两组学生相反,他们习惯先拒绝,再表述理由。此外,地位差距对3组研究对象在策略选择方面都产生了影响。

Al-Eryani(2007)比较了不同母语和文化背景的英语学习者拒绝语策略的使用情况。在该研究中,研究对象包括20名也门英语学习者、20名也门阿拉伯语使用者,以及20名美国英语母语使用者。数据收集方法为Beebe等(1990)设计的DCT。数据分析以语义套语为单位,数据编码使用Beebe等(1990)总结的拒绝策略分类法进行。结果发现,也门英语学习者和美国英语母语使用者使用的拒绝策略相似,但在策略使用顺序、语义套语内容上有所区别。具体地说,当交际对象社会地位较低时,也门英语学习者和美国英语母语使用者都在拒绝邀请时使用了相似的语义套语,并且使用语义套语的顺序接近。也门阿拉伯语使用者在拒绝时喜欢使用"Excuse"作为拒绝语的开头。然而,也门英语学习者和美国英语母语使用者在拒绝中则喜欢先表示"Regrets"或"Positive feelings"。也门英语语言水平高的学习者和美国英语母语使用者在拒绝策略使用顺序、频率和语义套语内容上较也门英语语言水平低的学习者更为接近。

Allami和Naeimi(2011)使用Beebe等(1990)设计的DCT研究了波斯英语学习者拒绝策略使用情况。研究对象为31名波斯语母语使用者、30名波斯英语学习者。30名波斯英语学习者根据其英语语言能力分为高、中、低3类。Allami和Naeimi(2011)将以上两组学生的数据和Kwon(2003)研究中37名美国英语母语使用者的研究数据进行了对比。所有收集到的拒绝策略数据采用Beebe等(1990)对拒绝策略的分类进行编码。研究结果显示,交际对象的社会地位和言语行为产出方式都会影响英语外语学习者的拒绝策略使用。英语母语参与者和以波斯语为母语的英语参与者在拒绝策略使用频率和语义套语方面都存在较大的区别。然而,英语母语参与者的拒绝策略使用受到交际对象社会地位的影响较小。此外,中高水平的英语外语学习者受到其母语社会文化负迁移的影响较大,语用失误较多;中低水平的英语外语学习者受到其母语社会文化负迁移的影响较小,语用失误较少。

Farnia和Abdul Sattar(2010)认为,英语是英语非母语使用者跨文化交际的工具。他们比较了马来西亚英语学习者和泰国英语学习者的拒绝言语行为实施情况。研究对象为马来西亚英语学习者和泰国英语学习者各20名，所有研究对象均为在校大学生。数据收集采用DCT的方法，DCT包含3个请求交际场景：①泰国妈妈请求帮忙照看她的孩子；②泰国妹妹请求帮忙完成家庭作业；③泰国哥哥请求和他一起做飞机模型。Farnia和Abdul Sattar（2010）发现，马来西亚和泰国大学生在拒绝年长或年幼的交际对象时，都采用了相似的拒绝策略，两组学生使用间接策略的频率高于直接策略。因此，在马来西亚学生和泰国学生用英语进行跨文化交际中，几乎没有出现交际失败的情况。但是，Farnia和Abdul Sattar（2010）发现了年龄因素会影响两组学生的策略选择和策略内容。

Kittisiriprasert（2011）将研究的焦点聚集在泰国学生用英语实施拒绝言语行为上。她的研究对象为19名泰国大学生。数据收集方法为DCT，DCT中包含12个场景，涵盖不同的社会地位和社会距离的交际对象。数据编码根据Beebe等（1990）的拒绝策略分类进行。研究结果表明，泰国学生在用英语进行拒绝时，既使用了直接策略，也使用了间接策略。使用的间接策略主要包括"Apologizing""Expressing positive opinion""Giving advice""Expressing gratitude"。在该研究中，Kittisiriprasert（2011）还发现学生还使用了一些不在Beebe等（1990）拒绝策略分类中的策略，如"Hesitation""Greetings""Accepting with condition""Showing intention and caring""Expressing negative opinion""Asking for sympathy""Promising"。除此以外，Kittisiriprasert（2011）的研究发现泰国英语使用者在实施拒绝言语行为时还有以下问题：①对语言功能的不正确使用；②使用不常用的英语表达方法；③表达中存在语法错误。Kittisiriprasert（2011）还指出这些问题的存在很可能都是其母语负迁移、英语语言知识匮乏以及英语使用经验不足等原因导致的。

Hong（2011）比较了英语母语使用者和非母语使用者如何拒绝中国教授的新年晚会邀请。共有60名大学生参加了此项研究，其中中国学生30名，美国学生30名。Hong（2011）通过中心行为语（head acts）和支撑语（supportive moves）进行语料分析。研究结果显示，两组学生的拒绝策略使用情况既有相似之处，也存在差异。首先，两组学生都使用了"Addressing with title""Explanation""Apologizing""Thanking""Direct refusal""Promising future event"和"Greeting"的拒绝策略。在这些拒绝策略中，两组学生使用"Thanking""Greeting""Explanation"和"Apologizing"的频率相似。中国的英语学习者使用直接策略的频率高于美国学生，并且中国学生从不使用"Explamation""Providing alternative"和"Indirect complaint"的拒绝策略。Hong（2011）认为中国学生不使用这些策略是他们缺乏英语语言的社会文化知识所致。此外，两组学生在策略使用上的差异还受到情景因素的影响，如师生间的地位差距。同时，亚洲国家习惯采取间接拒绝策略等因素也对学生的策略选择产生了影响。

Guo（2012）探索了中国和北美学生英语拒绝言语行为实施情况。他将Beebe等（1990）的拒绝言语行为DCT进行了修改。修改后的DCT包括8个拒绝言语行为场景。8个场景中，包含2个请求场景、2个邀请场景、3个帮助场景、1个建议场景。在场景设计中，Guo（2012）将强加程度、社会距离以及地位差距都纳入考虑。结果发现两组学生在拒绝策略使用上的相似之处多于不同之处。然而，值得一提的是，北美学生使用直接策略的频率高于中国学生；两组学生使用"Reason"策略的频率最高，但是北美学生在交际中的"Reason"内容更为广泛，表达更为直接。总的来说，中国学生使用"Reason"和"Statement of alternative"策略的频率最高，而美国学生使用"Regrets"和"Consideration of interlocutor's feelings"策略的频率最高。此外，两组学生在交际中对拒绝策略的选择都受到了交际场景、社会距离和地位差距的影响。例如，中国学生几乎不会拒绝社会地位高于自己的人，并且对话中的语言简洁，策略使用较少。此外，中国学生在交际中还很注意称呼语的使用，而北美学生在交际中更在乎个人权利。Guo（2012）认为，中国和北美学生的拒绝言语行为策略使用差异在很大程度上受到其不同母语文化的影响。

Al-Shboul等（2012）比较了不同文化背景的二语学习者拒绝言语行为实施情况。研究对象为6名约旦英语二语学习者和6名马来西亚英语二语学习者。数据收集方式为DCT，数据分析根据Beebe等（1990）总结的拒绝策略分类方法进行。结果表明，两组学生使用的拒绝策略种类和策略使用频率都相似。这是因为两种文化背景的英语学习者有相似的宗教信仰和集体主义文化取向。然而，无论交际对象的社会地位如何，约旦英语学习者在拒绝时更倾向于使用间接策略，而马来西亚英语学习者在拒绝地位更高或平等的人时更倾向于采用直接策略。此外，马来西亚英语学习者使用"Gratitude"和"Statement of philosophy"策略的频率明显高于约旦英语学习者，而约旦英语学习者使用"Promise of future acceptance"的频率明显高于马来西亚英语学习者。

Farnia和Wu（2012）比较了中国英语学习者和马来西亚英语学习者拒绝邀请时采用的策略。中国英语学习者均为国际生，马来西亚英语学习者均为在马来西亚学习的学生。数据收集方式为DCT，包含两个交际场景。交际对象的关系分别为平等关系（朋友间）和高-低社会地位关系（导师和说话者）。

结果显示，中国学生最常使用"Excuse""Explanation""Reason"策略，其次是"Statement of regret"策略；马来西亚学生最常使用"Statement of regret"策略，其次是"Excuse""Explanation""Reason"策略。两组学生第三常用的拒绝策略均为"Negative ability/willingness"。数据显示，在拒绝朋友时，中国学生采用"Expression of gratitude"和"Statement of regret"策略的频率明显比马来西亚学生高；马来西亚学生使用"Alerter"（即"sir"和"dear"）和"Repayment"的频率明显高于中国学生。在拒绝导师时，马来西亚学生使用"Statement of regret""Expression of negative ability""Greetings""Alternative"及"Repayment"策略的频率明显高于中国学生。Farnia 和 Wu（2012）还发现语法能力对两组学生的策略使用频率产生了一定的影响。此外，该研究还发现两组学生拒绝话语的计划和实施都受到其母语文化的影响。

Shishavan 和 Sharifian（2013）比较了波斯语（L1）和英语（L2）使用者拒绝策略使用情况。他们将性别和交际对象的社会地位作为变量，研究了86名约旦英语专业大学生的拒绝策略使用情况。数据收集采用 DCT 和小组访谈相结合的方法。数据分析基于修改过的 Beebe 等（1990）的拒绝策略分类。在数据分析时，Shishavan 和 Sharifian（2013）将拒绝话语分为中心行为语（head acts）和支撑语（supportive moves）进行分析。研究结果表明，波斯语（L1）和英语（L2）使用者在拒绝策略中心行为语使用上相似。在直接策略方面，他们都习惯使用"Statements of negative ability/willingness""Explicit refusals"和"Hedge performative"策略；在间接策略方面，他们都选择了"Statement of alternatives""Reasons and Explanations""Conditional acceptance""Letting the interlocutor off the hook"策略。此外，尽管波斯语（L1）和英语（L2）使用者在拒绝时选择使用的支撑语相似，并且这种策略选择的相似性不受性别和社会地位的影响，但两种语言使用者使用支撑语的频率是不同的。从小组访谈得知，英语（L2）使用者在实施拒绝言语行为时会将母语文化中的礼貌原则和由于社会距离产生的敬语影响移植到目标语中。

Boonkongsaen（2013）研究了泰国英语学习者和菲律宾英语学习者拒绝言语行为的实施情况。在该研究中，研究对象为30名泰国英语教师和30名菲律宾英语教师。数据收集采用 DCT 进行，DCT 共含有12个交际场景，分别为邀请、建议、帮助和请求场景。收集到的数据依据 Beebe 等（1990）的拒绝策略分类进行编码分析，并计算各种策略的使用频率。总的来说，Boonkongsaen（2013）发现泰国英语学习者和菲律宾英语学习者使用间接拒绝策略的频率都明显高于直接策略。但是，菲律宾学生采用直接策略的频率明显高于泰国学生。此外，两组学生使用"Explanation"的频率最高，其次为"Regret"策略。此外，泰国学生在拒绝策略的选择在很大程度受到话语引出手段和交际对象社会地位的影响。也就是说，泰国学生使用直接策略的频率明显低于菲律宾学生，尤其是当泰国学生交际对象的社会地位较高时。Boonkongsaen（2013）认为，该研究发现体现了两组学生用英语进行交际时，都受到了其母语文化的影响。泰国学生更多地使用间接策略，是因为泰国人在交际中对社会地位更加敏感。

Lin（2014）研究了中国学生和美国学生的英语拒绝策略使用情况。该研究的研究对象为30名中国母语普通话使用者、30名来自中国的英语学习者和30名来自美国的英语使用者。研究工具为调查问卷和DCT。DCT根据Beebe等（1990）对拒绝策略的分类进行编码。问卷调查结果显示，中国的英语学习者在拒绝别人时对面子威胁的敏感度比其他两组学生都强，因此，中国的英语学习者使用间接策略和附加语（adjuncts）的频率最高。在使用直接策略方面，3组学生都常用"Negative ability"和缓和策略。此外，"Explanation"策略是中国母语普通话使用者最常使用的间接策略。中国母语普通话使用者最常用的解释为家里有事或身体不适。Lin（2014）认为，这种现象的出现是受到了中国母语文化的影响，中国母语普通话使用者在拒绝时，习惯先进行解释，再表示遗憾；而中国英语学习者和美国英语母语使用者则更多在解释或否定能力（negative ability）后再表示遗憾。

在表2.4中，笔者从研究目的、研究对象、研究工具、数据分析以及研究结果等方面对前期拒绝言语行为的策略使用研究成果进行了总结。

表2.4 拒绝言语行为策略使用前期研究成果

1. Beebe等（1990）：Pragmatic transfer in ESL refusals	
Purpose（s）of the study	探究了英语二语学习者拒绝言语行为的语用迁移。
Participants	60名英语二语学习者。日语母语说日语的参与者20名，日语母语说英语的参与者20名，美国英语母语者20名。
Instruments	DCT，共含12个场景，包含拒绝请求、拒绝邀请、拒绝给予、拒绝建议各3个。每一类场景都包含对地位高、地位平等和地位低的交际对象各1个。
Data Analysis	（1）拒绝言语行为数据通过语义套语进行分析；（2）数据编码通过拒绝策略分类进行。

续表2.4

Results	(1) 日语母语的英语学习者在拒绝策略使用上主要有三类母语负迁移情况：语义套语顺序、语义套语使用频率、语义套语内容。 (2) 用日语参与的日语母语者和用英语参与的日语母语者间在拒绝地位比自己高或地位比自己低的交际对象时采用了不同的拒绝策略。 (3) 美国英语母语参与者在拒绝地位和自己相同的交际对象和比自己地位高的交际对象时采用了不同的拒绝策略。
2. Sairhun（1999）：English refusal strategies in Thai learners of English as a foreign language：a study of pragmatic transfer	
Purpose（s）of the study	研究了泰国英语学习者拒绝言语行为中语用迁移情况。
Participants	50名美国大学生和50名泰国大学生。
Instruments	DCT，12个场景，其中6个为请求场景，6个为建议场景。
Data Analysis	(1) 描述性统计分析； (2) 内容分析法。
Results	(1) 泰国学生在拒绝时多用间接策略，而美国学生则喜欢使用直接策略； (2) 泰国学生使用英语进行拒绝时，受到了母语负迁移的影响。
3. Kwon（2003）：Pragmatic transfer and proficiency in refusals of Korean EFL learners	
Purpose(s) of the study	研究韩国英语外语学习者的拒绝言语行为语用迁移情况。
Participants	118名研究对象，其中韩语母语使用者40名，美国英语使用者37名，韩语为母语的英语使用者111名。
Instruments	DCT。
Data Analysis	(1) 描述性统计分析； (2) 单因素方差分析； (3) 内容分析法。
Results	(1) 高水平的英语学习者由于其语言水平较高，受到语用迁移的影响最大； (2) 英语水平高的韩语母语使用者还能较好的迁移语调； (3) 英语语言水平高的学习者使用直接策略的频率更高； (4) 英语语言水平高的学习者在拒绝时比韩语母语使用者和英语母语使用者更加啰唆和委婉，对韩语拒绝策略和英语拒绝策略都存在过度使用现象。
4. Tanck（2004）：Speech act sets of refusal and complaint：a comparison of native and non-native English speakers' production	
Purpose（s）of the study	研究英语拒绝言语行为和抱怨言语行为实施情况。

续表2.4

Participants	12名英语母语使用者和13名英语外语学习者,13名英语外语学习者包括以中文、海地克里奥尔语、韩语、波兰语、俄语、塞尔维亚语、西班牙语和泰语为母语的学习者。
Instruments	DCT。
Data Analysis	(1) 描述性统计分析; (2) 独立样本T检验。
Results	(1) 英语母语使用者和英语外语学习者在拒绝邀请时都普遍使用了"Excuse""Expression of regret""Offer of alternative"策略; (2) 英语外语学习者比英语母语使用者较少使用"Excuses"或"Alternatives"策略; (3) 英语外语学习者比英语母语使用者较少使用"Regrets"或"Alternatives"策略。

5. Al-Kahtani(2005):Refusals realizations in three different cultures: a speech act theoretically-based cross-cultural study

Purpose(s) of the study	比较了英语母语使用者和英语外语学习者的拒绝策略。
Participants	3组不同语言文化背景的英语使用者,分别为10名美国英语母语使用者、10名阿拉伯英语学习者和10名日本英语学习者。
Instruments	DCT。
Data Analysis	(1) 依据Beebe等(1990)总结的拒绝策略分类; (2) 单因素方差分析; (3) 内容分析法。
Results	(1) 阿拉伯英语学习者和日本英语学习者在使用"Excuse"策略时不如美国英语母语使用者清晰; (2) 日本英语学习者使用"Statement of principle"和"Statement of philosophy"策略的频率高于其他两组研究对象; (3) 阿拉伯英语学习者和日本英语学习者在交际中比美国英语母语使用者更倾向于使用正式的表达方式。

6. Wannaruk(2005,2008):Pragmatic transfer in Thai EFL refusals

Purpose(s) of the study	研究泰国学生用英语进行拒绝时的语用迁移情况。
Participants	120名研究对象,其中40名泰国学生用泰语进行拒绝,40名泰国学生用英语进行拒绝,还有40名美国学生用英语实施拒绝言语行为。

续表2.4

Instruments	(1) DCT,12个场景,3个请求场景,3个建议场景,3个邀请场景以及3个提供帮助场景。每类场景都包含社会地位高、平等或低的交际对象各1个,每类场景中还含有熟悉和不熟悉社会距离的交际对象; (2) 访谈。
Data Analysis	(1) 内容分析法; (2) 单因素方差分析。
Results	(1) 在3个方面受到了其母语或母语文化的影响:①拒绝策略选择;②拒绝策略表达话语长度;③拒绝策略内容。 (2) 3组学生的策略选择都受到了交际对象社会地位和拒绝话语引出行为的影响。 (3) 英语语言水平高的泰国学生能够更加清楚完整的说明拒绝的原因,而英语水平低的泰国学生在进行解释时则更像是逐字逐句翻译母语。

7. Nguyen（2006）：Cross-cultural pragmatics: refusals of requests by Australian native speakers of English and Vietnamese learners of English

Purpose (s) of the study	研究英语母语使用者和非母语使用者实施拒绝言语行为时的异同。
Participants	40名澳大利亚英语母语使用者和40名越南英语外语学习者。
Instruments	DCT,包含19个日常生活交际场景,覆盖不同的社会距离及性别。
Data Analysis	(1) 内容分析法; (2) 独立样本T检验。
Results	(1) 越南英语学习者在交际中使用"Regrets""Statement of empathy""Explanation""Addressing term"策略的频率明显高于澳大利亚英语母语使用者; (2) 澳大利亚英语母语使用者在拒绝时更加直接,他们采用"Statement of principle""No"和"Unwillingness/doubt"策略的频率明显高于越南英语外语学习者; (3) 两组英语使用者拒绝策略使用的差异是由于其不同的文化背景导致的; (4) 越南英语学习者在策略选择时更易受到社会距离和地位差距的影响; (5) 在交际双方为异性时,两组英语使用者都较多采用"Regrets"策略。在拒绝同性时,越南英语学习者更倾向于使用"No"和"Statement of principle"策略,澳大利亚英语母语使用者则在拒绝异性时采用这两种策略的频率较高。

8. Han（2006）：On the classification of speech act refusals in Chinese: evidence and motivating factors

续表2.4

Purpose(s) of the study	(1) 研究中国英语学习者的社会文化迁移现象； (2) 探讨影响其社会文化迁移的因素。
Participants	50名中国英语学习者和50名英国英语母语使用者。
Instruments	(1) DCT； (2) 半结构化访谈。
Data Analysis	(1) 描述性统计分析； (2) 内容分析法。
Results	(1) 中国学生在选用语义套语时，受到母语社会文化迁移的影响； (2) 影响中国学生社会文化迁移的因素包括传统的社会心理观念、社会体制、政治因素，以及经济因素。

9. Geyang (2007): A pilot study on refusal to suggestions in English by Japanese and Chinese EFL learners

Purpose(s) of the study	调查了来自不同文化背景的英语学习者拒绝策略使用情况。
Participants	26名日本英语学习者、31名中国英语学习者和5名美国英语母语使用者。
Instruments	DCT。
Data Analysis	(1) 内容分析法； (2) 描述性统计分析； (3) 单因素方差分析。
Results	(1) 和日本英语学习者和中国英语学习者相比，美国的英语母语使用者更习惯直接表示拒绝； (2) 日本英语学习者比其他两组英语使用者使用了更多语义套语； (3) 3国学生使用语义套语的顺序不同； (4) 地位差距对3组研究对象在策略选择方面都产生了影响。

10. Al-Eryani (2007): Refusal strategies by Yemeni EFL learners

Purpose(s) of the study	比较不同母语和文化背景的英语学习者拒绝语策略使用情况。
Participants	20名也门英语学习者，20名也门阿拉伯语使用者，以及20名美国英语母语使用者。
Instruments	DCT。
Data Analysis	(1) 内容分析法； (2) 描述性统计分析； (3) 单因素方差分析。

续表2.4

Results	(1) 也门英语学习者和美国英语母语使用者使用的拒绝策略相似，但在策略使用顺序、语义套语内容上有所区别； (2) 也门英语语言水平高的学习者和美国英语母语使用者在拒绝策略使用顺序、频率和语义套语内容上较也门英语语言水平低的学习者更为接近。

11. Allami 和 Naeimi（2011）：A cross-linguistic study of refusals: an analysis of pragmatic competence development in Iranian EFL learners

Purpose(s) of the study	研究波斯英语学习者拒绝策略使用情况。
Participants	31名波斯语母语使用者和30名波斯英语学习者。
Instruments	DCT。
Data Analysis	(1) 内容分析法； (2) 描述性统计分析； (3) 单因素方差分析。
Results	(1) 交际对象的社会地位和言语行为产出方式都会影响英语外语学习者的拒绝策略使用； (2) 英语母语参与者和以波斯语为母语的英语参与者在拒绝策略使用频率和语义套语方面都存在较大的区别； (3) 英语母语参与者的拒绝策略使用受到交际对象社会地位的影响较小； (4) 中高水平的英语外语学习者受到其母语社会文化负迁移的影响较大，语用失误较多；中低水平的英语外语学习者受到其母语社会文化负迁移的影响较小，语用失误较少。

12. Farnia 和 Abdul Sattar（2010）：Intercultural communication: Malay and Thai university students' refusals to request

Purpose(s) of the study	比较了马来西亚英语学习者和泰国英语学习者的拒绝言语行为实施情况。
Participants	马来西亚英语学习者和泰国英语学习者各20名。
Instruments	DCT。
Data Analysis	(1) 内容分析法； (2) 描述性统计分析； (3) 独立样本T检验。
Results	(1) 马来西亚和泰国大学生在拒绝年长或年幼的交际对象时，都采用了相似的拒绝策略，两组学生使用间接策略的频率高于直接策略； (2) 年龄因素会影响两组学生的策略选择和策略内容。

13. Kittisiriprasert（2011）English refusal strategies used by Silpakorn University postgraduate students

续表2.4

Purpose(s) of the study	研究泰国学生用英语实施拒绝言语行为策略使用情况。
Participants	19名泰国大学生。
Instruments	DCT。
Data Analysis	(1) 内容分析法； (2) 描述性统计分析。
Results	(1) 泰国学生在用英语进行拒绝时，既使用了直接策略，也使用了间接策略。 (2) 泰国英语使用者在实施拒绝言语行为时还有以下问题：①对语言功能的不正确使用；②使用不常用的英语表达方法；③表达中存在语法错误。 (3) 泰国学生这些问题的存在很可能都是由于其母语负迁移，英语语言知识匮乏以及英语使用经验不足等原因导致的。

14. Hong (2011): Refusals in Chinese: how do L1 and L2 differ?

Purpose(s) of the study	比较英语母语使用者和非母语使用者如何拒绝中国教授的新年晚会邀请。
Participants	中国学生30名和美国学生30名。
Instruments	DCT。
Data Analysis	(1) 内容分析法； (2) 描述性统计分析； (3) 独立样本T检验。
Results	(1) 两组学生的拒绝策略使用情况既有相似之处，也存在差异； (2) 两组学生在策略使用上的差异还受到情景因素的影响； (3) 亚洲国家习惯采取间接拒绝策略等因素也对学生的策略选择产生了影响。

15. Guo (2012): Chinese and American refusal strategy: a cross-cultural approach

Purpose(s) of the study	探索了中国和北美学生英语拒绝言语行为实施情况。
Participants	DCT。
Instruments	中国大学生英语学习者和北美以英语为母语的大学生。
Data Analysis	(1) 内容分析法； (2) 描述性统计分析； (3) 独立样本T检验。

续表2.4

Results	(1) 两组学生在拒绝策略使用上的相似之处多于不同之处； (2) 北美学生使用直接策略的频率高于中国学生； (3) 两组学生在交际中对拒绝策略的选择都受到了交际场景、社会距离和地位差距的影响； (4) 中国和北美学生的拒绝言语行为策略使用差异在很大程度上受到其不同母语文化的影响。

16. Al-Shboul 等（2012）：An intercultural study of refusal strategies in English between Jordanian EFL and Malay ESL postgraduatestudents	
Purpose(s) of the study	比较不同文化背景的二语学习者拒绝言语行为实施情况。
Participants	6名约旦英语二语学习者和6名马来西亚英语二语学习者。
Instruments	DCT。
Data Analysis	(1) 内容分析法； (2) 描述性统计分析； (3) 独立样本T检验。
Results	(1) 两组学生使用的拒绝策略种类和策略使用频率都相似； (2) 无论交际对象的社会地位如何，约旦英语学习者在拒绝时更倾向于使用间接策略，而马来西亚英语学习者在拒绝地位更高或平等的人时更倾向于采用直接策略； (3) 马来西亚英语学习者使用"Gratitude"和"Statement of philosophy"策略的频率明显高于约旦英语学习者，而约旦英语学习者使用"Promise of future acceptance"的频率明显高于马来西亚英语学习者。

17. Farnia 和 Wu（2012）：An intercultural communication study of Chinese and Malaysian university students' refusal to invitation	
Purpose(s) of the study	比较了中国英语学习者和马来西亚英语学习者拒绝邀请时采用的策略。
Participants	中国英语学习者均为国际生，马来西亚英语学习者均为在马来西亚学习的学生。
Instruments	DCT。
Data Analysis	(1) 内容分析法； (2) 描述性统计分析； (3) 独立样本T检验。

续表2.4

Results	(1) 中国学生最常使用"Excuse""Explanation""Reason"策略，其次是"Statement of regret"策略；马来西亚学生最常使用"Statement of regret"策略，其次是"Excuse""Explanation""Reason"策略。 (2) 在拒绝朋友时，中国学生采用"Expression of gratitude"和"Statement of regret"策略的频率明显比马来西亚学生高；马来西亚学生使用"Alerter"（即"sir"和"dear"）和"Repayment"的频率明显高于中国学生。 (3) 在拒绝导师时，马来西亚学生使用"Statement of regret""Expression of negative ability""Greetings""Alternative"以及"Repayment"策略的频率明显高于中国学生。 (4) 语法能力和母语文化对两组学生的策略使用频率产生了一定的影响。
18. Shishavan 和 Sharifian（2013）：Refusal strategies in L1 and L2：a study of Persian-speaking learners of English	
Purpose(s) of the study	比较了波斯语（L1）和英语（L2）使用者拒绝策略使用情况。
Participants	86 名约旦英语专业大学生。
Instruments	(1) DCT； (2) 小组访谈。
Data Analysis	(1) 内容分析法； (2) 描述性统计分析； (3) 独立样本 T 检验。
Results	(1) 波斯语（L1）和英语（L2）使用者在拒绝策略中心行为语使用上相似； (2) 波斯语（L1）和英语（L2）使用者使用支撑语的频率不同； (3) 英语（L2）使用者在实施拒绝言语行为时会将母语文化中的礼貌原则和由于社会距离产生的敬语影响移植到目标语中。
19. Boonkongsaen（2013）：Filipinos and Thais saying "no" in English	
Purpose(s) of the study	研究泰国英语学习者和菲律宾英语学习者拒绝言语行为的实施情况。
Participants	30 名泰国英语教师和 30 名菲律宾英语教师。
Instruments	DCT。
Data Analysis	(1) 内容分析法； (2) 描述性统计分析； (3) 独立样本 T 检验。

续表2.4

Results	(1) 泰国英语学习者和菲律宾英语学习者使用间接拒绝策略的频率都明显高于直接策略； (2) 泰国学生在拒绝策略的选择在很大程度受到话语引出手段和交际对象社会地位的影响； (3) 两组学生用英语进行交际时，都受到了其母语文化的影响。
20. Lin（2014）：An interlanguage pragmatic study on Chinese EFL learners' refusal: perception and performance	
Purpose(s) of the study	研究中国学生和美国学生的英语拒绝策略使用情况。
Participants	30名中国母语普通话使用者、30名来自中国的英语学习者，以及30名来自美国的英语使用者。
Instruments	(1) 调查问卷； (2) DCT。
Data Analysis	(1) 内容分析法； (2) 描述性统计分析； (3) 单因素方差分析。
Results	(1) 中国的英语学习者使用间接策略和附加语（adjuncts）的频率最高； (2) 中国母语普通话使用者在拒绝时，习惯先进行解释，再表示遗憾，而中国英语学习者和美国英语母语使用者则更多在解释或否定能力（Negative ability）后再表示遗憾。

总的来说，以上对拒绝策略的研究都是围绕以下研究问题展开：①比较两门或两门以上语言使用者（如中文、泰语、马来语、英语等）对拒绝语策略的选择、使用频率、策略使用顺序及策略内容的异同；②比较英语母语使用者和英语非母语使用者对拒绝语策略的选择、使用频率、策略使用顺序及策略内容的异同。以上研究的主要发现有：①为了减少拒绝言语行为的面子威胁程度，间接策略使用的频率较高，尤其是如"Excuse""Explanation""Reason"策略的使用频率最高；②非英语母语使用者的拒绝言语行为实施反映出其在一定程度上受到母语文化的迁移；③影响拒绝策略使用的因素主要包括引出言语行为类型、社会距离、地位差距、母语文化、目标语水平、教学干预等；④英语母语使用者，如美国人或澳大利亚人使用直接拒绝策略的频率比英语非母语使用者高，尤其是亚洲英语非母语使用者。以上研究发现为本研究打下了坚实的基础，使本研究立足于比较不同英语非母语使用者的拒绝言语行为成为可能。

本章小结

本章首先回顾了和本研究相关的基本概念和基本理论，如合作原则、礼貌原则、语用学和交际能力、语用失败和跨文化交际、拒绝言语行为。其次回顾了拒绝言语行为研究的主要数据收集方法。最后对拒绝言语行为研究进行了综述。本研究根据以上理论和前人的研究经验和研究成果，设计了研究框架，下一章将对本研究的研究设计和研究方法进行详细论述。

第三章 研究方法

本研究旨在比较中泰缅大学生英语拒绝策略的使用情况。本章详细介绍了本研究使用的研究方法，包括研究设计（含研究对象、研究工具、数据收集、数据分析）和预研究（过程及结果）。

第一节 研究设计

本研究探讨中泰缅大学生英语中介语拒绝言语行为的策略使用情况。在本研究中，笔者共设计了 12 个拒绝言语行为交际场景，包含拒绝邀请、拒绝请求、拒绝建议、拒绝给予场景各 3 个，探索社会地位、地位差距和强加程度 3 个情景因素对交际策略使用的影响。本节将介绍本研究的研究设计，包括研究对象、研究工具、数据收集、数据分析几个方面的内容。

一、研究对象

本研究着眼于探索国籍、性别、英语语言能力以及社会地位、地位差距和强加程度对中泰缅大学生实施英语拒绝言语行为时策略使用的影响。Kasper 和 Dahl（1991）提出在进行言语行为研究时，每组的研究对象应不少于 30 人，如果每组的研究对象达不到 20 人，则属于个案研究。因为如果样本过小，其研究结果就达不到概括一组具有共同特征的研究对象的目的。基于以上考虑和实际情况，本研究将研究对象设定为中泰缅大学生各 60 名。中国学生全部来自贵州大学，泰国学生全部来自泰国苏兰拉里理工大学，缅甸学生全部来自缅甸曼德勒大学。所有学生均为在校大学生，年龄分布在 18 至 23 周岁。抽样原则为立意抽样和方便原则相结合。参与研究的学生所学专业涵盖英语专业、计算机科学专业、生物工程专业、机械工程专业、统计学专业、电子通信工程专业、哲学专业。

除了国籍，性别也是本研究的变量之一。因此，在确定研究对象时，笔者也通过立意抽样和方便原则相结合的方法，选取了男女同学各 90 名参与本次研究。

此外，英语语言水平是本研究考虑的因素之一。笔者为了了解研究对象的英语语言水平，请他们进行了英语口语水平自我评估问卷调查。该问卷的设计基于美国外语教学委员会（American Council on the Teaching of Foreign Languages）制定的《英语语言水平指导（2012）》进行。《英语语言水平指导（2012）》着眼于评估英语外语学习者的语言水平。其语言水平评估分为听、说、读、写能力。评估问卷设计为 Likert 五级量表形式，根据语言水平从低到高，分为 novice（1 分）、intermediate（2 分）、advanced（3 分）、superior（4 分）和 distinguished（5 分）。本研究探索中泰缅三国英语学习者拒绝策略使用情况，因此旨在了解学生的英语口语水平。此外，在日常教学中，中泰缅 3 国大学生更加重视读写能力的培养，其读写能力通常高于口语表达能力（Gallaher，2011）。

在本研究中，英语口语能力将被分为两个档次进行统计，根据学生自评情况，英语口语水平处于 level 1 到 level 3 的属于中低英语水平（lower intermediate level），level 4 到 level 5 的属于中高英语水平（upper intermediate level）。学生的口语能力自我评价量表见附录一。本研究通过对 180 名同学的英语口语能力进行自我评估以后，学生的英语口语水平及性别分布见表 3.1。

表 3.1　研究对象基本情况分布

Participants		Chinese $N=60$		Thai $N=60$		Burmese $N=60$	
		L (N)	U (N)	L (N)	U (N)	L (N)	U (N)
Male (N)	90	18	12	12	18	13	17
Female (N)	90	16	14	15	15	15	15
Total (N)	180	32	26	27	33	28	32

Note: "L" is lower intermediate, "U" is upper intermediate, "N" is number

从表 3.1 可见，参与本研究的 180 同学中，有中泰缅学生各 60 名；男生 90 名，女生 90 名；英语口语处于中低水平的学生共 87 名，处于中高水平的学生共 93 名。

二、研究工具

根据第二章对前期研究的回顾可知，任何数据收集工具都存在优点和不足。数据收集工具的选择基于研究目的和研究问题。根据本研究的研究目的和研究问题，本研究将书面语篇补全对话（WDCT）和半结构化访谈作为数据收集工具，这和多数拒绝言语行为的研究使用的研究工具一致。本研究选择将 WDCT 作为数据收集工具出于以下几点考虑：首先，WDCT 的数据收集方法较易操作，并且可以在短时间内收集大量数据（Barron，2003）；其次，WDCT 的数据收集方法可以将一些情景因素有效控制，如言语行为引出策略，以及说话双方的社会距离和地位差距等（Golato，2003；Schauer, Adolphs, 2006），这就使跨文化言语行为策略比较成为可能（Barron，2003）。半结构化访谈是本研究的另一数据收集工具，半结构化访谈可以作为 WDCT 数据收集的补充，以便更深入地了解学生在实施拒绝言语行为时的心理过程，以及了解学生在不同情景因素下采用的拒绝策略的出发点和原因。在本研究的 WDCT 设计过程中，笔者将以下几个因素纳入了考虑。

（一）情景设计

在本研究中，所有拒绝言语行为引出场景均为校园生活场景。本研究的校园生活场景内容设计从两个方面入手：①从前期相关研究中借用（Beebe, Takahashi, Uliss-Weltz, 1990；Amarien, 1997；Bacelar Da Silva, 2003；Tanck, 2004；Wannaruk, 2005；Nguyen, 2006；Geyang, 2007；Félix-Brasdefer, 2008；Duan, 2008；Farnia, Abdul Sattar, 2010；Martínez-Flor, Usó-Juan, 2011；Abdul Sattar et al., 2011；Guo, 2012；Farnia, Wu, 2012）；②从中泰缅三国大学生的真实校园生活场景选取。

本研究共设计了 12 个校园生活拒绝言语行为场景，包含拒绝请求、拒绝邀请、拒绝给予和拒绝建议的场景各 3 个，并将 3 个社会情景因素，即社会距离、地位差距以及强加程度纳入情景设计中。这 3 个社会情景因素对说话者实施言语行为产生重要影响（Brown, Levinson, 1987）。在本研究中，笔者将社会距离分为两种情况，即说话者和交际对象熟悉（familiar）和不熟悉（unfamiliar）的场景；笔者将地位差距分为说话者和交际对象同等地位（equal）和被拒绝对象地位高于说话者（higher）两种情况。此外，本研究将强加程度划分为强加程度强和强加程度弱两类。当学生拒绝学校领导、教授、老师时，强加程度强；当学生拒绝同学、朋友时，强加程度弱。在场景设计中，所有场景都贴近学生的学习生活，因此，在进行交际时，学生不需要扮演任何角色（Wannaruk，2008），而只需要像在日常生活中的真实场景下一样表现（Trosborg，1995）。本研究设计的12个交际场景见表3.2。

表 3.2 本研究的交际场景分布

Situation	Eliciting act	Description	Interlocutor		
			Social distance	Relative power	Ranking of imposition
1	Invitation	A college student invites another student, to whom he/she has met several times before, to a graduate thesis defense.	+	=	−
2	Invitation	A college teacher invites his college student to a workshop on career planning.	+	+	+
3	Invitation	A college teacher invites a new college student to lunch with other students.	−	+	+
4	Request	A college student requests another college student, whom he/she meets for the first time, to complete an interview for about 10 minutes.	+	=	−
5	Request	A classmate requests his/her classmate to check his/her homework.	+	=	−
6	Request	A professor requests a college student to attend an orientation for the new students.	−	+	+
7	Offer	A classmate offers help to his/her classmate in an assignment.	+	=	−

续表3.2

Situation	Eliciting act	Description	Interlocutor		
			Social distance	Relative power	Ranking of imposition
8	Offer	A professor offers a lecture attendance chance to a college student.	−	+	+
9	Offer	A college teacher offers a part-time teaching job to a college student.	+	+	+
10	Suggestion	A new college student suggests another new college student to join in a school activity.	−	=	−
11	Suggestion	An old friend suggests his/her old friend to take the entrance examination for a master degree.	+	=	−
12	Suggestion	A professor suggests a college student to present research in a conference.	−	+	+

Note：Social distance："+" familiar，"−" unfamiliar；Relative power："+" higher，"=" equal；Ranking of imposition："+" high，"−" low

（二）情景合理性

本研究着眼于比较中泰缅英语学习者实施拒绝言语行为时的策略使用情况。为了在研究中收集到学生在日常生活中可能使用的真实语料，笔者需要了解以上12个场景是否会出现在中泰缅大学生的日常生活当中。因此，在进行数据收集前，笔者对3国学生进行了半结构化访谈。访谈对象为21名参与研究的大学生，分别为中国大学生7名、泰国大学生7名、缅甸大学生7名。半结构化访谈采用英语进行，采取一对一的方式。每位被访谈者的访谈时间约为15分钟，访谈用录音笔录音。访谈预设问题4个，即：①Have you ever refused others in your life experience? ②In what kind of situations are you likely to refuse others? ③Have you refused your teachers or professors in your school life? ④Here are 12 situations，which require you to refuse invitations， requests, offers, and suggestions. Do you think those situations are possibly happen in your daily life? McKey 和 Gass（2005）提出，在访谈中对所有被访谈者设计同样的访谈问题，有助于研究者对访谈数据进行统计和比较。

访谈结束后，笔者对访谈数据进行了分析整理。笔者根据访谈数据了解每个场景在其日常生活中发生的可能性，以确定以上 12 个场景是否应用于本研究。如果超过 60% 的被访谈者认为该场景有可能发生，该场景则将被使用于数据收集。

根据统计结果，对接受访谈的 21 名同学的访谈结果进行统计后，笔者发现每个场景都有 60% 以上的同学表示会在现实生活中发生。同时，接受采访的学生还对以上场景提出了修改意见。如场景 1，学生建议将"A college student invites another student, to whom he/she has met several times before, to a graduate thesis defense" 修改为 "A college student invites another student, to whom he/she has met several times before, to his/her thesis defense"。表 3.3 列出了被访谈同学认为以上场景可能发生的比例。

表 3.3　交际场景在现实生活中发生的访谈结果

Situation	Eliciting act	Description	Percentage of interviewees who met the situation in daily life
1	Invitation	A college student invites another student, to whom he/she has met several times before, to a graduate thesis defense.	76%
2	Invitation	A college teacher invites his college student to a workshop on career planning.	71%
3	Invitation	A college teacher invites a new college student to lunch with other students.	86%
4	Request	A college student requests another college student, whom he/she meets for the first time, to complete an interview for about 10 minutes.	86%
5	Request	A classmate requests his/her classmate to check his/her homework.	90%
6	Request	A professor requests a college student to attend an orientation for the new students.	71%

续表3.3

Situation	Eliciting act	Description	Percentage of interviewees who met the situation in daily life
7	Offer	A classmate offers help to his/her classmate in an assignment.	81%
8	Offer	A professor offers a lecture attendance chance to a college student.	67%
9	Offer	A college teacher offers a part-time teaching job to a college student.	90%
10	Suggestion	A new college student suggests another new college student to join in a school activity.	95%
11	Suggestion	An old friend suggests his/her old friend to take the entrance examination for a master degree.	67%
12	Suggestion	A professor suggests a college student to present research in a conference.	67%

  笔者根据访谈结果对情景设计进行了调整，并设计 WDCT 交际内容。WDCT 的设计以以下模式进行：①简要介绍场景；②说话者 1 发起对话（邀请、请求、给予、建议），说话者 2（研究对象）发出回应。为了不干扰研究对象对每一个场景进行回应，笔者在数据收集前没有给予任何示例，只是明确告诉学生要对说话者 1 进行拒绝。设计完 WDCT 所有 12 个情景对话以后，笔者邀请了泰国苏兰拉里理工大学的 2 名美国教师进行校对，2 名美国教师均为英语系教师，均获得英语作为第二语言教学的相关专业硕士学位，并有长期在英语非母语国家教授英语的工作经验，以保证语言表达的准确性和自然。

  本研究的 WDCT 场景设计示例如下：

  Situation 4：A college student approaches you.

  Student：Excuse me. I'm a student here. I'm working on a research project on how college students consider about online shopping. Do you have 15 minutes to have an interview?

  You：_____

  Student：Alright, thank you.

  在进行正式研究以前，笔者对 WDCT 和半结构化访谈进行了预研究

（pilot study），详见本章第二节。预研究的目的在于了解 WDCT 的信度和效度、中泰缅大学生完成 WDCT 的时间、完成时间是否合理，访谈问题数量、顺序以及访谈时长是否合理。

三、数据收集

本研究共有 3 个数据收集工具，即英语口语水平自我评估量表（附录一）、WDCT 调查问卷（附录二）、半结构化访谈（附录三）。数据收集根据以下步骤进行：首先，通过英语口语水平自我评估量表请学生对自己的英语口语水平进行自我评估，评估结果见表 3.1。其次，所有学生需要完成 WDCT 调查问卷，该问卷共包含 12 个交际场景。学生首先要完成强加程度量表，然后使用拒绝言语行为补全对话。该问卷的完成时间大约为 40 到 60 分钟。最后，笔者随机从中泰缅三国参与研究的大学生中各抽取 10 名学生进行半结构化访谈，以了解他们实施拒绝言语行为的感受。半结构化访谈采用一对一的形式进行，访谈语言为英语，每位学生的访谈时间约为 25 分钟。

完成 WDCT 问卷以后，笔者共收到 152 份有效问卷、28 份无效问卷。28 份无效问卷中有 16 人使用了母语作答；12 人在完成 WDCT 问卷时，在部分情景中没有使用拒绝言语行为回答，而是直接接受。完成 152 份有效问卷的学生基本情况分布见表 3.4：

表 3.4 有效问卷研究对象基本情况分布

Participants		Chinese N=52			Thai N=51			Burmese N=49		
		L(N)	U(N)	Total	L(N)	U(N)	Total	L(N)	U(N)	Total
Male(N)	72	15	10	25	11	15	26	10	11	21
Female(N)	80	15	12	27	12	13	25	13	15	28
Total(N)	152	30	22	52	23	28	51	23	26	49

Note："L" is lower intermediate，"U" is upper intermediate，"N" is number

从表 3.4 可见，收回有效问卷的 152 名同学中，共有男生 72 名，女生 80 名；其中英语口语水平处于中低水平的学生共 76 名，处于中高水平的学生共 76 名。中泰缅三国的参与者分别为 52 名、51 名和 49 名。

四、数据分析

（一）数据编码

本研究收集了 WDCT 调查问卷数据和半结构化访谈数据。WDCT 调查问卷收集数据为学生实施 12 个拒绝言语行为时的策略使用情况。笔者首先对 WDCT 数据进行编码处理。编码根据语义套语和 Beebe 等（1990）设计的拒绝策略分类（附录四）进行。例如：在场景 2 中，某学生在拒绝系主任关于职业规划讲座的邀请时，说到"I am really very interested in it, but I am afraid I can't go. There are many courses in that afternoon. Sorry"。在分析时，该拒绝言语行为共有四个语义套语，每个语义套语都采用了不同的拒绝策略：

（1）I am really very interested in it...（Positive feeling）

（2）...but I am afraid I can't go.（Negative ability）

（3）There are many courses in that afternoon.（Explanation）

（4）Sorry.（Regret）

在编码处理时，有时会遇到学生在同一个场景中重复使用了语义套语或拒绝策略的情况，并且中间没有出现其他语义套语，同一语义套语或同一拒绝策略都只按一次统计。如：在情景 3 中，某学生拒绝老师和其他同学共进晚餐的邀请时说到"I am very sorry, so sorry. I have made an appointment with my old friends"。该拒绝言语行为使用了三个语义套语，三个拒绝策略：

（1）I am very sorry,...（Regret）

（2）So sorry.（Regret）

（3）I have made an appointment with my old friends.（Explanation）

在该拒绝言语行为中，（1）和（2）属于同一语义套语，因此在统计时只计算一次。同时（1）和（2）都使用了"Regret"的拒绝策略，统计时也不重复计算。

同样，如果在同一场景中，即使出现了重复使用了语义套语或拒绝策略的情况，并且中间出现了其他语义套语，同一语义套语或同一拒绝策略仍按使用一次进行统计。如：在场景 10 中，某学生拒绝同学提出了参加学校篮球比赛的建议，说到"I'm sorry, I am not good at playing basketball, sorry"。该拒绝言语行为使用了 3 个语义套语，3 个拒绝策略：

（1）I'm sorry...（Regret）

（2）I am not good at playing basketball...（Negative ability）

(3) Sorry. (Regret)

在该拒绝言语行为中，(1)和(3)属于同一语义套语，但是和(2)属于不同的语义套语，因此在统计时(1)和(3)计算一次。同时尽管(1)和(3)都使用了"Regret"的拒绝策略，但(2)属于"Negative ability"策略，统计时(1)和(3)不重复计算。

(二) 评分员间信度

本研究在进行编码处理时，邀请了两名评分员进行编码统计。两名评分员均具有英语相关专业博士学位，并有高校英语专业任教十年以上的工作经验。两名评分员经过培训以后，先对 10 份 WDCT 调查问卷分别评分，对有不同意见之处进行商讨，最后达成一致。接着，两名评分员分别对所有 WDCT 调查问卷进行分析，分析结果显示，两名评分员的评分一致性达到了 96.6%。对有不同意见之处，再次进行协商，当双方仍各持己见时，则请第三名评分员进行分析。第三名评分员具有英语相关专业博士学位，并且具有教授职称，在高校英语专业有长达 20 年的教学工作经验，以保证评分员间信度。

(三) 定量数据分析

根据本研究的研究问题，本研究采取定量研究和定性研究相结合的混合研究方式。在定量数据分析中，笔者首先通过描述性统计方法分析学生 WDCT 拒绝策略使用频率；其次通过单因素方差分析解中泰缅英语学习者拒绝策略使用有无差异，不同性别英语学习者拒绝策略使用有无差异，不同英语口语水平英语学习者拒绝策略使用有无差异，不同情境因素对学生拒绝策略使用有无影响。

(四) 定性数据分析

在本研究中，定性数据分析采用内容分析法，分析了解学生在完成 WDCT 时采用的语义套语和拒绝策略情况。此外，定性数据分析法还用于半结构化访谈数据分析，以了解学生在实施拒绝言语行为时的心理过程和使用拒绝策略的原因、学生完成不同交际场景下的 WDCT 采用拒绝策略情况。在研究开始以前，笔者对研究工具展开了预研究，以确保在研究中研究工具的正常使用。下一节将详细介绍预研究的过程和结果。

第二节 预研究

在预研究中，研究对象为中泰缅大学生各10名，共30名。这30名大学生将不参与主要研究。这些学生来自英语专业、机械工程专业、物理专业、计算机科学专业、食品工程专业和管理专业。30名学生中，包含男生12名，女生18名。抽样原则为立意抽样和随机抽样相结合。

在预研究中，数据收集方法为WDCT和半结构化访谈，访谈采取回顾性访谈的形式。对WDCT进行预研究的目的在于：①参与研究的中泰缅大学生是否能完全理解12个交际场景；②每个场景是否都能引出拒绝言语行为（Martínez-Flor, Usó-Juan, 2011）；③预设的WDCT完成时间是否合理。在进行WDCT数据收集以前，笔者先让学生阅读题目要求，再通读所有场景。学生在做WDCT以前可以向老师提出和WDCT有关的相关问题。

在完成WDCT以后，笔者立即随机抽取了12名同学进行了半结构化访谈，含中泰缅学生各3名。半结构化访谈采用一对一的形式进行，访谈语言为英语。对半结构化访谈进行预研究的主要目的在于：①了解学生完成WDCT时是否受到社会情景因素的影响；②访谈问题设置是否合理；③预设置的访谈时间是否合理；④确保录音设备正常工作。

通过预研究，笔者了解到个别WDCT交际场景的设计需要修改，以便更好地引出拒绝言语行为。例如，首先，在访谈中，有学生提到"The elicitations of some situations are not clear enough, which make them difficult to conduct the refusal speech act"。为了让学生更好地实施拒绝言语行为，笔者在题目要求里增加了说明。其次，为了让学生更好地理解交际对象的社会地位，笔者将一些场景中的"teacher"改为"the dean"或"the chair"。再次，在预研究中，少数学生将拒绝言语行为实施成了"同意"。访谈中两名学生提到WDCT里的"回答"（rejoinder）让他们感到模棱两可，认为在这样的前提下，他们既可以实施拒绝言语行为，也可以表示同意。因此，笔者在预研究后对一些情景的"回答"进行了修改，以便消除学生的误解。根据预研究情况，学生完成WDCT的时间为平均46分钟，笔者将主研究的WDCT部分完成时间定为60分钟。表3.5是修改后的12个交际场景，修改后的交际场景将用于主研究，用于主研究的WDCT见附录二。

表 3.5　主要研究 WDCT 情景

Situation	Eliciting Act	Description	Interlocutor		
			Social Distance	Relative Power	Ranking of Imposition
1	Invitation	A college student invites another student, to whom he/she has met several times before, to his/her graduate thesis defense.	+	=	−
2	Invitation	The chair of the department invites his/her college student to a workshop on career planning.	−	+	+
3	Invitation	A college teacher invites a college student to have dinner with other students.	+	+	+
4	Request	A college student requests another college student, whom he/she meets for the first time, to complete an interview for about 10 minutes.	−	=	−
5	Request	A tablemate requests his/her tablemate to check his/her homework.	+	=	−
6	Request	A professor requests a college student to attend an orientation for the new students.	−	+	+
7	Offer	A classmate offers help to his/her classmate in an assignment.	+	=	−
8	Offer	The dean of a school offers a lecture attendance chance to a college student.	−	+	+
9	Offer	A college teacher offers a part-time teaching job to a college student.	+	+	+

续表3.5

Situation	Eliciting Act	Description	Interlocutor		
			Social Distance	Relative Power	Ranking of Imposition
10	Suggestion	A new college student suggests another new college student to join in a school activity.	−	=	−
11	Suggestion	An old friend suggests his/her old friend to take the entrance examination for a master degree.	+	=	−
12	Suggestion	A professor suggests a college student to present research in a conference.	−	+	+

Note：Social distance：" + " familiar, " − " unfamiliar; Relative power: " + " higher, " = " equal; Ranking of imposition: " + " high, " − " low

在预研究中，笔者预设了如下访谈问题：①What did you notice when you responded in these situations? ② Did the status of interlocutors in the situations have effect on your responses? ③Did the relationship between you and the interlocutors affect your responses? ④ Did you have difficulties in finishing the DCT, if yes, what are they? 通过预研究，笔者了解到每位同学的访谈时间约为15分钟，录音设备能够正常工作，学生们都能逐一回答访谈问题。但是，通过预研究，笔者也了解到访谈问题还不能帮助本研究更深入了解学生的拒绝策略使用情况。因此，在主要研究时，笔者增加了访谈问题（附录三）。

本章小结

本章主要介绍了本研究的研究方法（包括研究对象、研究工具、数据收集、数据分析）以及预研究的设计和结果。本研究主要有两个数据收集工具：WDCT和半结构化访谈。WDCT含12个交际场景，半结构化访谈使用录音笔录音，再转换为文字。数据分析采用定量数据分析和定性数据分析相结合的方法。下一章将介绍本研究的研究结果。

第四章 研究结果

本章旨在根据本研究的研究问题逐一介绍研究结果,即:①不同国籍的中泰缅大学生在实施英语拒绝言语行为时,策略使用有何异同?②不同性别的中泰缅大学生在实施英语拒绝言语行为时,策略使用有何异同?③不同英语水平的中泰缅大学生在实施英语拒绝言语行为时,策略使用有何异同?④中泰缅大学生在实施英语拒绝言语行为时,其策略使用是否受到社会距离、地位差距、强加程度的影响?

第一节 不同国籍的中泰缅大学生英语拒绝策略比较

本节比较了不同国籍的中泰缅大学生英语拒绝言语行为策略使用情况。本节分别从拒绝邀请、拒绝请求、拒绝给予和拒绝建议4个方面进行统计,了解不同国籍的中泰缅三国英语学习者拒绝策略使用情况异同。

一、拒绝邀请

表4.1列出了在3个拒绝邀请场景中不同国籍的中泰缅英语学习者在各个拒绝策略上使用情况和总体拒绝策略使用情况,并比较了不同国籍的中泰缅英语学习者拒绝邀请时策略使用的异同。

3个拒绝场景分别为——场景1:A college student invites another student, to whom he/she has met several times before, to his/her graduate thesis defense;场景2:The chair of the department invites his/her college student to a workshop on career planning;场景3:A college teacher invites a new college student to have dinner with other students。

表 4.1 不同国籍的中泰缅大学生英语拒绝策略使用异同（拒绝邀请）

Refusal strategies		Situation 1 Count			Situation 1 Sig.	Situation 2 Count			Situation 2 Sig.	Situation 3 Count			Situation 3 Sig.	General Count			General Sig.
		C N=52	T N=51	B N=49		C N=52	T N=51	B N=49		C N=52	T N=51	B N=49		C N=52	T N=51	B N=49	
Direct	1. Performative	0	1	1	N.S.	0	0	0	—	0	1	1	N.S.	0	2	2	N.S.
	2. No	5	0	10	T<B	5	0	10	T<B	4	1	9	T<B	14	1	29	T<B
	3. Negative willingness/ability	51	37	19	C>T C>B T>B	51	39	22	C>T C>B T>B	49	35	18	C>T C>B T>B	151	111	59	C>T C>B T>B
	4. Regret	52	48	44	N.S.	49	50	46	N.S.	50	47	43	N.S	151	145	133	N.S.
	5. Wish	2	3	1	N.S.	0	0	0	—	2	1	1	N.S	4	4	2	N.S.
Indirect	6. Explanation	50	46	42	N.S.	49	47	44	N.S.	49	44	41	N.S	148	137	127	N.S.
	7. Alternative	4	5	4	N.S.	0	0	0	—	4	5	4	N.S	8	10	8	N.S.
	8. Set condition for future or past acceptance	4	6	6	N.S.	0	0	0	—	4	6	6	N.S	8	12	12	N.S.
	9. Promise of future acceptance	16	5	2	C>T C>B	15	7	5	C>B	15	4	2	C>T C>B	46	16	9	C>T C>B
	10. Statement of principle	4	4	3	N.S.	0	2	1	N.S.	4	4	3	N.S	8	10	7	N.S.
	11. Statement of philosophy	4	5	4	N.S.	0	0	0	—	3	4	3	N.S	7	9	7	N.S.
	12. Attempt to dissuade interlocutor	2	5	3	N.S.	0	1	0	N.S.	2	4	3	N.S	4	10	6	N.S.

续表 4.1

	Refusal strategies	Situation 1				Situation 2				Situation 3				General			
		Count			Sig.	Count			Sig.	Count			Sig.	Count			Sig.
		C N=52	T N=51	B N=49		C N=52	T N=51	B N=49		C N=52	T N=51	B N=49		C N=52	T N=51	B N=49	
Indirect	13. Acceptance that functions as a refusal	2	4	4	N.S.	0	0	0	N.S.	1	3	3	N.S.	3	7	7	N.S.
	14. Avoidance	5	3	2	N.S.	5	3	2	N.S.	4	3	2	N.S.	14	9	6	N.S.
	15. Positive opinion	13	5	2	C>B	17	7	3	C>T C>B	14	7	3	C>B	44	19	8	C>B
Adjuncts	16. Empathy	2	3	1	N.S.	0	1	0	N.S.	0	2	1	N.S.	2	6	2	N.S.
	17. Pause fillers	17	3	8	C>T	19	5	8	C>T C>B	19	4	10	C>T	55	12	26	C>T
	18. Gratitude	20	13	8	C>B	22	13	6	C>B	24	15	12	N.S.	66	41	26	C>B

Note: "C" is Chinese, "T" is Thai, "B" is Burman, "N.S." means "no significant difference", $p<0.05$

在拒绝邀请时，中国大学生使用了 Beebe 等（1990）对拒绝策略分类中的 17 种策略，泰国和缅甸大学生使用了 Beebe 等（1990）对拒绝策略分类中的所有 18 种策略。3 组学生使用频率最高的 3 种拒绝策略均为"Regret""Explanation"和"Negative willingness/ability"，中泰缅大学生使用以上策略的频数分别为 151、145、133，148、137、127 和 151、111、59。在"Regret"和"Explanation"拒绝策略的使用频率上，3 组学生没有明显区别。但是，3 组学生在使用"Negative willingness/ability"策略时，使用频率出现了显著性差异。中国大学生的使用频率明显高于泰国大学生和缅甸大学生，泰国大学生的使用频率明显高于缅甸大学生。3 组学生在实施"Regret"拒绝策略时，使用的语义套语内容比较相似，他们通常都用"I am sorry"或"What a pity"来表示抱歉或遗憾，如"I feel very sorry that I couldn't come"（S2，CS5），"What a pity"（S1，TS21），"I am sorry I can't join in you"（S3，BS10）。但是，在"Explanation"策略的表达方式上，三组学生仍然有所不同。例如：中国大学生在实施"Explanation"策略时，最常以家庭为由，"My grandpa will celebrate his birthday on that day"（S2，CS2），"My mum is sick, I have to go to the hospital on that time"（S1，CS25）；泰国大学生则习惯以学校有事为由进行拒绝，如"I would have class at that time"（S1，TS8），"Our club will prepare for a party this evening"（S3，TS36）；缅甸大学生则较为含蓄，通常不直接说出理由，而是含糊地进行解释，如"I have something important to do on next Friday"（S1，ES25），"I have an appointment that day"（S1，BS40）。在使用"Negative willingness/ability"策略进行拒绝时，3 国大学生的表达方式较为相似，如有中国大学生说"I'm afraid I can't join you"（S3，CS20），有泰国大学生说"I think it might be hard for me to attend the workshop"（S2，TS36），有缅甸大学生说"I don't think I can understand your topic"（S1，BS19）。

此外，在已使用的拒绝策略中，中国大学生使用频率最低的 3 种拒绝策略是"Empathy""Acceptance that functions as a refusal""Attempt to dissuade interlocutor"，使用频数分别为 2、3、4。如，使用"Empathy"策略时，有学生说"I think you will be very nervous"（S1，CS20）；在使用"Acceptance that functions as a refusal"策略时，有学生说"I think I will try to be there"（S1，CS45）；在使用"Attempt to dissuade interlocutor"策略时，有学生说"That's not a good idea"（S3，CS29）。泰国大学生使用频率最低的 3 种策略为"No""Performative"和"Wish"，使用频数分别为 1、2、4。在 3 种使用

频率最低的拒绝策略中,"No"和"Performative"策略都属于直接策略"Direct strategies",这说明从总体上看,泰国大学生较少使用直接策略。当泰国大学生使用"Performative"策略时会说"Can I refuse to go"(S1,TS19);当泰国大学生使用"Wish"策略时会说"I hope everything goes on smoothly with you"(S1,TS39)。在拒绝邀请时,缅甸大学生使用频率最低的3种拒绝策略为"Performative""Wish"和"Empathy",使用频率都是2。在使用"Performative"策略时,有缅甸大学生说"I refuse to attend your defense"(S1,BS22);在使用"Wish"策略时,有缅甸大学生说"Enjoy your dinner"(S3,BS37);在使用"Empathy"策略时,有缅甸大学生说"I know you will be unhappy"(S1,BS16)。

根据单因素方差分析结果,在18种拒绝策略中,不同国籍的中泰缅3组大学生共在6种拒绝策略使用频率上存在显著性差异,这些策略分别是"No""Negative willingness/ability""Promise of future acceptance""Positive opinion""Pause fillers""Gratitude"。其中,泰国大学生使用"No"策略的频率明显低于缅甸大学生,中国大学生使用"Negative willingness/ability"策略的频率明显高于泰国大学生和缅甸大学生。同时,泰国大学生使用该拒绝策略的频率也明显高于缅甸大学生,中国大学生使用"Promise of future acceptance"策略的频率明显高于泰国大学生和缅甸大学生,中国学大生使用"Positive opinion"策略的频率明显高于泰国大学生,中国大学生使用"Pause fillers"策略的频率明显高于泰国大学生,中国大学生使用"Gratitude"策略的频率明显高于缅甸大学生。

例如,学生使用"Promise of future acceptance"策略时,中泰缅三国大学生的语义套语内容没有明显区别。如有学生说"Maybe I can join you next time"(S3,CS5),"I promise I will join in your celebrate party"(S1,TS50);在表达"Positive opinion"时,CS19说"I'd love to come"(S1),TS39说"It must be full of fun"(S3),BS9说"The workshop must be very helpful"(S2)。学生们常用的"Pause fillers"有"Uhh"(S1,CS27)、"Well"(S2,TS22)等;学生使用"Gratitude"策略时会说"I really appreciate for your invitation"(S2,CS48),"Thank you very much for your invitation"(S1,TS42),"Thank you for giving me this chance"(S2,BS33)。

总的来说,在拒绝邀请时,中泰缅大学生在使用12种拒绝策略时,不同国籍的大学生使用频率相似,但他们在6种拒绝策略的使用频率上出现了显著差异。中国大学生在3种拒绝策略上的使用频率上明显高于泰国大学生;在4

种拒绝策略的使用频率上明显高于缅甸大学生；泰国大学生在1种拒绝策略的使用频率上明显高于缅甸大学生；缅甸大学生在1种拒绝策略的使用频率上明显高于泰国大学生。

二、拒绝请求

笔者比较了不同国籍的中泰缅大学生拒绝请求时的策略使用情况，3个拒绝请求场景分别是——场景4：A college student requests another college student, whom he/she meets for the first time, to complete an interview for about 10 minutes；场景5：A tablemate requests his/her tablemate to check his/her homework；场景6：A professor requests a college student to attend an orientation for the new students。表4.2比较了中泰缅大学生在三个请求场景中拒绝策略使用频率。

从表4.2可见，在拒绝请求时，不同国籍的中泰缅大学生都使用了Beebe等（1990）对拒绝策略分类中的13种策略，它们是："No" "Negative willingness/ability" "Regret" "Explanation" "Alternative" "Set condition for future or past acceptance" "Promise of future acceptance" "Attempt to dissuadeinterlocutor" "Acceptance that functions as a refusal" "Avoidance" "Positive opinion" "Gratitude" "Pause fillers"。不同国籍的3组大学生使用频率最高的3种拒绝策略均为"Regret" "Explanation"和"Negative willingness/ability"。中泰缅3组大学生使用"Regret"策略的频数分别为147、139、123，使用"Explanation"策略的频数分别为141、132、117，使用"Negative willingness/ability"策略的频数分别为142、99、50。如学生使用"Regret"策略时会说"I am sorry I can't help"（S4，TS16），"I am sorry I can't be there"（S6，TS33）；在使用"explanation"策略时，有学生说"I am afraid I can't have the interview since I am in a hurry"（S4，BS21），"I have another meeting at that time and it was arranged one week ago"（S6，CS50），"I am not good at this"（S5，TS18）；在使用"Negative willingness/ability"策略进行拒绝时，有学生说"I don't understand it"（S5，CS36），"I don't think I can help the freshman in the orientation"（S6，BS27），"I had no experience on online shopping"（S4，BS22）。

表 4.2 不同国籍的中泰缅大学生英语拒绝策略使用异同（拒绝请求）

	Refusal strategies	Situation 4				Situation 5				Situation 6				General			
		Count			Sig.	Count			Sig.	Count			Sig.	Count			Sig.
		C N=52	T N=51	B N=49		C N=52	T N=51	B N=49		C N=52	T N=51	B N=49		C N=52	T N=51	B N=49	
Direct	1. Performative	0	0	0	—	0	0	0	—	0	0	0	—	0	0	0	—
	2. No	6	0	8	T<B	7	1	9	T<B	8	2	10	N.S	21	3	27	T<B
	3. Negative willingness/ability	49	34	17	C>T C>B T>B	47	33	16	C>T C>B T>B	46	32	17	C>T C>B T>B	142	99	50	C>T C>B T>B
	4. Regret	51	47	43	N.S.	49	46	41	N.S.	47	46	39	N.S.	147	139	123	N.S
Indirect	5. Wish	0	0	0	—	0	0	0	—	0	0	0	—	0	0	0	—
	6. Explanation	48	45	40	N.S.	47	44	39	N.S.	46	43	38	N.S.	141	132	117	N.S
	7. Alternative	5	6	5	N.S.	4	6	4	N.S.	4	5	4	N.S.	13	17	13	N.S
	8. Set condition for future or past acceptance	5	7	7	N.S.	4	6	4	N.S.	5	7	5	N.S.	14	20	16	N.S
	9. Promise of future acceptance	17	6	2	C>T C>B	15	6	2	C>T C>B	15	7	4	C>B	47	19	8	C>T C>B
	10. Statement of principle	0	0	0	—	0	0	0	—	0	0	0	—	0	0	0	—
	11. Statement of philosophy	0	0	0	—	0	0	0	—	0	0	0	—	0	0	0	—
	12. Attempt to dissuade interlocutor	3	6	4	N.S.	3	5	4	N.S.	2	4	4	N.S.	8	15	12	N.S

续表 4.2

Refusal strategies		Situation 4				Situation 5				Situation 6				General			
		Count			Sig.	Count			Sig.	Count			Sig.	Count			Sig.
		C N=52	T N=51	B N=49		C N=52	T N=51	B N=49		C N=52	T N=51	B N=49		C N=52	T N=51	B N=49	
Indirect	13. Acceptance that functions as a refusal	3	5	5	N.S.	3	4	4	N.S.	4	6	4	N.S.	10	15	13	N.S.
	14. Avoidance	6	4	3	N.S.	5	3	4	N.S.	6	4	5	N.S.	17	11	12	N.S.
	15. Positive opinion	12	6	3	C>B	11	7	4	N.S.	10	8	5	N.S.	33	21	12	N.S.
	16. Empathy	0	0	0	—	0	0	0	—	0	0	0	—	0	0	0	—
Adjuncts	17. Pause fillers	16	4	9	C>T	16	4	8	C>T	16	5	8	C>T	48	13	25	C>T
	18. Gratitude	19	14	8	N.S.	18	13	9	N.S.	18	12	8	N.S.	55	39	25	N.S.

Note: "C" is Chinese, "T" is Thai, "B" is Burman, "N.S." means "no significant difference", $p<0.05$.

此外，从表 4.2 可见，在已使用的 13 种拒绝策略中，在拒绝请求时，中国大学生使用频率最低的 3 种策略是 "Attempt to dissuade interlocutor"、"Acceptance that functions as a refusal" 和 "Alternative" 策略，中国大学生使用以上 3 种策略的频数分别为 8、10、13。例如，在使用 "Attempt to dissuade interlocutor" 策略时，有学生说 "I am not interested in that"（S4，CS23）；使用 "Acceptance that functions as a refusal" 策略时，有学生说 "I really don't want to miss it"（S6，CS29）；学生在使用 "Alternative" 策略时说 "I think Cherry could attend"（S6，CS35）。泰国大学生使用频率最低的 3 种策略为 "No"、"Avoidance" 和 "Pause fillers"，泰国大学生使用这 3 种拒绝策略的频数分别为 3、11、13。例如，在使用 "Avoidance" 策略时，学生多采用了 "Repetition of part of the request"、"Topic switch" 和 "Silence" 的方式，如学生说 "Ten minutes?"（S4，TS27）；在使用 "Pause fillers" 策略时，泰国大学生常用 "Silence" 的方式进行表达。拒绝请求时，在已使用的 13 种策略中，缅甸大学生使用频率最低的 4 种策略是 "Promise of future acceptance"、"Attempt to dissuade interlocutor"、"Positive opinion"、"Avoidance"，缅甸大学生使用这 4 种拒绝策略的频数分别为 8、12、12、12。例如，缅甸大学生在使用 "Promise of future acceptance" 策略时会说 "I will ask you for help next time"（S5，BS12）；在使用 "Attempt to dissuade interlocutor" 策略时会说 "That's a bad idea"（S4，BS48）；在使用 "Acceptance that functions as a refusal" 策略时，有学生会说 "I will check whether I will be free that day"（S6，BS28）；在使用 "Avoidance" 策略时，常采用 "Nonverbal" 中的 "Silence" 或 "Do nothing" 的方式进行表达。

根据单因素方差分析结果，在已使用的 13 种拒绝策略中，不同国籍的中泰缅大学生共在 4 种策略的使用频率上存在显著性差异，这些拒绝策略分别是 "No"、"Negative willingness/ability"、"Promise of future acceptance" 和 "Pause fillers"。其中，泰国大学生使用 "No" 策略的频率明显低于缅甸大学生，中国大学生使用 "Negative willingness/ability" 策略的频率明显高于泰国大学生和缅甸大学生。同时，泰国大学生使用这一拒绝策略的频率也明显高于缅甸大学生，中国大学生使用 "Promise of future acceptance" 策略的频率明显高于泰国大学生和缅甸大学生，中国大学生使用 "Pause fillers" 策略的频率明显高于泰国大学生。例如，有学生使用 "Promise of future acceptance" 策略时会说 "Maybe I can help you with the interview tomorrow"（S4，CS22），"I will help you next time"（S5，TS20）；学生们常用的 "Pause fillers"策略以"silence"或"nonverbal"方式表达的居多,也有学生使用"Well"的方式进行表达(S5,CS29)。

总之,在拒绝请求时,不同国籍的中泰缅大学生都采用了 Beebe 等(1990)总结的 13 类拒绝策略。在使用其中 9 种拒绝策略时,不同国籍的中泰缅大学生的使用频率相似,但他们在 4 种拒绝策略的使用频率上出现了显著性差异。泰国大学生使用"No"策略的频率明显低于缅甸大学生,中国大学生使用"Negative willingness/ability"策略的频率明显高于泰国大学生和缅甸大学生。同时,泰国大学生使用该拒绝策略的频率也明显高于缅甸大学生,中国大学生使用"Promise of future acceptance"策略的频率明显高于泰国大学生和缅甸大学生,中国大学生使用"Pause fillers"策略的频率明显高于泰国大学生。

三、拒绝给予

表 4.3 比较了不同国籍的中泰缅大学生在拒绝给予时的策略使用情况。本研究共设计了 3 个拒绝给予场景——场景 7:A classmate offers help to his/her classmate in an assignment;场景 8:The dean of a school offers a lecture attendance chance to a college student;场景 9:A college teacher offers a part-time teaching job to a college student。

表 4.3　不同国籍的中泰缅大学生英语拒绝策略使用异同（拒绝给予）

Refusal strategies		Situation 7 C N=52	Situation 7 T N=51	Situation 7 B N=49	Sig.	Situation 8 C N=52	Situation 8 T N=51	Situation 8 B N=49	Sig.	Situation 9 C N=52	Situation 9 T N=51	Situation 9 B N=49	Sig.	General C N=52	General T N=51	General B N=49	Sig.
Direct	1. Performative	0	0	0	—	0	0	0	—	0	0	0	—	0	0	0	—
	2. No	0	0	0	—	0	0	0	—	0	0	0	—	0	0	0	—
	3. Negative willingness/ability	47	34	19	C>T C>B T>B	45	34	21	C>B T>B	43	34	21	C>B T>B	135	102	61	C>B T>B
Indirect	4. Regret	49	46	42	N.S.	47	45	41	N.S.	45	44	39	N.S	141	135	122	N.S.
	5. Wish	0	0	0	—	0	0	0	—	0	0	0	—	0	0	0	—
	6. Explanation	47	44	38	N.S.	45	44	37	N.S.	43	43	35	N.S.	135	131	110	N.S.
	7. Alternative	0	0	0	—	0	0	0	—	0	0	0	—	0	0	0	—
	8. Set condition for future or past acceptance	6	8	8	N.S.	7	8	7	N.S.	7	10	8	N.S.	20	26	23	N.S.
	9. Promise of future acceptance	18	7	4	C>T C>B	16	7	6	N.S.	15	8	8	N.S	49	22	18	C>B
	10. Statement of principle	0	0	0	—	0	0	0	—	0	0	0	—	0	0	0	—
	11. Statement of philosophy	0	0	0	—	0	0	0	—	0	0	0	—	0	0	0	—
	12. Attempt to dissuade interlocutor	0	0	0	—	0	0	0	—	0	0	0	—	0	0	0	—

续表 4.3

	Refusal strategies	Situation 7				Situation 8				Situation 9				General			
		Count			Sig.	Count			Sig.	Count			Sig.	Count			Sig.
		C N=52	T N=51	B N=49		C N=52	T N=51	B N=49		C N=52	T N=51	B N=49		C N=52	T N=51	B N=49	
Indirect	13. Acceptance that functions as arefusal	3	5	7	N.S.	4	6	7	N.S.	5	7	8	N.S.	12	18	22	N.S.
	14. Avoidance	7	5	4	N.S.	8	6	5	N.S.	9	7	6	N.S.	24	18	15	N.S.
	15. Positive opinion	13	7	4	N.S.	14	8	5	N.S.	14	9	7	N.S.	41	24	16	N.S.
	16. Empathy	0	0	0	—	0	0	0	—	0	0	0	—	0	0	0	—
Adjuncts	17. Pause fillers	17	5	10	C>T	17	6	11	C>T	17	7	13	N.S.	51	18	34	C>T
	18. Gratitude	19	15	8	N.S.	19	16	10	N.S.	19	15	10	N.S.	57	46	28	N.S.

Note: "C" is Chinese, "T" is Thai, "B" is Burman, "N.S." means "no significant difference", $p<0.05$

从表 4.3 可见，在拒绝给予时，不同国籍的中泰缅大学生使用了 Beebe 等 (1990) 对拒绝策略分类中的 10 种策略，这些策略分别是 "Negative willingness/ability" "Regret" "Explanation" "Set condition for future or past acceptance" "Promise of future acceptance" "Acceptance that functions as a refusal" "Avoidance" "Positive opinion" "Gratitude" "Pause fillers"。不同国籍的中泰缅大学生使用频率最高的策略均为 "Regret" 策略，其次为 "Explanation" 策略和 "Negative willingness/ability" 策略。中泰缅大学生使用 "Regret" 策略的频数分别为 141、135、122，3 组学生使用该策略的频率没有显著性差异。中泰缅大学生使用 "Explanation" 策略的频数分别为 135、131、110，3 组学生在该策略的使用频率上没有显著性差异。3 组学生使用 "Negative willingness/ability" 策略的频数分别为 135、102、61，在该拒绝策略的使用频率上，中国大学生和泰国大学生的使用频率都明显高于缅甸大学生。如有学生使用 "Regret" 策略时说 "I am sorry I want to try by myself" （S7，CS29）， "I am sorry I can't do the job" （S9，BS46）；在使用 "Explanation" 策略时，有学生说 "I am afraid I can't take the job since I am preparing for the examination of the teacher qualification" （S9，CS50）；"I have an appointment with the doctor at that time" （S8，TS35）；在使用 "Negative willingness/ability" 策略时，有学生说 "I am not good at maths myself" （S9，CS10），"I can't accept your help" （S7，TS19）。此外，在已使用的拒绝给予的策略中，中国大学生使用频率最低的 3 种策略是 "Acceptance that functions as a refusal" "Set condition for future or past acceptance" 和 "Avoidance"，中国大学生在这 3 种策略上的使用频数分别是 12、20、24。例如，在使用 "Acceptance that functions as a refusal" 策略时，有中国大学生说 "I will come if I can finish my homework at that time" （S8，CS51）；在使用 "Set condition for future or past acceptance" 策略时，有学生说 "I hope I will still have this chance if I could pass the final exam" （S9，CS30）；有中国大学生使用 "Avoidance" 策略时，说 "Do you want to go swimming after class" （S7，CS31）。泰国大学生在拒绝给予时，使用频率最低的 3 种策略是 "Acceptance that functions as a refusal" "Avoidance" 和 "Pause fillers"，泰国大学生使用这 3 种拒绝策略的频数都是 18。如，在使用 "Acceptance that functions as a refusal" 策略时，有泰国大学生说 "I really want your help" （S7，TS6）；在使用 "Avoidance" 策略时，有学生说， "Let me consider about it" （S9，TS29）；在使用 "Pause fillers" 策略时，泰国大学生常用

"Urr""Right"等进行表达。缅甸大学生在拒绝给予时,在已使用的拒绝策略中,频率最低的3种为"Avoidance""Positive opinion"和"Promise of future acceptance"。缅甸大学生使用这3种拒绝策略的频率分别为15、16、18。例如,在使用"Avoidance"策略时,有缅甸大学生说"Let me consider about it"(S9,BS29);在使用"Positive opinion"策略时,有缅甸大学生说"I really want to earn some money"(S9,BS23);使用"Promise of future acceptance"策略时,有缅甸大学生说"I promise I will receive your help next time when I have difficulty"。

根据单因素方差分析结果,在以上10种学生使用的拒绝策略中,中泰缅3组大学生共在3种策略的使用频率上存在显著性差异,除"Negative willingness/ability"策略外,还有"Promise of future acceptance"和"Pause fillers"策略。不同国籍的中泰缅大学生使用"Promise of future acceptance"策略的频数分别为49、22、18,在该策略的使用频率上,中国大学生明显高于缅甸大学生;中泰缅大学生使用"Pause fillers"策略的频数分别为51、18、34,在该策略的使用频率上,中国大学生明显高于泰国大学生。例如,有学生使用"Promise of future acceptance"策略时用到的语义套语如"Can I accept your help next time"(S7,CS45),"I will attend next time"(S8,TS30)。

总之,在拒绝给予时,中泰缅大学生都采用了Beebe等(1990)总结的18种拒绝策略中的10类,在使用其中7种拒绝策略时,中泰缅大学生的使用频率相似,但他们在3种拒绝策略的使用频率上出现了显著性差异。

四、拒绝建议

表4.4比较了不同国籍的中泰缅大学生在拒绝建议时的策略使用频率。本研究共设计了3个建议场景——场景10:A new college student suggests another new college student to join in a school activity;场景11:An old friend suggests his/her old friend to take the entrance examination for a master degree;场景12:A professor suggests a college student to present research in a conference。

表 4.4 不同国籍的中泰缅大学生英语拒绝策略使用异同（拒绝建议）

	Refusal strategies	Situation 10				Situation 11				Situation 12				General			
		Count			Sig.	Count			Sig.	Count			Sig.	Count			Sig.
		C N=52	T N=51	B N=49		C N=52	T N=51	B N=49		C N=52	T N=51	B N=49		C N=52	T N=51	B N=49	
Direct	1. Performative	0	0	0	—	0	0	0	—	0	0	0	—	0	0	0	—
	2. No	0	0	0	—	0	0	0	—	0	0	0	—	0	0	0	—
	3. Negative willingness/ability	45	33	19	C>T C>B T>B	43	33	19	C>B T>B	42	32	20	C>B	130	98	58	C>B T>B
	4. Regret	0	0	0	—	0	0	0	—	0	0	0	—	0	0	0	—
	5. Wish	0	0	0	—	0	0	0	—	0	0	0	—	0	0	0	—
Indirect	6. Explanation	46	43	37	N.S.	44	42	37	N.S.	45	43	38	N.S.	135	128	112	N.S.
	7. Alternative	0	0	0	—	0	0	0	—	0	0	0	—	0	0	0	—
	8. Set condition for future or past acceptance	8	8	9	N.S.	8	8	9	N.S.	9	9	11	N.S.	25	25	29	N.S.
	9. Promise of future acceptance	19	8	5	C>T C>B	19	10	6	C>B	20	12	7	C>B	58	30	18	C>B
	10. Statement of principle	0	0	0	—	0	0	0	—	0	0	0	—	0	0	0	—
	11. Statement of philosophy	0	0	0	—	0	0	0	—	0	0	0	—	0	0	0	—
	12. Attempt to dissuade interlocutor	3	5	7	N.S.	3	7	8	N.S.	4	9	8	N.S.	10	21	23	N.S.

续表 4.4

Refusal strategies			Situation 10				Situation 11				Situation 12				General			
			Count			Sig.	Count			Sig.	Count			Sig.	Count			Sig.
			C N=52	T N=51	B N=49		C N=52	T N=51	B N=49		C N=52	T N=51	B N=49		C N=52	T N=51	B N=49	
Indirect		13. Acceptance that functions as a refusal	3	5	7	N.S.	5	5	9	N.S.	5	6	10	N.S.	13	16	26	N.S.
		14. Avoidance	8	6	5	N.S.	8	7	7	N.S.	8	8	8	N.S.	24	21	20	N.S.
		15. Positive opinion	14	8	5	N.S.	15	9	6	N.S.	16	11	7	N.S.	45	28	18	N.S.
		16. Empathy	0	0	0	—	0	0	0	—	0	0	0	—	0	0	0	—
Adjuncts		17. Pause fillers	17	6	10	C>T	19	7	11	C>T	20	9	11	N.S.	56	22	32	N.S.
		18. Gratitude	20	16	9	N.S.	20	18	9	N.S.	20	19	11	N.S.	60	53	29	C>T

Note: "C" is Chinese, "T" is Thai, "B" is Burman, "N.S." means "no significant difference", $p<0.05$

从表 4.4 可见，在拒绝建议时，不同国籍的中泰缅大学生使用了 Beebe 等（1990）对拒绝策略分类中的 10 种策略，这些拒绝策略分别是"Negative willingness/ability""Explanation""Set condition for future or past acceptance""Promise of future acceptance""Attempt to dissuade interlocutor""Acceptance that functions as a refusal""Avoidance""Positive opinion""Pause fillers"和"Gratitude"。

在拒绝建议时，中国大学生使用频率最高的 3 组策略为"Explanation""Negative willingness/ability""Gratitude"，中国大学生使用这 3 种策略的频数分别为 135、130、60。例如，在使用"Explanation"策略时，有学生说"I have already joined in the football club"（S10，CS10）；在使用"Negative willingness/ability"策略时，有中国大学生说"I'd better not present my research since I am not capable to do that"（S12，CS30）；在使用"Gratitude"策略时，有学生说"Thank you for your suggestion"（S10，CS37）。泰国大学生在拒绝建议时，使用频率最高的 3 种策略为"Explanation""Negative willingness/ability"和"Gratitude"，泰国大学生使用这 3 种策略的频数分别为 128、98、53。例如，在使用"Explanation"策略时，有学生说"In fact, I want to have a job after my graduation"（S11，TS48）；在使用"Negative willingness/ability"策略时，有泰国大学生说"I don't think I can pass the examination"（S11，TS13）；在使用"Gratitude"策略时，有学生说"I really appreciate for your suggestion"（S12，TS36）。拒绝建议时，缅甸大学生使用频率最高的策略为"Explanation""Negative willingness/ability"和"Pause fillers"。缅甸大学生使用这 3 种拒绝策略的频数分别为 112、58、32。例如，在使用"Explanation"策略时，有缅甸大学生说"I have joined in several activities"（S10，BS41）；在使用"Negative willingness/ability"策略时，有缅甸大学生说"I have never thought about that."（S11，BS37）；缅甸大学生使用"Pause fillers"策略的频率也相对较高，在使用该策略时，缅甸大学生常使用如"Oh""Right"等方式进行表达。

根据表 4.4 的数据统计结果，在已使用的策略中，中国大学生在拒绝建议时使用频率最低的 3 种策略是"Attempt to dissuade interlocutor""Acceptance that functions as a refusal"和"Avoidance"，使用频数分别为 10、13、24。例如，在使用"Attempt to dissuade interlocutor"策略时，有学生说"It doesn't suit me"（S11，CS9）；在使用"Acceptance that functions as a refusal"策略时，有学生说"I will think about that"（S11，CS33）；中国大

学生在使用"Avoidance"策略时,常常采取"Nonverbal"的表达方式,如"Silence""Do nothing""Physical departure"等。拒绝建议时,在已使用的策略中,泰国大学生使用频率最低的3种策略是"Acceptance that functions as a refusal""Attempt to dissuade interlocutor"和"Avoidance",使用频数分别为16、21、21。例如,泰国大学生在使用"Acceptance that functions as a refusal"策略时说"I don't like those activities"(S10,TS29);当使用"Attempt to dissuade interlocutor"策略时,泰国大学生说"It's bad"(S12,TS21);在使用"Avoidance"策略时,泰国大学生常使用"Topic switch"的方式,如"I am in a hurry for a meeting"(S12,TS47)。缅甸大学生在拒绝建议时,使用频率最低的3种策略是"Promise of future acceptance""Positive opinion"和"Avoidance",使用频数分别为18、18、20。例如,在使用"Promise of future acceptance"策略时,有缅甸大学生说"I will join in some school activities after I pass the final exam"(S10,BS41);在使用"Positive opinion"策略时,有缅甸大学生说"I'd love to give the presentation"(S12,BS22);在使用"Avoidance"策略时,缅甸大学生多采用"Silence"的表达方式。

根据单因素方差分析结果,在以上10种学生使用的拒绝策略中,不同国籍的中泰缅大学生共在3种策略使用频率上存在显著性差异,它们是"Negative willingness/ability""Promise of future acceptance"和"Pause fillers"。在使用"Negative willingness/ability"策略时,中国大学生和泰国大学生的使用频率都明显高于缅甸大学生;不同国籍的中泰缅大学生使用"Promise of future acceptance"策略的频数分别为58、30、18,在该策略的使用频率上,中国大学生明显高于缅甸大学生;中泰缅大学生使用"Pause fillers"策略的频数分别为56、22、32,在该策略的使用频率上,中国大学生明显高于泰国大学生。例如,在使用"Promise of future acceptance"策略时,有学生说"I want to have a job first, and when I have enough money, I will consider about that?"(S11,CS29),"I hope I can do it next time, then I can do it better"(S12,BS32);学生们使用"Pause fillers"时,常用"Well""Er"来进行表达。

总之,在拒绝建议时,不同国籍的中泰缅大学生都采用了Beebe等(1990)总结的18种拒绝策略中的10类,在使用其中7种拒绝策略时,中泰缅大学生的使用频率相似,但他们在3种拒绝策略的使用频率上出现了显著性差异。在使用"Negative willingness/ability"策略时,中国大学生和泰国大学生的使用频率都明显高于缅甸大学生；在使用"Promise of future acceptance"策略的频率上，中国大学生明显高于缅甸学生；在使用"Pause fillers"策略的频率上，中国大学生明显高于泰国大学生。

第二节 不同性别的中泰缅大学生英语拒绝策略比较

本节比较了不同性别的中泰缅大学生实施英语拒绝言语行为时的策略使用情况。本节分别从拒绝邀请、拒绝请求、拒绝给予和拒绝建议4个方面的策略使用频率进行统计，了解不同性别中泰缅英语学习者拒绝策略使用频率情况的异同。

一、拒绝邀请

表4.5列出了在3个拒绝邀请场景中不同性别的中泰缅英语学习者拒绝策略使用情况和总体使用情况，并比较了不同性别中泰缅英语学习者拒绝邀请时策略使用的异同。

表 4.5 不同性别的中泰缅大学生英语拒绝策略使用异同（拒绝邀请）

	Refusal strategies	Situation 1 Count M N=72	Situation 1 Count F N=80	Situation 1 Sig.	Situation 2 Count M N=72	Situation 2 Count F N=80	Situation 2 Sig.	Situation 3 Count M N=72	Situation 3 Count F N=80	Situation 3 Sig.	General Count M N=72	General Count F N=80	General Sig.
Direct	1. Performative	1	1	N.S.	0	0	—	1	1	N.S.	2	2	N.S.
	2. No	13	2	M>F	13	2	M>F	12	2	M>F	38	6	M>F
	3. Negative willingness/ability	49	58	N.S.	48	64	M<F	48	54	N.S.	145	176	N.S.
	4. Regret	64	80	M<F	67	78	N.S.	61	79	M<F	192	237	N.S.
	5. Wish	2	4	N.S.	0	0	—	1	3	N.S.	3	7	N.S.
Indirect	6. Explanation	61	77	M<F	62	78	M<F	58	76	M<F	181	231	M<F
	7. Alternative	11	2	M>F	0	0	—	11	2	M>F	22	4	M>F
	8. Set condition for future or past acceptance	6	10	N.S.	0	0	—	6	10	N.S.	12	20	N.S.
	9. Promise of Future acceptance	10	13	N.S.	17	10	N.S.	10	11	N.S	37	34	N.S.
	10. Statement of principle	5	6	N.S.	3	0	N.S.	5	6	N.S	13	12	N.S.
	11. Statement of philosophy	4	9	N.S.	0	0	—	2	8	N.S	6	17	N.S.
	12. Attempt to dissuade interlocutor	2	8	N.S.	1	0	N.S.	2	7	N.S	5	15	N.S.
	13. Acceptance that functions as a refusal	4	6	N.S.	0	0	—	4	3	N.S.	8	9	N.S.
	14. Avoidance	4	6	N.S.	4	6	N.S.	3	6	N.S	11	18	N.S.

续表4.5

Refusal strategies		Situation 1 Count			Situation 2 Count			Situation 3 Count			General Count		
		M N=72	F N=80	Sig.	M N=72	F N=80	Sig.	M N=72	F N=80	Sig.	M N=72	F N=80	Sig.
Adjuncts	15. Positive opinion	3	17	M<F	7	20	M<F	3	21	M<F	13	58	N.S.
	16. Empathy	2	4	N.S.	1	0	N.S.	2	1	N.S.	5	5	N.S.
	17. Pause fillers	4	24	M<F	4	28	M<F	7	26	M<F	15	78	M<F
	18. Gratitude	0	41	M<F	0	41	M<F	7	44	M<F	7	126	M<F

Note: "M" is male, "F" is female, "N.S." means "no significant difference", $p<0.05$

表4.5比较了在3个邀请场景中,不同性别的中泰缅英语学习者拒绝策略使用情况。在拒绝邀请时,不同性别的中泰缅大学生都使用了Beebe等(1990)对拒绝策略分类中的所有18种策略。两组学生使用频率最高的3种拒绝策略为"Regret"策略,其次为"Explanation"策略和"Negative willingness/ability"策略。男生和女生使用"Regret"策略的频数分别为192、237,使用"Explanation"策略的频数分别为181、231,使用"Negative willingness/ability"策略的频数分别为145、176。在使用"Regret"策略时,不同性别的2组学生的语义套语内容多以"I am sorry"和"What a pity"开头,如学生使用"Regret"策略时说"What a pity that I couldn't come"(S1,MS52);"I feel so sorry I can't join in you"(S3,FS70)。但是,在使用"Explanation"策略的表达方式上,不同性别学生提出的理由有所不同。例如:男生在实施"Explanation"时,最常以与朋友或熟人有约为由,如"I have an appointment with my classmate that day"(S1,MS12);女生则习惯以家庭或学校有事为由进行拒绝,如"I have to eat with my family this evening"(S3,FS68),"We have English corner that day"(S1,FS29)。学生在使用"Negative willingness/ability"策略时说"I can't have dinner with you this evening"(S3,BS18)。

此外,在已经使用的拒绝邀请的策略中,男生使用频率最低的策略有"Performative""Wish""Attempt to dissuade interlocutor"和"Empathy";男生使用以上策略的频数分别为2、3、5、5。例如,男生使用"Performative"策略时说"I should refuse to go to your defense"(S1,MS15);使用"Wish"策略的学生说"Good luck in your defense"(S1,MS61);使用"Attempt to dissuade interlocutor"策略时,学生说"I am not interested in that"(S2,MS29);使用"Empathy"策略的学生说"It's a hard process"(S1,MS11)。女生在拒绝邀请时,在已使用的拒绝策略中,使用频率最低的3种策略是"Performative""Alternative"和"Empathy",女生在以上3种拒绝策略上的使用频数分别为2、4、5。例如,女生使用"Performative"策略时说"I have to refuse you to for that"(S3,FS18);在使用"Alternative"策略时,有女生说"I may recommend Kornwipa to go to the workshop"(S2,FS58);在使用"Empathy"策略时,有女生说"I know You will have a hard time"(S1,FS61)。

根据单因素方差分析结果,在18种拒绝策略中,男女学生共在5种拒绝策略的使用频率上存在显著性差异,这些策略分别是"No""Explanation"

"Alternative" "Gratitude" 和 "Pause fillers"。其中，女生使用 "Explanation" "Gratitude" "Pause fillers" 策略的频率都明显高于男生，男生使用 "No" "Alternative" 策略的频率明显高于女生。例如，在使用 "Gratitude" 策略进行拒绝时，无论是男生还是女生，最常用的语义套语开头都多为 "Thank you..."，或 "I am really appreciated..."。如，学生会说 "Thank you so much to let me know the workshop"（S2，FS26），"I really feel so appreciated for having this chance to eat with you"（S3，MS16）；学生使用 "Alternative" 策略时会说 "Why don't you ask our monitor to attend the workshop"（S2，MS55），"Maybe I'd better have class at that time"（S1，MS62）。

总的来说，在拒绝邀请时，不同性别的中泰缅大学生都采用了 Beebe 等（1990）总结的 18 种拒绝策略，在使用其中 13 种拒绝策略时，不同性别中泰缅大学生的使用频率相似，但在 5 种拒绝策略的使用频率上出现了显著性差异。女生在 3 种拒绝策略的使用频率上明显高于男生，男生在两种拒绝策略的使用频率上明显高于女生。

二、拒绝请求

表 4.6 比较了在拒绝请求时，不同性别的中泰缅英语学习者拒绝策略使用频率上的异同。

从表 4.6 可见，在拒绝请求时，不同性别的中泰缅大学生均使用了 Beebe 等（1990）对拒绝策略分类中的 13 种策略，它们分别是："No" "Negative willingness/ability" "Regret" "Explanation" "Alternative" "Set condition for future or past acceptance" "Promise of future acceptance" "Attempt to dissuade interlocutor" "Acceptance that functions as a refusal" "Avoidance" "Positive opinion" "Gratitude" 和 "Pause fillers"。

表 4.6 不同性别的中泰缅大学生英语拒绝策略使用异同（拒绝请求）

	Refusal strategies	Situation 1 Mean M N=72	F N=80	Sig.	Situation 2 Mean M N=72	F N=80	Sig.	Situation 3 Mean M N=72	F N=80	Sig.	General Mean M N=72	F N=80	Sig.
Direct	1. Performative	0	0	—	0	0	—	0	0	—	0	0	—
	2. No	12	2	M>F	14	3	M>F	16	4	M>F	42	9	M>F
	3. Negative willingness/ability	45	55	N.S.	44	52	N.S.	42	53	N.S.	131	160	N.S
	4. Regret	62	79	M<F	59	77	M<F	57	75	M<F	178	231	M<F
	5. Wish	0	0	—	0	0	—	0	0	—	0	0	—
Indirect	6. Explanation	58	75	M<F	58	72	N.S.	56	71	N.S.	172	218	M<F
	7. Alternative	12	4	M>F	10	4	N.S.	8	5	N.S.	30	13	N.S.
	8. Set condition for future or past acceptance	6	13	N.S.	4	10	N.S.	7	10	N.S.	17	33	N.S.
	9. Promise of Future acceptance	10	15	N.S.	9	14	N.S.	9	17	N.S.	28	46	N.S.
	10. Statement of principle	0	0	—	0	0	—	0	0	—	0	0	—
	11. Statement of philosophy	0	0	—	0	0	—	0	0	—	0	0	—
	12. Attempt to dissuade interlocutor	2	11	M<F	2	10	M<F	2	8	N.S.	6	29	M<F
	13. Acceptance that functions as a refusal	5	8	N.S.	5	6	N.S.	7	7	N.S.	17	21	N.S.
	14. Avoidance	4	9	N.S.	3	9	N.S.	5	10	N.S.	12	28	N.S.

续表4.6

Refusal strategies		Situation 1			Situation 2			Situation 3			General		
		Mean		Sig.	Mean		Sig.	Mean		Sig.	Mean		Sig.
		M N=72	F N=80		M N=72	F N=80		M N=72	F N=80		M N=72	F N=80	
Adjuncts	15. Positive opinion	3	18	M<F	3	19	M<F	4	19	M<F	10	56	M<F
	16. Empathy	0	0	—	0	0	N.S.	0	0	—	0	0	—
	17. Pause fillers	4	25	M<F	6	22	M<F	7	22	M<F	17	69	M<F
	18. Gratitude	1	40	M<F	1	39	M<F	3	35	M<F	5	114	M<F

Note: "M" is male, "F" is female, "N.S." means "no significant difference", $p<0.05$

不同性别的两组大学生使用频率最高的3种拒绝策略均为"Regret""Explanation""Negative willingness/ability"。男生使用"Regret"策略的频数为178，女生使用该策略的频数达到了231；男生使用"Explanation"策略的频数为172，女生使用该策略的频数为218；在"Negative willingness/ability"策略的使用上，男生的使用频数为131，女生的使用频数为160。例如，当学生使用"Regret"策略时，无论是男生还是女生，都常用"I am sorry"来表示抱歉；但是在使用"Explanation"策略时，男女生的"Explanation"内容是不同的，女生常以家庭或在外兼职为由进行拒绝，如"I have to go back now"（S5，MS12），"I have a part-time job that day"（S6，FS32）；而男生则常以朋友或学校为由进行拒绝，如"My friend is waiting for me"（S4，MS40），"We have a football game with class 2"（S5，FS19）；在"Negative willingness/ability"策略的使用上，男女生都常常直接用"I can't...""I am not good at..."等。如在使用该策略时，有学生说"I have to say I can't attend the orientation"（S6，FS70）。

此外，在所有使用的13种拒绝策略中，男生使用频率最低的3种策略是"Gratitude""Attempt to dissuade interlocutor"和"Positive opinion"，男生使用这3种策略的频数分别为5、6、10。例如，在使用"Gratitude"策略时，有男生说"I really appreciate for having this chance"（S4，MS67）；使用"Attempt to dissuade interlocutor"策略时，有学生说"Please don't ask me to do such kind of things"（S5，MS56）；使用"Positive opinion"策略时，有男生说"That's great"（S6，MS12）。拒绝请求时，在已使用的策略中，女生使用频率最低的3种策略是"No""Alternative"和"Acceptance that functions as a refusal"，使用频率分别为9、13、21。如：使用"Alternative"策略的女生会说"I think my friend could help you"（S4，FS71），使用"Acceptance that functions as a refusal"策略的学生会说"I really want to come"（S6，FS38）。

根据单因素方差分析结果，在13种已使用的拒绝策略中，不同性别的中泰缅大学生共在7种策略使用频率上存在显著性差异，它们是"No""Regret""Explanation""Attempt to dissuade interlocutor""Positive opinion""Pause fillers"和"Gratitude"。其中，男生使用"No"策略的频率明显高于女生；女生使用"Regret""Explanation""Attempt to dissuade interlocutor""Positive opinion""Pause fillers"和"Gratitude"策略的频率明显高于男生。例如，在使用"Attempt to dissuade interlocutor"策略进行拒绝

时，有学生说 "I am not good at this"（S5，FS11），"I have no time on it"（S4，MS27）；在使用 "Positive opinion" 策略时，有学生说 "I'd love to"（S6，FS62），"I hope I can help you to check your homework"（S5，FS22）；学生们使用 "Gratitude" 策略时说 "Thank you for your trust"（S5，MF67）。

  总之，在拒绝请求时，不同性别的中泰缅大学生都采用了 Beebe 等（1990）总结的 18 种拒绝策略中的 13 类，在使用其中 6 种拒绝策略时，中泰缅学生的使用频率相似，但有 7 种拒绝策略的使用频率出现了显著性差异。男生使用 "No" 策略的频率明显高于女生，女生使用 "Regret" "Explanation" "Attempt to dissuade interlocutor" "Positive opinion" "Pause fillers" 和 "Gratitude" 策略的频率明显高于男生。

三、拒绝给予

  表 4.7 比较了在拒绝给予时，不同性别的中泰缅大学生拒绝策略的使用情况。

  从表 4.7 可见，在拒绝给予时，不同性别的中泰缅大学生均使用了 Beebe 等（1990）对拒绝策略分类中的 10 种策略，它们分别是 "Negative willingness/ability" "Regret" "Explanation" "Set condition for future or past acceptance" "Promise of future acceptance" "Acceptance that functions as a refusal" "Avoidance" "Positive opinion" "Pause fillers" 和 "Gratitude"。

  2 组学生使用频率最高的 3 种拒绝策略均为 "Regret" "Explanation" "Negative willingness/ability"。男生使用 "Regret" 策略的频数为 178，女生使用该策略的频数达到了 220；男生使用 "Explanation" 策略的频数为 159，女生使用该策略的频数为 218；在 "Negative willingness/ability" 策略的使用上，男生的使用频数 132，女生的使用频数为 166。如学生使用 "Regret" 策略时，常常用 "How pitiful I am"（S8，MS55）来表示抱歉；在使用 "Explanation" 策略时，有学生用了 "I want to spend more time on study"（S9，FS66），"I want to do it independently"（S7，MS52）进行表达；在使用 "Negative willingness/ability" 策略时，有学生说 "I have no experience in teaching children"（S9，FS36），"I am afraid I can't understand what people will talk about"（S8，FS28）。

表 4.7 不同性别的中泰缅大学生英语拒绝策略使用异同（拒绝给予）

	Refusal strategies	Situation 7 Mean M N=72	F N=80	Sig.	Situation 8 Mean M N=72	F N=80	Sig.	Situation 9 Mean M N=72	F N=80	Sig.	General Mean M N=72	F N=80	Sig.
Direct	1. Performative	0	0	—	0	0	—	0	0	—	0	0	—
	2. No	0	0	—	0	0	—	0	0	—	0	0	—
	3. Negative willingness/ability	44	56	N.S.	44	56	N.S.	44	54	N.S.	132	166	N.S.
	4. Regret	61	76	M<F	60	73	N.S.	57	71	N.S.	178	220	N.S.
	5. Wish	0	0	—	0	0	—	0	0	—	0	0	—
	6. Explanation	55	74	M<F	53	73	M<F	50	71	M<F	159	218	M<F
	7. Alternative	0	0	—	0	0	—	0	0	—	0	0	—
Indirect	8. Set condition for future or past acceptance	8	14	N.S.	9	13	N.S.	9	16	N.S.	26	43	N.S.
	9. Promise of Future acceptance	13	16	N.S.	13	16	N.S.	15	16	N.S.	41	48	N.S.
	10. Statement of principle	0	0	—	0	0	—	0	0	—	0	0	—
	11. Statement of philosophy	0	0	—	0	0	—	0	0	—	0	0	—
	12. Attempt to dissuade interlocutor	0	0	—	0	0	—	0	0	—	0	0	—
	13. Acceptance that functions as a refusal	6	9	N.S.	7	10	N.S.	10	10	N.S.	23	29	N.S.
	14. Avoidance	4	12	N.S.	7	12	N.S.	7	15	N.S.	18	39	N.S.

续表4.7

Refusal strategies		Situation 7 Mean			Situation 8 Mean			Situation 9 Mean			General Mean		
		M N=72	F N=80	Sig.	M N=72	F N=80	Sig.	M N=72	F N=80	Sig.	M N=72	F N=80	Sig.
Adjuncts	15. Positive opinion	5	19	M<F	8	19	M<F	9	21	M<F	22	59	M<F
	16. Empathy	0	0	—	0	0	—	0	0	—	0	0	—
	17. Pause fillers	5	27	M<F	7	27	M<F	9	28	M<F	21	82	M<F
	18. Gratitude	3	39	M<F	4	41	M<F	5	39	M<F	12	119	M<F

Note: "M" is male, "F" is female, "N.S." means "no significant difference", $p<0.05$

此外，在所有使用的 10 种拒绝策略中，男生拒绝给予时使用频率最低的策略为"Gratitude""Avoidance"和"Pause fillers"，使用频数分别为 12、18、21。例如，在使用"Gratitude"策略时，许多学生用"Thank you"（S8，MS67）来表示感谢；在使用"Avoidance"策略时，许多男生采用了"Repetition of part of request"的表达方法，如"A part-time job"（S9，MS29）；在使用"Pause fillers"策略时，男生常用如"Urr""Chai"等表达方式。女生使用频率最低的 3 种策略是"Acceptance that functions as a refusal""Avoidance"和"Set condition for future or past acceptance"，使用频数分别为 29、39、43。例如，女生使用"Acceptance that functions as a refusal"策略时说"I will ask my mum"（S9，FS78）；在使用"Avoidance"策略时，女生常使用"Nonverbal"的表达方式，如"Silence""Do nothing"等；使用"Set condition for future or past acceptance"策略时，学生说"If you had told me earlier, I wouldn't have made arrangements that day"（S8，FS72）。

根据单因素方差分析结果，拒绝给予时，在 10 种使用的拒绝策略中，不同性别的中泰缅大学生共在 4 种策略使用频率上存在显著性差异，它们是"Explanation""Positive opinion""Pause fillers"和"Gratitude"。男生使用以上 4 种策略的频率明显低于女生。男女学生使用"Explanation""Positive opinion""Pause fillers"和"Gratitude"策略的频数分别为 159、218、23、59、21、82 和 12、119。例如，在使用"Positive opinion"策略进行拒绝时，学生说"I am really very interested in teaching"（S9，FS20），"I am eager for a part-time job"（S9，MS61）；在使用"Pause fillers"策略时，学生们常使用如"Er""Right"等表示思考；在使用"Gratitude"策略时，有学生说"I am grateful to have this opportunity"（S8，FF23）。

总之，在拒绝给予时，不同性别的中泰缅大学生都采用了 Beebe 等（1990）总结的 18 种拒绝策略中的 10 类，在使用其中 6 种拒绝策略时，不同性别的中泰缅大学生的使用频率相似；但在 4 种拒绝策略的使用频率上出现了显著差异，男生的使用频率均明显低于女生。

四、拒绝建议

表 4.8 比较了在拒绝建议时不同性别的中泰缅大学生拒绝策略的使用情况。

表 4.8 不同性别的中泰缅大学生英语拒绝策略使用异同（拒绝建议）

Refusal strategies		Situation 10 Mean			Situation 11 Mean			Situation 12 Mean			General Mean		
		M N=72	F N=80	Sig.	M N=72	F N=80	Sig.	M N=72	F N=80	Sig.	M N=72	F N=80	Sig.
Direct	1. Performative	0	0	—	0	0	—	0	0	—	0	0	—
	2. No	0	0	—	0	0	—	0	0	—	0	0	—
	3. Negative willingness/ability	41	56	N.S.	40	55	N.S.	38	56	M<F	119	167	N.S.
	4. Regret	0	0	—	0	0	—	0	0	—	0	0	—
	5. Wish	0	0	—	0	0	—	0	0	—	0	0	—
Indirect	6. Explanation	53	73	M<F	52	71	M<F	54	72	M<F	159	216	M<F
	7. Alternative	0	0	—	0	0	—	0	0	—	0	0	—
	8. Set condition for future or past acceptance	10	15	N.S.	10	15	N.S.	12	17	N.S.	32	47	N.S.
	9. Promise of Future acceptance	14	18	N.S.	15	20	N.S.	16	23	N.S.	45	61	N.S.
	10. Statement of principle	0	0	—	0	0	—	0	0	—	0	0	—
	11. Statement of philosophy	0	0	—	0	0	—	0	0	—	0	0	—
	12. Attempt to dissuade interlocutor	6	9	N.S.	7	11	N.S.	9	12	N.S.	22	32	N.S.
	13. Acceptance that functions as a refusal	6	9	N.S.	8	11	N.S.	8	13	N.S.	22	33	N.S.
	14. Avoidance	4	15	M<F	6	16	M<F	8	16	N.S.	18	47	M<F

续表4.8

Refusal strategies		Situation 10			Situation 11			Situation 12			General		
		Mean		Sig.	Mean		Sig.	Mean		Sig.	Mean		Sig.
		M N=72	F N=80		M N=72	F N=80		M N=72	F N=80		M N=72	F N=80	
Adjuncts	15. Positive opinion	8	19	M<F	9	21	M<F	11	23	M<F	28	63	M<F
	16. Empathy	0	0	—	0	0	—	0	0	—	0	0	—
	17. Pause fillers	5	28	M<F	8	29	M<F	10	30	M<F	23	87	M<F
	18. Gratitude	6	39	M<F	7	40	M<F	9	41	M<F	22	120	M<F

Note: "M" is male, "F" is female, "N.S." means "no significant difference", $p<0.05$

从表 4.8 可见，在拒绝建议时，不同性别的中泰缅大学生均使用了 Beebe 等（1990）总结的拒绝策略分类中的 10 类，它们分别是："Negative willingness/ability""Explanation""Set condition for future or past acceptance""Promise of future acceptance""Attempt to dissuade interlocutor""Acceptance that functions as a refusal""Avoidance""Positive opinion""Pause fillers"和"Gratitude"。

男生使用频率最高的 3 种拒绝策略为"Explanation""Negative willingness/ability"和"Promise of Future acceptance"，使用频数分别为 159、119、45。女生使用频率最高的 3 种拒绝策略为"Explanation""Negative willingness/ability"和"Gratitude"，使用频数分别为 216、167、120。例如，男生在使用"Explanation"策略时说"I have joined in three school clubs already"（S10，MS71），女生在使用该策略时说"I want to focus on my study"（S10，FS62）；在使用"Negative willingness/ability"策略时，男生说"I am not good at my major"（S11，MS56），女生在使用该策略时说"My research is not innovative at all"（S12，FS39）；在使用"Promise of Future acceptance"策略时，男生说"I think I should take the entrance exam after I earn some money"（S11，MS10）。女生在使用"Gratitude"策略时，大多采用"Thank you for your suggestion"的表达方法。

此外，在所有使用的 10 种拒绝策略中，男生使用频率最低的策略有"Avoidance""Attempt to dissuade interlocutor""Acceptance that functions as a refusal"和"Gratitude"，使用频数分别为 18、22、22、22。女生使用频率最低的 3 种拒绝策略为"Attempt to dissuade interlocutor""Acceptance that functions as a refusal"和"Set condition for future or past acceptance"，使用频数分别为 32、33、47。例如，在使用"Attempt to dissuade interlocutor"策略时，有男生说"Don't ask me to join in that kind of activity"（S10，MS57）；女生在使用该策略时会说"I have never considered about that"（S11，FS11）。在使用"Acceptance that functions as a refusal"策略时，有男生说"I will think about it"（S11，MS66），有女生说"Maybe I could consider about it seriously"（S12，FS29）。此外，"Gratitude"也是男生使用频率较低的策略，在使用该策略时，有男生说"Thank you for your advice"（S10，MS49）。男生使用频率较低的策略还有"Pause fillers"，在使用该策略时，男生常用"Err""Well"等进行表达。与男生不同的是，女生使用频率较低的策略还有"Avoidance"和"Set condition for future or past acceptance"。在使用"Avoidance"策略时,女生常常采取"Silence"或"Topic switch"的方式进行表达;在使用"Set condition for future or past acceptance"策略时,有女生说"If my mum allows, I will join in some school activities"(S10,FS62)。

根据单因素方差分析结果,在 10 种已使用的拒绝建议策略中,不同性别的中泰缅大学生共在 5 种策略使用上存在显著性差异,它们是"Explanation""Avoidance""Positive opinion""Pause fillers"和"Gratitude"。男女同学使用以上拒绝策略的频数分别为 159、216,18、47,28、63,23、87 和 22、120。在这 5 种策略的使用频率上,男生均明显低于女生。例如,在使用"Positive opinion"策略时,有男生说"I really want to join in school activities"(S10,MS17);有女生说"It must be very challenging"(S11,FS37)。

总之,在拒绝建议时,不同性别的中泰缅大学生都采用了 Beebe 等(1990)总结的 18 种拒绝策略中的 10 类,在使用其中 5 种拒绝策略时,不同性别的中泰缅大学生的使用频率相似;但有 5 种拒绝策略的使用频率出现了显著差异;男生的使用频率均明显低于女生。

第三节 不同英语水平的中泰缅大学生英语拒绝策略比较

本节比较了不同英语水平的中泰缅大学生英语拒绝言语行为策略使用情况。本节分别从拒绝邀请、拒绝请求、拒绝给予和拒绝建议 4 个方面进行统计,以了解不同英语水平中泰缅英语学习者拒绝策略使用情况的异同。

一、拒绝邀请

表 4.9 列出了在 3 个拒绝邀请场景中不同英语水平的中泰缅英语学习者拒绝策略使用情况和总体使用情况,并比较了不同英语水平的中泰缅英语学习者拒绝邀请时策略使用的异同。

表4.9 不同英语水平的中泰缅大学生英语拒绝策略使用异同（拒绝邀请）

	Refusal strategies	Situation 1 Mean L N=76	Situation 1 Mean U N=76	Situation 1 Sig.	Situation 2 Mean L N=76	Situation 2 Mean U N=76	Situation 2 Sig.	Situation 3 Mean L N=76	Situation 3 Mean U N=76	Situation 3 Sig.	General Mean L N=76	General Mean U N=76	General Sig.
Direct	1. Performative	2	0	N.S.	0	0	—	2	0	N.S	4	0	N.S.
	2. No	8	7	N.S.	8	7	N.S.	8	6	N.S	24	20	N.S.
	3. Negative willingness/ability	50	57	N.S.	53	59	N.S.	48	54	N.S	151	170	N.S.
	4. Regret	69	75	L<U	70	75	N.S.	67	73	N.S	206	223	N.S.
	5. Wish	3	3	N.S.	0	0	—	3	1	N.S	6	4	N.S.
	6. Explanation	67	71	N.S.	67	73	N.S.	64	70	N.S	198	214	N.S.
	7. Alternative	10	3	L>U	0	0	—	10	3	L>U	20	6	L>U
Indirect	8. Set condition for future or past acceptance	7	9	N.S.	0	0	—	7	9	N.S	14	18	N.S.
	9. Promise of Future acceptance	8	15	N.S.	9	18	N.S.	8	13	N.S	25	46	N.S.
	10. Statement of principle	6	5	N.S.	2	1	N.S.	6	5	N.S	14	11	N.S.
	11. Statement of philosophy	6	7	N.S.	0	0	—	5	5	N.S	11	12	N.S.
	12. Attempt to dissuade interlocutor	6	4	N.S.	0	1	N.S.	6	3	N.S	12	8	N.S.
	13. Acceptance that functions as a refusal	5	5	N.S.	0	0	—	3	4	N.S	8	9	N.S.
	14. Avoidance	5	5	N.S.	5	5	N.S.	5	4	N.S	15	14	N.S.

续表4.9

Refusal strategies		Situation 1 Mean			Situation 2 Mean			Situation 3 Mean			General Mean		
		L N=76	U N=76	Sig.	L N=76	U N=76	Sig.	L N=76	U N=76	Sig.	L N=76	U N=76	Sig.
Adjuncts	15. Positive opinion	7	13	N.S.	10	17	N.S	10	14	N.S	27	44	N.S.
	16. Empathy	3	3	N.S.	0	1	N.S	1	2	N.S	4	6	N.S.
	17. Pause fillers	15	13	N.S.	16	16	N.S	17	16	N.S	48	45	N.S.
	18. Gratitude	15	26	L<U	15	26	L<U	19	32	L<U	49	84	L<U

Note: "L" is lower intermediate, "U" is upper intermediate, "N.S." means "no significant difference", $p<0.05$

从表4.9可见，在3个邀请场景中，英语水平处于"lower intermediate"的学生共使用了Beebe等（1990）总结的拒绝策略分类中所有18种策略，包含3项直接策略、11项间接策略、4项附加语策略。英语水平处于"upper intermediate"的学生使用了其中的17种拒绝策略，该组学生没有使用的拒绝策略为"Performative"。

不同英语水平的两组中泰缅大学生使用频率最高的策略均为"Regret"策略，其次为"Explanation"策略，第三为"Negative willingness/ability"策略。英语水平处于"lower intermediate"和"upper intermediate"的学生使用"Regret""Explanation"和"Negative willingness/ability"策略的频数分别为206、223，198、214和151、170。在使用"Regret"策略时，学生说"I feel so regretted that I couldn't come"（S2，US39）；学生在实施"Explanation"策略时说"I am a little busy"（S3，LS16），"I will leave for a trip that day"（S1，LS28）；学生在使用"Negative willingness/ability"策略时，有的说"I can't join in you"（S3，LS72）。

此外，在拒绝邀请时，英语水平处于"lower intermediate"的学生使用频率最低的三种拒绝策略为"Performative""Empathy"和"Wish"，使用频数分别为4、4、6。例如，在使用"Performative"策略时，有学生说"I have to refuse you"（S3，LS11）；在使用"Empathy"策略时，有学生说"I know you will feel nervous"（S1，LS68）；有的学生在使用"Wish"策略时，说"I wish you can pass it"（S1，LS20）。英语水平处于"upper intermediate"的学生使用频率最低的3种拒绝策略为"Wish""Alternative"和"Empathy"，使用频数分别为4、6、6。例如，在使用"Wish"策略时，有学生说"I wish you pass the defense smoothly"（S1，US22）；在使用"Alternative"策略时，有学生说"John is more suitable for this workshop"（S2，US41）；当学生使用"Empathy"策略时，有学生说"I know you will be disappointed"（S1，US61）。

根据单因素方差分析结果，在18种拒绝策略中，不同英语水平的中泰缅大学生共在两种拒绝策略使用上存在显著性差异，它们是"Alternative"和"Gratitude"。其中，英语水平处于"lower intermediate"的学生使用"Alternative"策略的频率明显高于英语水平处于"upper intermediate"的学生，英语水平处于"upper intermediate"的学生使用"Gratitude"策略的频率明显高于英语水平处于"lower intermediate"的学生。例如，当学生使用"Alternative"策略时会说"I can help you prepare for the defense"（S1，

LS25），"Maybe I will come to congratulate your success after the defense"（S1，US71）；在使用"Gratitude"策略进行拒绝时，有学生说"I really thank you for the invitation"（S3，US75），"Thank you very much to ask me to go to the workshop"（S2，LS31）。

总的来说，在拒绝邀请时，不同英语水平的中泰缅大学生都采用了Beebe等（1990）总结的13种拒绝策略，在使用其中的16种拒绝策略时，不同英语水平的中泰缅学生的使用频率相似；但有两种拒绝策略的使用频率出现了显著差异。英语水平处于"lower intermediate"的学生使用"Alternative"策略的频率明显高于英语水平处于"upper intermediate"的学生，英语水平处于"upper intermediate"的学生使用"Gratitude"策略的频率明显高于英语水平处于"lower intermediate"的学生。

二、拒绝请求

表4.10呈现了不同英语水平的中泰缅大学生拒绝请求时的策略使用异同。表4.10比较了在三个请求场景中，不同英语水平的中泰缅大学生拒绝策略使用情况。在拒绝请求时，不同英语水平中泰缅大学生都使用了Beebe等（1990）的拒绝策略分类中的13种策略，分别是"No" "Negative willingness/ability" "Regret" "Explanation" "Alternative" "Set condition for future or past acceptance" "Promise of future acceptance" "Attempt to dissuade interlocutor" "Acceptance that functions as a refusal" "Avoidance" "Positive opinion" "Gratitude"和"Pause fillers"。

在拒绝请求时，不同英语水平的中泰缅大学生使用频率最高的3种拒绝策略为"Regret" "Explanation"和"Negative willingness/ability"。英语水平处于"lower intermediate"和"upper intermediate"的学生使用"Regret" "Explanation"和"Negative willingness/ability"策略的频数分别为191、218、195、195和136、155。在使用"Regret"策略时，学生说"What a pity that I can't help"（S4，LS70），"I am sorry that I do not know this"（S5，LS22）；学生在实施"Explanation"策略时说"I have to leave now"（S5，LS17），"I have a class meeting that day"（S6，US26）；有学生采用"Negative willingness/ability"策略时说"I don't understand these exercises"（S5，LS39）。

表 4.10 不同英语水平的中泰缅大学生英语拒绝策略使用异同（拒绝请求）

	Refusal strategies	Situation 4 Mean			Situation 5 Mean			Situation 6 Mean			General Mean		
		L N=76	U N=76	Sig.	L N=76	U N=76	Sig.	L N=76	U N=76	Sig.	L N=76	U N=76	Sig.
Direct	1. Performative	0	0	—	0	0	—	0	0	—	0	0	—
	2. No	8	6	N.S.	9	8	N.S.	11	9	N.S.	28	23	N.S.
	3. Negative willingness/ability	48	52	N.S.	44	52	N.S.	44	51	N.S.	136	155	N.S.
	4. Regret	67	74	L<U	64	72	L<U	60	72	L<U	191	218	L<U
	5. Wish	0	0	—	0	0	—	0	0	—	0	0	—
Indirect	6. Explanation	66	67	N.S.	66	64	N.S.	63	64	N.S.	195	195	N.S.
	7. Alternative	12	4	L>U	10	4	N.S.	10	3	L>U	32	11	L>U
	8. Set condition for future or past acceptance	8	11	N.S.	5	9	N.S.	7	10	N.S.	20	30	N.S.
	9. Promise of Future acceptance	9	16	N.S.	8	15	N.S.	10	16	N.S.	27	47	N.S.
	10. Statement of principle	0	0	—	0	0	—	0	0	—	0	0	—
	11. Statement of philosophy	0	0	—	0	0	—	0	0	—	0	0	—
	12. Attempt to dissuade interlocutor	7	6	N.S.	6	6	N.S.	4	6	N.S.	17	18	N.S.
	13. Acceptance that functions as a refusal	7	6	N.S.	5	6	N.S.	6	8	N.S.	18	20	N.S.
	14. Avoidance	6	7	N.S.	5	7	N.S.	7	8	N.S.	18	22	N.S.

续表4.10

Refusal strategies		Situation 4			Situation 5			Situation 6			General		
		Mean		Sig.	Mean		Sig.	Mean		Sig.	Mean		Sig.
		L N=76	U N=76		L N=76	U N=76		L N=76	U N=76		L N=76	U N=76	
Adjuncts	15. Positive opinion	8	13	N.S.	9	13	N.S.	10	13	N.S.	27	39	N.S.
	16. Empathy	0	0	—	0	0	—	0	0	—	0	0	—
	17. Pause fillers	14	15	N.S.	14	14	N.S.	13	16	N.S.	41	45	N.S.
	18. Gratitude	15	26	L<U	15	25	L<U	12	26	L<U	42	77	L<U

Note: "L" is lower intermediate, "U" is upper intermediate, "N.S." means "no significant difference", $p<0.05$

此外，拒绝请求时，在所有使用的拒绝策略中，英语水平处于"lower intermediate"的学生使用频率最低的3种策略为"Attempt to dissuade interlocutor""Acceptance that functions as a refusal"和"Avoidance"，使用频率分别为17、18、18。例如，在使用"Attempt to dissuade interlocutor"策略时，有学生说"I can't let my friend wait for me"（S4，LS27）；使用"Acceptance that functions as a refusal"策略时，有学生说"I will have a try"（S5，LS10）；在使用"Avoidance"策略时，学生常使用"Silence"和"Nonverbal"策略，还有一些学生采用了"Topic switch"策略。例如，有学生说"Do not forget to tell me your opinion on Friday's gathering"（S5，LS53）。英语水平处于"upper intermediate"的学生使用频率最低的3种策略为"Alternative""Attempt to dissuade interlocutor""Acceptance that functions as a refusal"使用频率分别为11、18、20。例如，在使用"Alternative"策略时，有学生说"You should check by yourself first, if you have difficulties after that, maybe you can ask me for help"（S5，US29）；在使用"Attempt to dissuade interlocutor"策略时，有学生说"Don't ask me to have the interview"（S4，US56）；在使用"Acceptance that functions as a refusal"策略时有学生说"You want me to do that?"（S5，US63）。

根据单因素方差分析结果，在使用的13种拒绝策略中，不同英语水平的中泰缅学生共在3种拒绝策略使用上存在显著性差异，它们是"Regret""Alternative"和"Gratitude"策略。其中，英语水平处于"lower intermediate"的学生使用"Alternative"策略的频率明显高于英语水平处于"upper intermediate"的学生，英语水平处于"upper intermediate"的学生使用"Regret"和"Gratitude"策略的频率明显高于英语水平处于"lower intermediate"的学生。例如，有学生在使用"Alternative"策略时说"I can ask my friend for your interview"（S4，US72），"Maybe our monitor could come"（S6，US22）。

总的来说，在拒绝请求时，不同英语水平的中泰缅大学生都使用了13种拒绝策略。在使用其中10种拒绝策略时，不同英语水平的两组中泰缅大学生的使用频率相似。但是，在3种拒绝策略的使用频率上，不同英语水平的中泰缅大学生出现了显著差异。两组学生使用频率较高的策略为"Regret""Explanation"和"Negative willingness/ability"策略。使用频率较低的为"Avoidance""Acceptance that functions as a refusal""Attempt to dissuade interlocutor"策略。英语水平处于"lower intermediate"的学生使用

"Alternative"策略的频率明显高于英语水平处于"upper intermediate"的学生,英语水平处于"upper intermediate"的学生使用"Regret"和"Gratitude"策略的频率明显高于英语水平处于"lower intermediate"的学生。

三、拒绝给予

表 4.11 比较了不同英语水平的中泰缅大学生拒绝给予时的策略使用情况。表 4.11 分别比较了在 3 个给予场景中,不同英语水平的中泰缅英语学习者进行拒绝时的策略使用情况。在拒绝给予时,不同英语水平的中泰缅大学生都使用了 Beebe 等(1990)对拒绝策略分类中的 10 种策略。它们分别是"Negative willingness/ability""Regret""Explanation""Set condition for future or past acceptance""Promise of future acceptance""Acceptance that functions as a refusal""Avoidance""Positive opinion""Pause fillers"和"Gratitude"。

在拒绝给予时,不同英语水平的两组中泰缅大学生使用频率最高的 3 种拒绝策略为"Regret""Explanation"和"Negative willingness/ability"。英语水平处于"lower intermediate"和"upper intermediate"使用"Regret""Explanation"和"Negative willingness/ability"策略的频数分别为 184、214、181、195 和 146、152。在使用"Regret"策略时,学生常使用"I am sorry""I am terribly sorry"等进行表达;有学生在实施"Explanation"策略时说"I think I can handle it"(S7,LS9),"I will be a salesgirl"(S6,US19);有学生在使用"Negative willingness/ability"策略时说"I am afraid that I can't do this job"(S9,LS72),"I am not be able to accept your help"(S7,US61)。

表 4.11 不同英语水平的中泰缅大学生英语拒绝策略使用异同（拒绝给予）

	Refusal strategies	Situation 7 Frequency L N=76	Situation 7 Frequency U N=76	Situation 7 Sig.	Situation 8 Frequency L N=76	Situation 8 Frequency U N=76	Situation 8 Sig.	Situation 9 Frequency L N=76	Situation 9 Frequency U N=76	Situation 9 Sig.	General Frequency L N=76	General Frequency U N=76	General Sig.
Direct	1. Performative	0	0	—	0	0	—	0	0	—	0	0	—
	2. No	0	0	—	0	0	—	0	0	—	0	0	—
	3. Negative willingness/ability	49	51	N.S.	49	51	N.S.	48	50	N.S.	146	152	N.S.
	4. Regret	63	74	L<U	62	71	L<U	59	69	L<U	184	214	L<U
	5. Wish	0	0	—	0	0	—	0	0	—	0	0	—
Indirect	6. Explanation	62	67	N.S	61	65	N.S.	58	63	N.S.	181	195	N.S.
	7. Alternative	0	0	—	0	0	—	0	0	—	0	0	—
	8. Set condition for future or past acceptance	10	12	N.S	10	12	N.S.	12	13	N.S.	32	37	N.S.
	9. Promise of Future acceptance	12	17	N.S	11	18	N.S.	13	18	N.S.	36	53	N.S.
	10. Statement of principle	0	0	—	0	0	—	0	0	—	0	0	—
	11. Statement of philosophy	0	0	—	0	0	—	0	0	—	0	0	—
	12. Attempt to dissuade interlocutor	0	0	—	0	0	—	0	0	—	0	0	—
	13. Acceptance that functions as a refusal	7	8	N.S	7	10	N.S.	8	12	N.S.	22	30	N.S.
	14. Avoidance	7	9	N.S	9	10	N.S.	12	10	N.S.	28	29	N.S.

续表4.11

Refusal strategies		Situation 7			Situation 8			Situation 9			General		
		Frequency		Sig.	Frequency		Sig.	Frequency		Sig.	Frequency		Sig.
		L N=76	U N=76		L N=76	U N=76		L N=76	U N=76		L N=76	U N=76	
Adjuncts	15. Positive opinion	9	15	N.S	9	18	N.S.	10	20	L<U	28	53	N.S.
	16. Empathy	0	0	—	0	0	—	0	0	—	0	0	—
	17. Pause fillers	14	18	N.S	13	21	N.S.	16	21	N.S.	43	60	N.S.
	18. Gratitude	16	26	L<U	16	29	L<U	16	28	L<U	48	83	L<U

Note: "L" is lower intermediate, "U" is upper intermediate, "N.S." means "no significant difference", $p<0.05$

此外，拒绝给予时，在已使用的拒绝策略中，英语水平处于"lower intermediate"的学生使用频率最低的 3 种策略是"Acceptance that functions as a refusal""Avoidance"和"Positive opinion"，使用频数分别为 22、28、28。例如，学生在使用"Acceptance that functions as a refusal"策略时说"How nice if I could take this part-time job"（S9，LS75）；使用"Avoidance"策略的学生采用了"Hedging""Topic switch""Postponement"等方法。如，学生采用"Hedging"的表达方式时说"I am not sure whether I could be there or not"（S8，LS58），有使用"Postponement"表达方式的学生说"I should think about it"（S7，LS51）；使用"Positive opinion"策略时，有学生说"I really appreciate for this chance"（S8，LS39）。英语水平处于"lower intermediate"的学生在拒绝给予时，使用频率最低的 3 种策略为"Avoidance""Acceptance that functions as a refusal""Set condition for future or past acceptance"，使用频数分别为 29、30、37。例如，在使用"Acceptance that functions as a refusal"策略时，有学生说"I even want to listen to the lecture in my dream"（S8，US67）；使用"Avoidance"策略时，学生常常用"Topic switch"和"Joke"的方法进行表达，如"My friend is waiting for me"（S8，US28）；使用"Set condition for future or past acceptance"策略时，有学生说"If I still could not do it tomorrow, I will ask you for help"（S7，LS21），"I would do part-time job if I could pass my TEM-4"（S9，US11）。

根据单因素方差分析结果，在使用的 10 种拒绝策略中，不同英语水平的中泰缅学生共在 2 种拒绝策略使用频率上存在显著性差异，它们是"Regret"策略和"Gratitude"策略。英语水平处于"lower intermediate"的学生和"upper intermediate"使用这 2 种策略的频数分别为 184、214、48、83。英语水平处于"lower intermediate"的学生在这两种策略上的使用频率明显低于英语水平处于"upper intermediate"的学生。例如，有学生在使用"Alternative"策略时说"I can ask my friend for your interview"（S4，US72），"Maybe our monitor could come"（S6，US22）。

总的来说，在拒绝给予时，不同英语水平的中泰缅大学生都采用了 10 种拒绝策略。在使用其中 8 种拒绝策略时，两组英语水平的中泰缅大学生使用频率相似，但是，不同英语水平的学生在 2 种拒绝策略的使用频率上出现了显著性差异。英语水平处于"lower intermediate"的学生使用这两种拒绝策略的频率明显低于英语水平处于"upper intermediate"的学生。

四、拒绝建议

表 4.12 比较了不同英语水平的中泰缅大学生拒绝建议时的策略使用情况。

表 4.12 比较了在 3 个建议场景中，不同英语水平的中泰缅大学生进行拒绝时的策略使用情况。在拒绝建议时，不同英语水平的中泰缅大学生都使用了 Beebe 等（1990）拒绝策略分类中的 10 类。它们分别是"Negative willingness/ability""Explanation""Set condition for future or past acceptance""Promise of future acceptance""Attempt to dissuade interlocutor""Acceptance that functions as a refusal""Avoidance""Positive opinion""Pause fillers""Gratitude"。

在拒绝建议时，不同英语水平的中泰缅大学生使用频率最高的 3 种拒绝策略为"Explanation""Negative willingness/ability"和"Gratitude"。英语水平处于"lower intermediate"和"upper intermediate"的学生使用"Explanation""Negative willingness/ability"和"Gratitude"策略的频数分别为 176、199，139、147 和 55、87。有学生在实施"Explanation"策略时说"I will go to the private school for a teaching job at the weekend"（S10，LS37），"I am not ready for the presentation"（S12，US29）；有学生采用"Negative willingness/ability"策略时说"I don't think I can pass the exam"（S11，LS49），"I am not able to join in the activity you mentioned"（S10，US55）；在使用"Gratitude"策略时，有学生说"I really appreciate for your suggestion"（S12，US49）。

表 4.12 不同英语水平的中泰缅大学生英语拒绝策略使用异同（拒绝建议）

Refusal strategies		Situation 10 Frequency L N=76	Situation 10 Frequency U N=76	Situation 10 Sig.	Situation 11 Frequency L N=76	Situation 11 Frequency U N=76	Situation 11 Sig.	Situation 12 Frequency L N=76	Situation 12 Frequency U N=76	Situation 12 Sig.	General Frequency L N=76	General Frequency U N=76	General Sig.
Direct	1. Performative	0	0	—	0	0	—	0	0	—	0	0	—
	2. No	0	0	—	0	0	—	0	0	—	0	0	—
	3. Negative willingness/ability	47	50	N.S.	47	48	N.S.	45	49	N.S.	139	147	N.S.
	4. Regret	0	0	—	0	0	—	0	0	—	0	0	—
	5. Wish	0	0	—	0	0	—	0	0	—	0	0	—
Indirect	6. Explanation	60	66	N.S.	58	65	N.S.	58	68	L<U	176	199	N.S.
	7. Alternative	0	0	—	0	0	—	0	0	—	0	0	—
	8. Set condition for future or past acceptance	12	13	N.S.	12	13	N.S.	13	16	N.S.	37	42	N.S.
	9. Promise of Future acceptance	13	19	N.S.	17	18	N.S.	21	18	N.S.	51	55	N.S.
	10. Statement of principle	0	0	—	0	0	—	0	0	—	0	0	—
	11. Statement of philosophy	0	0	—	0	0	—	0	0	—	0	0	—
	12. Attempt to dissuade interlocutor	7	8	N.S.	8	10	N.S.	8	13	N.S.	23	31	N.S.
	13. Acceptance that functions as a refusal	7	8	N.S.	9	10	N.S.	9	12	N.S.	25	30	N.S.
	14. Avoidance	9	10	N.S.	10	12	N.S.	12	12	N.S.	31	34	N.S.

续表4.12

Refusal strategies		Situation 10			Situation 11			Situation 12			General		
		Frequency		Sig.	Frequency		Sig.	Frequency		Sig.	Frequency		Sig.
		L N=76	U N=76		L N=76	U N=76		L N=76	U N=76		L N=76	U N=76	
Adjuncts	15. Positive opinion	11	16	N.S.	13	17	N.S.	14	20	N.S.	38	53	N.S.
	16. Empathy	0	0	—	0	0	—	0	0	—	0	0	—
	17. Pause fillers	16	17	N.S.	17	20	N.S.	18	22	N.S.	61	59	N.S.
	18. Gratitude	17	28	N.S.	18	29	N.S.	20	30	N.S.	55	87	N.S.

Note: "L" is lower intermediate, "U" is upper intermediate, "N.S." means "no significant difference", $p<0.05$

此外，拒绝建议时，在已使用的拒绝策略中，英语水平处于"lower intermediate"的学生使用频率最低的 3 种策略是"Attempt to dissuade interlocutor""Acceptance that functions as a refusal"和"Avoidance"，使用频数分别为 23、25、31。例如，在使用"Attempt to dissuade interlocutor"策略时，有学生说"This idea is not good at all"（S11，LS45）；使用"Acceptance that functions as a refusal"策略时，有学生说"How excited if I could pass the entrance exam"（S11，LS51）；使用"Avoidance"策略时，一些学生采用了"Hedging"和"Topic switch"的表达方法。如有学生采用"Hedging"方法时说"I will try to finish the research before the conference"（S12，LS32），使用"Topic switch"方法时，有学生说"My teacher asks me to go to his office now"（S10，LS21）。拒绝建议时，英语水平处于"upper intermediate"的学生使用频率最低的 3 种策略是"Acceptance that functions as a refusal""Attempt to dissuadeinterlocutor"和"Avoidance"使用频数分别为 30、31、34。例如，在使用"Acceptance that functions as a refusal"策略时，有学生说"I will ask my friend whether they would like to come"（S10，US29）；使用"Attempt to dissuade interlocutor"策略时，有学生说"I won't be happy in further study"（S11，US37）；使用"Avoidance"策略时，英语水平处于"upper intermediate"的学生常使用"Verbal"的表达方式，如"Repetition or part of request""Postponement"等。在使用"Repetition or part of request"时，有学生说"Present my research？"（S12，US46）；在使用"Postponement"时，有学生说"Let me consider about it"（S11，US18）。根据单因素方差分析结果，在使用的 10 种拒绝建议的策略中，不同英语水平的中泰缅大学生在拒绝策略使用频率上没有显著性差异。

总的来说，在拒绝建议时，不同英语水平的中泰缅大学生都采用了 10 种拒绝策略。不同英语水平的两组学生使用频率最高的 3 种拒绝策略均为"explanation""Negative willingness/ability"和"Gratitude"，使用频率最低的 3 种策略均为"Acceptance that functions as a refusal""Avoidance"和"Attempt to dissuade interlocutor"。两组英语水平的中泰缅达学生在 10 种拒绝策略上的使用频率相似，不存在显著性差异。

第四节 中泰缅大学生英语拒绝策略总体使用情况

表4.13对中泰缅大学生的英语拒绝策略使用频率进行了总结,并在总体上比较了不同国籍、不同性别、不同英语水平的中泰缅大学生的拒绝策略使用情况。

从表4.13及表4.1、表4.2、表4.3、表4.4的分析结果可见,中泰缅大学生在实施拒绝言语行为时,中国学生共使用了17种拒绝策略,泰缅学生共使用了18种拒绝策略。学生对Beebe等(1990)总结的18种拒绝策略的使用频数分布在0至1824次之间,即假设没有学生在12个拒绝场景中使用该策略,则该策略的使用频数为0。如果每个学生在每个场景中都使用了该策略,则该策略的使用频数为1824次。现将策略使用频率分为高中低3个等级,使用频率处于0～0.608(含0.608)的策略为使用频率低,使用频数处于609至1216(含1216)的属于使用频率中等,使用频数处于1217至1824属于使用频率高。根据这一标准,从表4.13可见,总的来说,中泰缅学生使用频率低的拒绝策略共有15种,分别为"Performative""No""Wish""Alternative""Set condition for future or past acceptance""Promise of future acceptance""Statement of principle""Statement of philosophy""Attempt to dissuade interlocutor""Acceptance that functions as a refusal""Avoidance""Positive opinions""Empathy""Gratitude"和"Pause fillers";中泰缅大学生使用频率中等的拒绝策略共有2种,即"Negative willingness/ability"和"Regret";中泰缅大学生使用频率高的拒绝策略只有1种,即"Explanation"。

表 4.13 中泰缅大学生英语拒绝策略总体使用情况

	Refusal strategies	Nationality Count C N=52	T N=51	B N=49	Sig.	Gender Count M N=72	F N=80	Sig.	Language proficiency Count L N=76	U N=76	Sig.	Total Count
Direct	1. Performative	0	2	2	N.S.	2	2	N.S.	4	0	N.S	4
	2. No	35	4	56	T<B	80	15	M>F	52	43	N.S	95
	3. Negative willingness/ability	558	410	228	C>T C>B T>B	527	669	N.S.	572	624	L<U	1196
Indirect	4. Regret	439	419	378	N.S.	548	688	N.S.	581	655	N.S	1236
	5. Wish	4	4	2	N.S.	3	7	N.S.	6	4	N.S	10
	6. Explanation	559	528	466	N.S.	670	883	M<F	750	803	N.S	1553
	7. Alternative	21	27	21	N.S.	52	17	M>F	52	17	L>U	69
	8. Set condition for future or past acceptance	67	83	80	N.S.	87	143	N.S.	103	127	N.S	230
	9. Promise of Future acceptance	200	87	53	C>T C>B	150	190	N.S.	139	201	N.S	340
	10. Statement of principle	8	10	7	N.S.	13	12	N.S.	14	11	N.S	25
	11. Statement of philosophy	7	9	7	N.S.	6	17	N.S.	11	12	N.S	23
	12. Attempt to dissuade interlocutor	22	46	41	N.S.	33	76	N.S.	52	57	N.S	109

续表 4.13

Refusal strategies		Nationality Count			Sig.	Gender Count		Sig.	Language proficiency Count		Sig.	Total Count
		C N=52	T N=51	B N=49		M N=72	F N=80		L N=76	U N=76		
Indirect	13. Acceptance that functions as refusal	38	56	68	N.S.	70	92	N.S.	73	89	N.S	162
	14. Avoidance	79	59	53	N.S.	59	132	N.S.	92	99	N.S	191
	15. Positive opinion	163	92	54	N.S.	73	236	M<F	120	189	N.S	309
	16. Empathy	2	6	2	N.S.	5	5	N.S.	4	6	N.S	10
Adjuncts	17. Pause fillers	210	65	117	C>T	76	316	M<F	183	209	N.S	392
	18. Gratitude	238	179	108	N.S.	46	479	M<F	194	331	L<U	525

Note: C is Chinese, T is Thai, B is Burnese, M is male, F is femalee, L is lower intermediate, U is upper intermediate, N.S. means "no significant difference", $p<0.05$

此外，表4.13还比较了中泰缅学生以国籍、性别、英语水平为变量的拒绝策略使用频率。从表4.13可见，中国学生使用频率低的拒绝策略共有13种，分别为"Performative""No""Wish""Alternative""Set condition for future or past acceptance""Promise of Future acceptance""Statement of principle""Statement of philosophy""Attempt to dissuade interlocutor""Acceptance that functions as a refusal""Avoidance""Positive opinion"和"Empathy"；中国学生使用频率中等的拒绝策略有3种，它们是"Regret""Pause fillers"和"Gratitude"；中国学生使用频率高的拒绝策略有2种，它们是"Negative willingness/ability"和"Explanation"。泰国学生使用频率低的拒绝策略有15种，分别为"Performative""No""Wish""Alternative""Set condition for future or past acceptance""Promise of future acceptance""Statement of principle""Statement of philosophy""Attempt to dissuade interlocutor""Acceptance that functionsas a refusal""Avoidance""Positive opinion""Empathy""Pause fillers"和"Gratitude"；泰国学生使用频率中等的拒绝策略有1种，即"Regret"；泰国学生使用频率高的拒绝策略有2种，分别是"Explanation"和"Negative willingness/ability"。根据统计结果，缅甸学生使用频率低的拒绝策略有15种，它们分别是"Performative""No""Wish""Alternative""Set condition for future or past acceptance""Promise of future acceptance""Statement of principle""Statement of philosophy""Attempt to dissuade interlocutor""Acceptance that functions as a refusal""Avoidance""Positive opinion""Empathy""Pause fillers"和"Gratitude"；缅甸学生使用频率中等的拒绝策略有2种，它们是"Regret"和"Negative willingness/ability"；缅甸学生使用频率高的拒绝策略有1种，即"Explanation"。中泰缅大学生在使用的18种交际策略中，其中14种策略的使用频率没有显著性差异，但在4种策略的使用频率上出现了显著性差异。存在使用频率显著性差异的策略是"No""Negative willingness/ability""Promise of Future acceptance"和"Pause fillers"。具体地说，泰国学生使用"No"策略的频率明显低于缅甸学生；中国学生使用"Negative willingness/ability"策略的频率明显高于泰国学生和缅甸学生，泰国学生使用该策略的频率明显高于缅甸学生；中国学生使用"Promise of future acceptance"策略的频率明显高于泰国学生和缅甸学生；中国学生使用"Pause fillers"策略的频率明显高于泰国学生。

根据表4.13及表4.5、表4.6、表4.7、表4.8的分析结果，从性别上看，男女同学都使用了 Beebe 等（1990）总结的 18 种拒绝策略。其中，男生使用频率低的策略有 15 种，分别是 "Performative" "No" "Wish" "Alternative" "Set condition for future or past acceptance" "Promise of future acceptance" "Statement of principle" "Statement of philosophy" "Attempt to dissuade interlocutor" "Acceptance that functions as a refusal" "Avoidance" "Positive opinion" "Empathy" "Pause fillers" 和 "Gratitude"；男生使用频率中等的拒绝策略有 2 种，它们是 "Regret" 和 "Negative willingness/ability"；男生使用频率高的策略有 1 种，即 "Explanation"。在 18 种拒绝策略中，女生使用频率低的策略有 14 种，它们是 "Performative" "No" "Wish" "Alternative" "Set condition for future or past acceptance" "Promise of Future acceptance" "Statement of principle" "Statement of philosophy" "Attempt to dissuade interlocutor" "Acceptance that functions as a refusal" "Avoidance" "Positive opinion" "Empathy" 和 "Pause fillers"；女生使用频率中等的拒绝策略有 2 种，分别是 "Regret" 和 "Gratitude"；女生使用频率高的拒绝策略有 2 种，它们是 "Negative willingness/ability" 和 "Explanation"。根据表 4.13，不同性别的两组学生在 12 种拒绝策略的使用频率上没有显著差异，但在 6 种策略的使用频率上出现了显著差异，它们是 "No" "Explanation" "Alternative" "Positive opinion" "Pause fillers" 和 "Gratitude"。其中，男生在 "No" 策略的使用频率上明显高于女生，女生在 "Explanation" "Alternative" "Positive opinion" "Pause fillers" 和 "Gratitude" 策略的使用频率上明显高于男生。

根据表 4.13 及表 4.9、表 4.10、表 4.11、表 4.12 的分析结果，从不同英语水平中泰缅大学生拒绝策略使用情况来看，英语水平处于 "lower intermediate" 的学生使用了 Beebe 等（1990）总结的 18 种拒绝策略；英语水平处于 "higher intermediate" 的同学都使用了 Beebe 等（1990）总结的除 "Performative" 外的 17 种拒绝策略。其中，英语水平处于 "lower intermediate" 的学生使用频率低的策略有 15 种，分别是 "Performative" "No" "Wish" "Alternative" "Set condition for future or past acceptance" "Promise of future acceptance" "Statement of principle" "Statement of philosophy" "Attempt to dissuade interlocutor" "Acceptance that functions as a refusal" "Avoidance" "Positive opinion" "Empathy" "Pause fillers" 和 "Gratitude"；英语水平处于 "lower intermediate" 的学生使用频率中等的拒绝策略有 2 种，它们是 "Regret" 和 "Negative willingness/ability"；英语水平处于 "lower intermediate" 的学生使用频率高的策略有 1 种，即

"Explanation"。在 18 种拒绝策略中，英语水平处于"higher intermediate"的同学使用频率低的策略有 14 种，它们是"Performative""No""Wish""Alternative""Set condition for future or past acceptance""Promise of future acceptance""Statement of principle""Statement of philosophy""Attempt to dissuade interlocutor""Acceptance that functions as a refusal""Avoidance""Pause fillers""Empathy"和"Positive opinion"；英语水平处于"Higher intermediate"的同学使用频率中等的拒绝策略有 2 种，分别是"Regret"和"Gratitude"；英语水平处于"upper intermediate"的同学使用频率高的拒绝策略有 2 种，它们是"Negative willingness/ability"和"Explanation"策略。根据表 4.13，在 18 种拒绝策略的使用上，不同英语水平的两组学生在 15 种拒绝策略的使用上没有显著差异，但在 3 种策略的使用频率上出现了显著差异，它们是"Regret""Alternative"和"Gratitude"。其中，英语水平处于"lower intermediate"的学生在"Alternative"策略的使用频率上明显高于英语水平处于"upper intermediate"的同学，英语水平处于"lower intermediate"的学生在"Regret"和"Gratitude"策略的使用频率上明显低于英语水平处于"higher intermediate"的同学。

总的来说，中泰缅学生使用拒绝策略的频率不高，不同国籍、不同性别、不同英语水平的学生在一些拒绝策略使用频率上存在显著性差异。中国学生的拒绝策略使用频率高于泰国学生和缅甸学生，泰国学生的拒绝策略使用频率高于缅甸学生；女生的拒绝策略使用频率高于男生；英语水平高的学生的拒绝策略使用频率高于英语水平低的学生。下一节将分析不同情境因素下中泰缅学生英语拒绝策略使用情况。

第五节　不同情境因素下中泰缅大学生英语拒绝策略使用情况

本节拟回答研究问题：中泰缅大学生在英语拒绝言语行为策略使用时，如何受到情景因素的影响？在本研究中，情景因素包括社会距离（social distance）、地位差距（relative power）、强加级别（ranking of imposition）。本节将比较中泰缅 3 国学生实施拒绝言语行为时，在策略选择上是否受到以上 3 个情景因素的影响。

为了比较中泰缅大学生在用英语中介语实施拒绝言语行为时是否受到社会距离、地位差距、强加级别三个情景因素的影响，笔者邀请了两名美国教师先将12个交际场景分别划分为：社会距离为熟悉（＋）（即说话者和老师、朋友、室友间的社会距离），社会距离为不熟悉（－）（即说话者和部门领导、院长、新朋友或硕博士生的社会距离）；地位差距大（＋）（即部门领导、院长、老师和说话者之间地位差距），地位差距小或无（＝）（即同学、新朋友、室友和说话者的社会差距）；强加程度强（＋）（即部门领导、院长、老师对说话者的邀请、请求、给予、建议），强加程度弱（－）（即同学、新朋友、室友、陌生人对说话者的邀请、请求、给予、建议）。

一、社会距离

根据表3.4，在本研究的12个交际场景中，从社会距离看，共有6个场景的交际双方属于关系熟悉，分别为场景1（邀请）、场景3（邀请）、场景5（请求）、场景7（给予）、场景9（给予）、场景11（建议）。交际双方关系熟悉的场景包含了拒绝邀请、拒绝请求、拒绝给予和拒绝建议；还有6个场景的交际双方为关系不熟悉，分别是场景2（邀请）、场景4（请求）、场景6（请求）、场景8（给予）、场景10（建议）、场景12（建议）。这6个场景也包含了拒绝邀请、拒绝请求、拒绝给予和拒绝建议。表4.14比较了在不同社会距离场景下，中泰缅学生拒绝策略使用频率情况。

表4.14 不同社会距离场景下中泰缅大学生英语拒绝策略使用情况

	Refusal strategies	Social Distance（＋）Mean	Social Distance（－）Mean	Sig.
Direct	1. Performative	4	0	＋＜－
	2. No	46	49	N. S.
	3. Negative willingness/ability	598	598	N. S.

续表4.4

	Refusal strategies	Social Distance（＋）Mean	Social Distance（－）Mean	Sig.
Indirect	4. Regret	685	551	N. S.
	5. Wish	10	0	＋＞－
	6. Explanation	775	778	N. S.
	7. Alternative	40	29	＋＞－
	8. Set condition for future or past acceptance	118	112	N. S.
	9. Promise of future acceptance	162	178	N. S.
	10. Statement of principle	22	3	N. S.
	11. Statement of philosophy	23	0	N. S.
	12. Attempt to dissuade interlocutor	49	60	N. S.
	13. Acceptance that functions as a refusal	82	80	N. S.
	14. Avoidance	91	100	N. S.
Adjuncts	15. Positive opinion	150	159	N. S.
	16. Empathy	9	1	N. S.
	17. Pause fillers	195	197	N. S.
	18. Gratitude	265	260	N. S.

Note："＋" familiar，"－" unfamiliar；$p<0.05$

根据表4.14，中泰缅大学生在使用英语中介语实施拒绝言语行为时，采用了Beebe等（1990）总结的所有18种拒绝策略。表4.14反映出学生在不同社会距离的交际场景中，对不同拒绝策略的使用频率也有所不同。从表4.14可见，中泰缅大学生在交际双方社会距离亲密的场景中，使用频率最高的3种拒绝策略是"Explanation""Regret"和"Negative willingness/ability"，学生使用这3种拒绝策略的频数分别为775、685、598。在交际双方社会距离亲密的场景中，学生使用频率最低的3种拒绝策略为"Performative""Empathy""Wish"，使用频数分别为4、9、10。在交际双方社会距离疏远的场景中，学生使用频率最高的3种拒绝策略为"Explanation""Regret"和"Negative willingness/ability"，使用频数分别为778、551、598。在交际双方社会距离疏远的场景中，学生使用频率最低的3种拒绝策略为"Empathy""Statement of principle"和"Alternative"，使用频数分别为1、3、29。当交际双方关系疏远时，学生没有使用"Performative""Wish"和"Statement of philosophy"策略。由此可见，无论是在交际双方社会关系亲密的场景中，或是交际双方关系疏远的场景中，中泰缅学生使用频率最高的拒绝策略均为"Explanation""Regret"和"Negative willingness/ability"策略。但是，从不同的社会距离来看，学生使用频率最低的拒绝策略则略有不同。

在访谈中，有学生表示，当拒绝别人时，无论关系远近，都应该先表示遗憾，并说明原因（IS2，IS5，IS6，IS8，IS12，IS15，IS18）。因此，学生在进行拒绝时，使用"Regret"+"Explanation""Regret"+"Negative willingness/ability""Regret"+"Negative willingness/ability"+"Explanation"语义套语的情况最为常见。

例如，有学生在拒绝教授请求参加新生见面会（场景6）时，使用了"Regret"+"Negative willingness/ability"+"Explanation"的语义套语：

S116：I am so sorry（Regret）that I can't attend the orientation（Negative ability），because my mother is in hospital（Explanation）.

又如，在拒绝老同学提出的参加研究生入学考试建议（场景11）时，有学生使用了"Regret"+"Explanation"的语义套语：

S27：What a pity（Regret）that I have no such a plan，because I have to get a job as soon as I graduate to support my family（Explanation）.

再如，在拒绝老师提出的和其他同学一起共进晚餐的邀请（场景3）时，有学生使用了"Regret"+"Negative willingness/ability"的语义套语：

S89：I am really sorry（Regret）that I can't have dinner with you today（Negative ability）.

从社会距离的角度进行分析，无论在社会距离亲密的场景中，还是在社会距离疏远的情境中，学生使用"Empathy"和"Performative"拒绝策略的频率都很低。在访谈中，学生们提到几乎不使用"Performative"策略是因为"It's not polite to refuse people directly, whether they are close to me or not"（IS3，IS10，IS17），"If I refuse people directly, they will be hurt"（IS9，IS11，IS18，IS19）。此外，在提到"Empathy"策略时，很多学生表示在拒绝时不会用到这一策略，因为没有必要对交际对方表示同情。在关系亲密的场景中，学生使用"Wish"策略的频率也很低，当问及这点的时候，有学生认为"It's not easy to show our wishes to people in most situations where it indicates the relationship between the speaker and I are close to each other, and it seems that 'wish' do not suit those situations"（IS20）。问及"Statement of principle"策略时，学生认为几乎没有使

用这种策略是因为很多拒绝场景没有涉及原则问题，不需要使用到该策略（IS1，IS8，IS10，IS12）。此外，在关系疏远的交际场景中，学生没有使用"Wish"和"Statement of philosophy"策略。在访谈中，学生普遍认为当和交际对象关系疏远时，不适合使用这两种交际策略，因为"When refuse people who are not familiar with us, we just need to show our regret or gratitude"（IS11，IS19），"It seems we don't have to say too much with people unfamiliar with us"（IS10，IS20）。

从表 4.14 可见，中泰缅大学生对拒绝策略的使用频率和社会距离存在一定的关系。在已使用的 18 种拒绝策略中，根据交际场景的社会距离亲疏程度，中泰缅大学生在 3 种拒绝策略的使用频率上出现了显著性差异。这 3 种拒绝策略分别是"Performative""Wish"和"Alternative"。其中，在"Performative"策略的使用频率上，学生在和交际对象关系亲密的场景下使用频率明显高于学生和交际对象关系疏远的场景。在关系亲密的场景中，学生使用"Performative"策略的频数为 4；在关系疏远的场景中，学生使用该拒绝策略的频数为 0。也就是说，在交际双方关系疏远的场景下，学生几乎没有使用"Performative"策略。而在交际双方关系亲密的场景中，有个别学生使用了该策略，使用该策略时，有学生说"I refuse to accept your interview"（S4，S125）。此外，在"Wish"策略和"Alternative"策略的使用上，学生在和交际对象关系亲密的场景下使用频率明显低于学生和交际对象关系疏远的场景。在关系亲密的场景中，学生使用"Wish"策略的频数为 10，使用"Alternative"策略的频数为 40；在关系疏远的场景中，学生使用以上两种拒绝策略的频数分别为 0 和 29。在交际双方关系疏远时，中泰缅大学生没有使用"Wish"策略，在交际双方关系亲密的场景中，少量学生使用了该策略。有学生使用该策略时说"I wish the committee members will be happy with your thesis"（S1，S121）。尽管在不同社会距离场景下，中泰缅学生都使用了"Alternative"策略，但在交际双方关系亲密的交际场景中，学生使用该策略的频率仍要明显高于交际双方关系疏远的交际场景。例如，有学生使用该策略时说"I think I can find a job first instead of continuing my study"（S11，S89）。

二、地位差距

从表 3.4 可见，在本研究的 12 个交际场景中，从地位差距看，共有 6 个场景的交际双方存在高低地位关系，分别为场景 2（邀请）、场景 3（邀请）、场景 6（请求）、场景 8（给予）、场景 9（给予）、场景 12（建议）。交际双方地位高低的场景分布于拒绝邀请、拒绝请求、拒绝给予和拒绝建议中；另有 6

个场景的交际双方为平等地位关系,分别是场景1(邀请)、场景4(请求)、场景5(请求)、场景7(给予)、场景10(建议)、场景11(建议)。这6个场景包含了拒绝邀请、拒绝请求、拒绝给予和拒绝建议。表4.15比较了中泰缅大学生拒绝策略使用是否受到了地位差距的影响。

表4.15 不同地位差距场景下中泰缅大学生英语拒绝策略使用情况

	Refusal strategies	Relative Power(+) Count	Relative Power(=) Count	Sig.
Direct	1. Performative	2	2	N.S.
	2. No	49	46	N.S.
	3. Negative willingness/ability	601	595	N.S
Indirect	4. Regret	678	558	+<=
	5. Wish	4	6	N.S.
	6. Explanation	774	779	N.S.
	7. Alternative	26	43	+<=
	8. Set condition for future or past acceptance	109	121	N.S.
	9. Promise of future acceptance	173	167	N.S.
	10. Statement of principle	14	11	N.S.
	11. Statement of philosophy	10	13	N.S.
	12. Attempt to dissuade interlocutor	41	68	+<=
	13. Acceptance that functions as a refusal	79	83	N.S.
	14. Avoidance	99	92	N.S.
Adjuncts	15. Positive opinion	165	144	N.S.
	16. Empathy	4	6	N.S.
	17. Pause fillers	205	187	+>=
	18. Gratitude	269	256	N.S.

Note:"+" higher,"=" equal; $p<0.05$

表4.15列出了在不同的地位差距情景下,中泰缅大学生英语拒绝策略的使用情况。当交际情景的地位差距为"高-低"地位时,即交际对象的社会地位高于说话者时,中泰缅大学生使用频率最高的3种拒绝策略为"Explanation""Regret"和"Negative willingness/ability"。学生使用这3种拒绝策略的频数分别为774、678、601。在交际双方地位差距为高低地位时,

中泰缅学生使用频率最低的3种拒绝策略为"Performative""Wish"和"Empathy",使用频数分别为2、4、4。在交际情景中,当交际双方社会地位没有差距时,中泰缅大学生使用频率最高的3种拒绝策略是"Explanation""Negative willingness/ability""Regret",使用频数分别为779、595、558。在交际双方地位平等的交际场景中,中泰缅学生使用频率最低的3种拒绝策略为"Performative""Wish"和"Empathy",使用频数分别为2、6、6。

中泰缅大学生在拒绝策略的使用频率上,根据交际对方社会地位比自己高或和自己平等的情景,在4种拒绝策略的使用频率上出现了显著性差异。这4种拒绝策略为"Regret""Alternative""Attempt to dissuade interlocutor"和"Pause fillers"。当交际场景中出现交际对方比学生社会地位高的情况时,学生使用"Regret"策略和"Pause fillers"策略的频率明显高于交际对方社会地位和学生平等的情景。当交际对方的社会地位高于说话者时,说话者使用以上2种策略上的频数分别为678、205。当交际双方的社会地位相当时,学生使用以上拒绝策略的频数分别为558、187。从数据上看,无论在交际场景中交际对方地位比说话者高或是平等的情况下,中泰缅大学生使用"Regret"策略的频率都是比较高的。然而,在其他2种出现使用频率显著差异的拒绝策略使用上,即"Alternative"和"Attempt to dissuade interlocutor"策略,学生与交际对方社会地位平等场景下的使用频率明显高于交际对方社会地位高于学生的场景。当交际对方的社会地位高于说话者时,说话者使用以上2种拒绝策略的平均频数分别为26、41;当交际双方的社会地位平等时,在进行拒绝时,中泰缅学生使用以上策略的平均频数分别为43、68。

三、强加程度

表3.4显示了在本研究的12个交际场景中,从强加程度看,共有6个场景强加程度强,分别为场景2(邀请)、场景3(邀请)、场景6(请求)、场景8(给予)、场景9(给予)、场景12(给予)。交际双方地位高低的场景分布于拒绝邀请、拒绝请求、拒绝给予和拒绝建议中;另有6个场景强加程度弱,分别是场景1(邀请)、场景4(请求)、场景5(请求)、场景7(给予)、场景10(建议)、场景11(建议)。这6个场景包含了拒绝邀请、拒绝请求、拒绝给予和拒绝建议。表4.16比较了中泰缅学生拒绝策略使用是否受到了地位差距的影响。

表4.16 不同强加程度场景下中泰缅大学生英语拒绝策略使用情况

	Refusal strategies	Degree of Imposition(+) Mean	Degree of Imposition(=) Mean	Sig.
Direct	1. Performative	2	2	N.S.
	2. No	49	46	N.S.
	3. Negative willingness/ability	601	595	N.S.
Indirect	4. Regret	678	558	+>=
	5. Wish	4	6	N.S.
	6. Explanation	774	779	N.S.
	7. Alternative	26	43	+<=
	8. Set condition for future or past acceptance	109	121	N.S.
	9. Promise of Future acceptance	173	167	N.S.
	10. Statement of principle	14	11	N.S.
	11. Statement of philosophy	10	13	N.S.
	12. Attempt to dissuade interlocutor	41	68	+<=
	13. Acceptance that functions as a refusal	79	83	N.S.
	14. Avoidance	99	92	N.S.
Adjuncts	15. Positive opinion	165	144	N.S.
	16. Empathy	4	6	N.S.
	17. Pause fillers	205	187	+<=
	18. Gratitude	269	256	N.S.

Note: "+" high, "-" low; $p<0.05$

表4.16表现了不同强加程度场景下中泰缅学生拒绝策略使用情况。从表4.16可见，当交际情景中的交际对象强加程度强时，中泰缅大学生使用频率最高的3种拒绝策略为"Explanation""Regret"和"Negative willingness/ability"，使用频数分别为774、678、601。在交际对象在表达邀请、请求、给予和建议强加程度强时，中泰缅大学生使用频率最低的3种拒绝策略为"Performative""Wish"和"Empathy"，使用频数分别为2、4、4。在交际情景中，当交际对象强加程度弱时，中泰缅大学生使用频率最高的3种拒绝策略是"Explanation""Negative willingness/ability"和"Regret"，使用频数分别

为779、595、558。在交际对象强加程度弱的交际场景中,中泰缅大学生使用频率最低的拒绝策略为"Performative""Wish""Empathy",使用平均频数分别为2、6、6。

表4.16体现了在不同的强加程度的交际情景下,中泰缅大学生英语拒绝策略的使用情况。根据强加程度不同,中泰缅大学生在4种拒绝策略的使用频率上出现了显著性差异。这4种拒绝策略为"Regret""Alternative""Attempt to dissuade interlocutor""Pause fillers"。当交际场景中交际对方表达邀请、请求、给予和建议的强加程度强时,学生使用"Regret"策略和"Pause fillers"策略的频率明显高于交际对方强加程度弱的情景。当交际对方强加程度强时,说话者使用以上策略的频数分别为678、205。当交际对方强加程度弱时,学生使用以上策略的频数分别为558、187。然而,在其他2种出现使用频率显著差异的拒绝策略使用上,即"Alternative"和"Attempt to dissuade interlocutor",在交际对方强加程度弱的场景下,学生的使用频率明显高于交际对方强加程度强的场景。当交际对方强加程度强时,说话者使用以上两种拒绝策略的平均频数分别为26、41;当交际对方强加程度弱,在进行拒绝时,中泰缅大学生使用以上策略的平均频数分别为43、68。

本章小结

本章是本书的研究结果部分,共分为五小节,分别描述了不同国籍的中泰缅大学生英语拒绝策略使用情况、不同性别的中泰缅大学生英语拒绝言语行为策略使用情况、不同英语水平的中泰缅大学生英语拒绝言语行为策略使用情况、中泰缅大学生英语拒绝策略总体使用情况,以及中泰缅大学生英语拒绝策略使用受到社会距离、地位差距、强加程度的情景因素影响情况。本章中的各小节主要比较了不同分组下的中泰缅大学生的各种拒绝策略使用频率,并举例说明了使用频率高和使用频率低的拒绝策略语义套语使用情况。下一章是本书研究结果的讨论部分,将详细分析中泰缅大学生拒绝策略使用异同产生的原因。

第五章 讨 论

本章就4个研究问题的研究结果逐一展开讨论。首先，本章讨论了不同国籍的中泰缅大学生在校园生活场景中英语拒绝策略使用的异同；其次，本章讨论了不同性别的中泰缅大学生英语拒绝策略的使用情况；再次，本章讨论了不同英语水平的中泰缅大学生英语拒绝策略使用异同；最后，本章就不同情景因素下中泰缅大学生的英语拒绝策略使用情况进行了讨论。

第一节 不同国籍的中泰缅大学生英语拒绝策略使用异同讨论

一、不同国籍的中泰缅大学生英语拒绝策略使用异同

根据上一章呈现的研究结果，不同国籍的中泰缅大学生在拒绝策略使用上既存在共性，也存在一些差异。总的来说，在拒绝邀请的3个情景中，中泰缅大学生在12种拒绝策略上的使用频率相似，但有6种策略出现了使用频率显著性差异。其中，中国大学生拒绝策略的使用频率明显高于泰国大学生和缅甸大学生，且均体现在间接策略的使用上。具体表现在：①中国大学生在3种拒绝策略的使用频率上明显高于泰国大学生，分别是"Negative willingness/ability" "Promise of future acceptance" 和 "Pause fillers"；②中国大学生在4种拒绝策略的使用频率上明显高于缅甸大学生，分别是"Negative willingness/ability"，"Promise of future acceptance" "Positive opinion" 和 "Gratitude" ③泰国大学生在1种拒绝策略的使用频率上明显高于缅甸大学生，即 "Negative willingness/ability" 策略；④缅甸大学生在1种拒绝策略的使用频率上明显高于泰国大学生，即 "No" 策略。

中泰缅 大学生英语拒绝策略 探索

拒绝请求时，不同国籍的中泰缅大学生都采用了 Beebe 等（1990）总结的 18 种拒绝策略中的 13 类，在使用其中 9 种拒绝策略时，中泰缅大学生的使用频率相似，但有 4 种拒绝策略的使用频率出现了显著性差异。这 4 种拒绝策略既包含直接策略，也包含间接策略，具体表现在：①中国大学生在 2 种间接拒绝策略的使用频率上明显高于泰国大学生和缅甸大学生，即"Negative willingness/ability"和"Promise of future acceptance"策略；②中国大学生使用"Pause fillers"策略的频率明显高于泰国大学生；③泰国大学生使用直接策略"No"的频率明显高于缅甸大学生。

拒绝给予时，不同国籍的中泰缅大学生都使用了 Beebe 等（1990）总结的 18 种拒绝策略中的 10 类，不同国籍的三组学生在其中 7 类拒绝策略的使用频率上相似，但在 3 种拒绝策略的使用频率上出现了显著性差异，具体表现在：①中国大学生在使用"Negative willingness/ability"和"Promise of future acceptance"策略的频率上明显高于缅甸大学生；②中国大学生在"Pause fillers"策略的使用频率上明显高于泰国大学生；③泰国大学生在"Negative willingness/ability"策略的使用频率上明显高于缅甸大学生。

拒绝建议时，不同国籍的中泰缅大学生都采用了 Beebe 等（1990）总结的 18 种拒绝策略中的 10 类，在使用其中 7 种拒绝策略时，中泰缅大学生的使用频率相似，但有 3 种拒绝策略的使用频率出现了显著性差异，出现显著性差异的拒绝策略包含了直接策略，间接策略和附加语策略，具体表现在：①中国大学生使用"Negative willingness/ability"策略和"Promise of future acceptance"策略的频率明显高于缅甸大学生；②中国大学生使用"Pause fillers"策略的频率明显高于泰国大学生；③泰国大学生使用"Negative willingness/ability"策略的频率明显高于缅甸大学生。

从总体上看，中国大学生共使用了 17 种拒绝策略，泰国大学生和缅甸大学生共使用了 18 种拒绝策略。中国大学生使用频率低的拒绝策略共有 13 种，包含直接策略 2 种、间接策略 10 种、附加语策略 1 种；使用频率中等的策略有 3 种，含 1 种间接策略和两种附加语策略；使用频率高的策略有 2 种，含 1 种直接策略和 1 种间接策略。泰国大学生使用频率低的拒绝策略有 15 种，含 2 种直接策略、10 种间接策略和 3 种附加语策略；泰国大学生使用频率中等的拒绝策略 1 种，即属于间接策略的"Regret"策略；泰国大学生使用频率高的拒绝策略有 2 种，含 1 种直接策略和 1 种间接策略。缅甸大学生在所有使用的策略中，使用频率低的拒绝策略有 15 种，包括了两种直接策略、10 种间接策略、3 种附加语策略；缅甸大学生使用频率中等的拒绝策略有 2 种，包含 1 种直接策略和 1 种间接策略；缅甸大学生使用频率高的拒绝策略有 1 种，即属于间接策略的"Explanation"策略。此外，从总体上看，中泰缅大学生在 18 种拒绝策略的使用上，有 4 种策略的使用频率出现了显著性差异，他们是"No""Negative willingness/ability""Promise of future acceptance"和"Pause fillers"策略。其中，中国大学生使用"Negative willingness/ability"和"Promise of future acceptance"策略的频率明显高于泰国大学生和缅甸大学生，中国大学生使用"Pause fillers"策略的频率明显高于泰国大学生，泰国大学生使用"Negative willingness/ability"策略的频率明显高于缅甸大学生，缅甸大学生使用"No"策略的频率明显高于泰国大学生。

二、不同国籍的中泰缅大学生英语拒绝策略使用相似性讨论

根据本研究的研究结果，不同国籍的中泰缅大学生拒绝策略总体使用频率都较低，不同国籍的 3 国大学生使用频率最高的 3 种拒绝策略均为"Negative willingness/ability""Regret"和"Explanation"。这可以从中泰缅 3 国的文化背景进行解释。中泰缅 3 国学生长期受到佛家思想的影响，往往表现得谦虚和礼貌。因此，在对别人进行拒绝时，总是会尽可能减轻对交际对象面子威胁的程度，他们认为这 3 种拒绝策略都能帮助交际对象保留面子，使对方较易接受"被拒绝"的情形。

"Negative willingness/ability"策略是表明不情愿、能力不够或反对意见的拒绝策略（Shishavan，Sharifian，2013）。尽管"Negative willingness/ability"策略属于直接策略（Beebe，Takahashi，Uliss-Weltz，1990），但并不像其他直接拒绝策略，如"No"一样对交际对象进行简单草率拒绝（Wannaruk，2008）。这也是中泰缅大学生实施"Negative willingness/ability"策略频率高的原因。因为中泰缅大学生受其文化传统的影响，养成了谦虚的习惯。在实施拒绝言语行为时，尤其以否定能力进行拒绝的方式很常见。此外，在实施"Negative willingness/ability"策略时，中泰缅大学生使用了一些词汇或短语缓和词（Felix-Brasdefer，2004），以缓解对交际对象的面子威胁的程度（Liu，2004）。如学生在实施"Negative willingness/ability"策略时，使用了以下缓和词："I'm afraid…""I think…""Maybe…"等。中泰缅大学生使用"Negative willingness/ability"策略进行拒绝时，常常使用如下表达方式："I think I am not capable enough to do the work of the part-time job well.""Maybe my family can't support me to continue my study economically"。

"Regret"策略是中泰缅大学生使用频率最高的拒绝策略之一。"Regret"

策略常常被使用在拒绝话语的开头或是结尾。Sairhun（1999）认为"Regret"是拒绝语中基本的元素，在她的研究中，泰国学生和美国学生几乎在每一个拒绝请求的场景中都使用了该策略。在本研究中，中泰缅大学生在使用"Regret"策略时，其表达方式可以分为以下3类：

（1）表达"Apology"。不同国籍的中泰缅大学生都使用了该表达方式。学生们常用"Sorry""Sorry for that""I'm sorry about that""I apologize for...""I'm sorry to tell you that..."来表达"Apology"。值得一提的是，中泰缅大学生在表达"Apology"时，有时会使用加强词（intensifiers）来加强语气。这一发现和 Sairhun（1999）、Kwon（2003）、Prachanant（2006）、Kittisiriprasert（2011）的研究结果一致。例如，在本研究中，学生使用了"really""must""have to""very much""extremely""terribly""so""awfully"等。除使用加强词外，一些学生还重复使用了"Regret"策略，即同时将该策略使用在拒绝的开头和结尾，以加强遗憾的语气，例如，"Sorry, I really couldn't attend your defence, I'm sorry"，"I'd like to join in your dinner, but I'm sorry that I have to go home. I'm sorry again"。

（2）表示"pity"。中泰缅大学生都使用了这一表达方式，以表达他们不能接受邀请、请求、给予、建议的遗憾和失望。Hong（2011）指出，中国人常常将"pity"作为实施拒绝言语行为的方式。例如，中泰缅三国大学生使用了"It's a pity...""What a pity...""It's bad..."等表达"Regret"。例如，有学生在使用"Regret"拒绝策略时说"It's a pity that I can't go to your defense...", "It's so bad that I can't go to the orientation"。

（3）请求原谅。在表示"Regret"时，中泰缅大学生中有个别同学使用了请求原谅的表达方式。具体体现在拒绝教授的请求参加新生见面会的交际场景中，学生使用了"Forgive me"的表达方式。美国人也会使用这种"Regret"策略的表达方式来表示不能接受交际对象的请求（Sairhun，1999）。在访谈中，使用这一表达方式的学生表示"It's a chance the professor gives to me, so I hope he wouldn't be angry for my refusal"。此外，有些学生使用这一表达方式可能源于他们的英语基础不够好，不知如何合理地进行拒绝。

"Explanation"策略是中泰缅大学生使用频率最高的拒绝策略之一。正如 Hassani 等（2011）所说，"Explanation"策略是全球公认的体现礼貌原则的拒绝策略。但是，根据交际情景的不同，语言学习者实施"Explanation"策略时采用的理由也会有所不同。在拒绝邀请时，中泰缅大学生使用的"Explanation"理由通常是提前有约会或是安排好的事情。例如，学生在拒绝参加同学的答辩邀请时说"I have an appointment with my grandparents that day"（TS17），在拒绝系主任邀请参加工作坊时说"I have class that time"（BS19），在拒绝老师邀请共进晚餐时说"I have already promised my parents I will have dinner with them today"（CS33）。这一研究结果和 Sairhun（1999）和 Lin（2014）的研究发现不谋而合，Sairhun（1999）的研究发现泰国大学生在实施拒绝言语行为时习惯以家庭成员为理由；Lin（2014）也发现中国大学生在实施拒绝言语行为时，常常以与家人有约为理由。

在拒绝请求时，中泰缅大学生拒绝接受采访的邀请时通常以"忙"或"赶时间"为由。在这个交际场景中，一些学生在访谈中提出，由于邀请者是陌生人，他们在拒绝时会有一些压力，也不愿意也认为没有必要给出具体的理由。然而，在拒绝同桌请求帮忙检查作业时，多数学生表达了自己能力不够，如"I am not good at this subject"（CS, 21）。学生们认为表示自己能力不够可以在很大程度上缓解对交际对象的面子威胁，很好地保留对方的面子。在拒绝教授邀请参加新生见面会时，学生们则更习惯以事先安排好的事由为由拒绝，这些事由有私事，也有学校的其他安排，如课程、活动等。在采访中，学生表示，拒绝学校老师或教授等的邀请、请求、给予、建议时，他们感觉还是有一定压力的，以学校安排为由，不但可以在很大程度上减轻面子威胁的程度，还可以缓解自己拒绝邀请的压力（IS3，IS7，IS9，IS17，IS19）。

拒绝给予时，多数学生在拒绝同学给予完成任务的帮助时，都采用了不想麻烦同学的理由。这和中泰缅三国的传统习惯有关。在拒绝系主任给予的听讲座的机会时或老师给予的兼职教师机会时，多数学生以自己学习繁忙或在学校有别的活动安排为由进行拒绝。在 Wannaruk（2008）的研究中，她也发现泰国学生在拒绝老师或学校领导给予的工作和事务时，常常也常以学习任务重为由。例如，在拒绝老师给予的兼职时，有学生说"I want to concentrate on preparing for my examination of TEM-4"（CS50）。

在拒绝建议时，几乎所有使用"Explanation"策略的中泰缅大学生在拒绝新同学邀请参加学校活动时，都采用了学习太忙或活动过多为由，例如，"I have joined in some other activities"（TS38），"I need to spend more time on study"（BS40）。在拒绝老朋友提出的考研建议时，多数使用"Explanation"策略的中泰缅大学生都以想工作挣钱补贴家用为由。在采访中，学生提到这一方面和长期的学习压力有关，"I want to work first before I continue my further study"（BS29）；一方面和家庭的经济状况相关，"I am the eldest child in my family, so I have to earn money to support my family"（TS1）。中泰缅大

学生拒绝教授提出的在会议上发言的建议时，多数学生都表示自己还未完成研究。这和 Wannaruk（2008）的研究发现相似。Wannaruk（2008）在研究中发现在拒绝导师提出的参加新加坡举办的学术会议中陈述论文时，所有参与研究的中泰学生都表示研究还未完成。

总的来说，在实施"Explanation"拒绝策略时，学生根据交际场景的不同，常以有别的安排、学习任务重或没有准备好为由。中泰缅大学生使用"Explanation"拒绝策略的频率很高。在采访中，学生提到频繁使用这一策略是因为在拒绝时给予对方合理的理由可以缓解对方的尴尬情绪，还可以缓解在拒绝时对交际对方造成的面子威胁伤害。此外，学生提到使用"Explanation"策略进行拒绝还想向对方表示"拒绝"并不是主观上不愿接受，而是不得已而为之，希望能得到对方的理解。

不同国籍的中泰缅大学生使用频率最低的3种策略都包含"Performative"和"Wish"策略。"Performative"属于直接策略，泰缅大学生使用这一策略的频率都很低，中国大学生没有使用该策略。在访谈中，学生提到采用诸如"I refuse..."的话语拒绝别人过于直接，对交际对方构成了面子威胁，也很不礼貌，而且会对交际双方的关系构成影响，因此，中泰缅3国学生都有表示，在实施拒绝言语行为时，几乎不会使用到该策略。"Wish"策略属于间接策略。在访谈中，学生提到在拒绝别人时，一般只会想到抱歉、解释等策略进行拒绝，而很少使用"Wish"策略，"If I refuse my friend's suggestion to take the entrance examination for a master degree, I don't know what wish I could have"（BS33）。

三、不同国籍的中泰缅大学生英语拒绝策略使用差异性讨论

中泰缅3国大学生在6种拒绝策略的使用上出现了显著性差异，中国大学生使用"Negative willingness/ability"策略的频率明显高于泰国大学生和缅甸大学生。中国人将自谦视为一种美德。同时，中国人还认为采用对自己能力否定的方式进行拒绝，不会伤害交际对象的面子，也是对对方进行的礼貌性拒绝。因此，在拒绝别人时，常常采取自我否定的方式。中国大学生采用"Negative willingness/ability"策略的频率明显高于泰国大学生和缅甸大学生也是受到这一传统文化的影响。

中国大学生使用"Promise of future acceptance"策略的频率也明显高于泰国大学生和缅甸大学生，"Future acceptance"实质上是"the employment of promise to delay acceptance"（Wannaruk，2008）。在本研究中，这一拒绝

策略常常被中泰缅大学生用于实施拒绝言语行为的最后,以留给交际对方他们的拒绝是不确定的,也许以后还可以弥补的印象。采用"Promise of future acceptance"策略时,本研究中的中泰缅大学生主要采取了以下两种方式:①改变时间,即承诺将在以后某个时间接受,如"I will take a part-time job after I pass the TEM-4";②附加条件,即如果某种条件具备,拒绝就可以不实现,如"If I have time, I will go to your defense"。在访谈中,有中国大学生认为使用"Promise of future acceptance"策略,能缓解对交际对方的面子威胁程度,并能向对方传递仍乐意接受邀请、请求、给予、建议的想法。在中国学生看来,拒绝别人是一件难以开口的事,给予别人将来的承诺,会缓解自己拒绝别人时的不安情绪。

此外,中国大学生使用"Pause fillers"策略的频率也明显高于泰国大学生。总的来说,不同国籍的中泰缅大学生使用该策略的频率都不低。在采访中,有中国大学生提到"Pause fillers"策略反映了在拒绝交际对象时内心的犹豫,同时也反映了他们为了不直接粗鲁地拒绝别人,大脑中需要思考如何对语言进行组织的过程。此外,中国大学生还提到之所以频繁地使用"Pause fillers"策略,也是因为自己的英语水平不高,在实施拒绝言语行为时,需要花时间回忆词汇的选择和语法的使用。例如,在访谈中,有中国大学生提到"It's not that easy for me to express myself in English, so I need time to think how to use English to express my meaning"(IS1,IS3)。在本研究中,中泰缅大学生常用的"Pause fillers"策略表现为回答时使用"Well""Oh""Hmm""Right"等。

尽管泰国大学生使用"Pause fillers"策略的频率相对较低,Panichkul(2003)指出泰国人经常使用"Pause fillers"策略,泰国人使用该策略的表达方式为使用以"/ue/""/oe/""/a/""/o/"等发音的词语表示语气暂缓。但是,这些"Pause fillers"策略的表现形式在泰语中的发音是不出声的,泰国人在使用英语时,很可能将这些"Pause fillers"策略的表达方式迁移到英语中,在进行数据整理和分析的时候,因为这些表达方式的发音在英语中没有对应的拼写,泰国学生可能没有体现在WDCT中。在统计时,就可能被忽略,没有计入该策略使用的统计。另一种可能性和本研究的研究工具有关,本研究采用了书面补全对话方式收集数据,正如Wannaruk(2008)所说,如果采用角色扮演的数据收集工具,泰国学生使用的一些语气词就能被收集到。

中国大学生使用"Positive opinion"和"Gratitude"策略的频率明显高于缅甸大学生。Lin(2014)在他的研究中也发现中国学生,尤其是中国的EFL

学习者较喜欢使用"Positive opinion"策略。和"Negative ability/Willingness"策略相反,"Positive opinion"策略用于表达说话者对邀请、请求、给予和建议的兴趣和向往等。在本研究中,笔者发现中泰缅大学生习惯将该策略和"Explanation"策略同时使用,并且放在拒绝语的开头。这一研究结果和Felix-Brasdefer(2004)的研究结果一致,Felix-Brasdefer(2004)在研究中也发现学生常将"Positive opinion"策略用于拒绝言语行为的开头,用以表达同意、愿意等任何积极的态度。缅甸大学生使用"Positive opinion"策略的频率明显低于中国大学生。在访谈中,缅甸大学生提到,在拒绝时,他们会避免使用该策略,这是因为他们担心在拒绝中使用该策略后,会在随后的交流中被迫接受。此外,缅甸大学生使用该策略的频率较低还因为在现实交际中,缅甸大学生表示很少有机会用英语表达"Positive opinion",因此对相关词汇和短语不熟悉。在使用该策略时,中泰缅大学生常用的表达方式有"I'd like to, but…""Yes, but…""I want to, but…"等。例如,在拒绝老师提供的做兼职教师的建议时,有学生说"I'd love to, but I have to spend a lot of time on study"(CS22)。

在"Gratitude"策略的使用上,不同国籍的中泰缅大学生的频率都不低。中泰缅大学生使用该策略时常常采用"Thank you""That's very kind of you""I'm very appreciated"等方式进行表达。在本研究中,中泰缅大学生常常将"Gratitude"和"Explanation"策略同时使用。Sairhun(1999)和Wannaruk(2008)也发现中泰两国学生习惯将这两种拒绝策略同时使用。中泰缅大学生为了强调他们对于邀请、请求、给予、建议的感谢,常常使用加强词,如"… for your kindness""… for thinking of me""… for giving me the chance"等。此外,一些学生在同一交际情境中重复使用了"Gratitude"策略,这也许是因为他们想对交际对方表示由衷的感谢或是因为他们想礼貌地结束交流。中国大学生使用"Gratitude"策略的频率明显高于缅甸大学生。在Guo(2012)的研究中,他也发现中国大学生在该策略上的使用频率较其他国家英语学习者高。在一些其他学者(Nelson, Al Batal, El Bakary, 2002; Kwon, 2003; Guo, 2012)的研究中,他们发现英语母语使用者在实施拒绝言语行为时使用该策略的频率高于非英语母语使用者,中国大学生使用该策略的频率高于缅甸大学生也许是源于中国大学生更善于模仿英语母语使用者,在拒绝时使用"Gratitude"策略以表示感谢(Kwon, 2003)。在采访中,中国大学生也表示尽管根据中国的文化传统,在拒绝别人时一般不会先对交际对象的邀请或建议等表示感谢。但是,由于在学习英语的过程中,他们受到了英语国家文化的影响,久而久之也养成了先表示感激的习惯。尤其是英语专业的学生,他们几乎在所有拒绝之前都表示了感谢。

泰国大学生多数受到佛家思想的影响,常常会表示谦虚。泰国大学生使用"Negative willingness/ability"策略的频率明显高于缅甸大学生很可能是长期受其宗教信仰影响的缘故。在访谈中,泰国大学生提到"I refuse people because I am incapable to do so"(ISI5),"I don't think I have the ability to satisfy the request"(ISI2)。在访谈中,泰国大学生表示,否定自己的能力是自谦的表现,这也是受到了泰国传统文化的影响。即使在用英语实施拒绝言语行为,他们也认为通过否定自己的能力表示自谦可以缓解对交际对象的面子威胁程度,保留对方的面子。

缅甸大学生使用"No"策略的频率明显高于泰国大学生。在以往的研究中(Tanck,2004;Nguyen,2005;Wannaruk,2008;Lin,2014),学者们发现英语外语使用者极少使用该策略,这和本研究的研究结果一致。语言使用者并不想使用这样的直接策略,因为容易对交际对方造成面子威胁,多数英语使用者都希望在交际中保持和谐关系(Kittisiriprasert,2011)。拒绝言语行为本身就是一种面子威胁行为(Brown,Levinson,1987)。因此,采用直接策略"No"就显得不够礼貌且可能伤害交际对方的感情(Wannaruk,2008;Tian,2014)。在本研究中,当学生使用"No"策略时,常常会伴随使用一些缓和策略,如"Explanation""Regret"和"Gratitude",以减少拒绝的负面影响(Kwon,2003)。在本研究中,缅甸大学生使用"No"策略的频率明显高于泰国大学生。在访谈中,很多缅甸大学生表示之所以使用该策略,很大程度上是自己的英语交际能力不强造成的,因为自己不知道该如何用英语进行拒绝,干脆直接说了"No",以达到拒绝目的。

第二节 不同性别的中泰缅大学生英语拒绝策略使用异同讨论

一、不同性别的中泰缅大学生英语拒绝策略使用异同情况

根据第四章的研究结果,不同性别的中泰缅大学生都使用了 Beebe 等(1990)总结的 18 种拒绝策略。总的来说,在拒绝邀请的 3 个情景中,不同性

别的中泰缅大学生在 13 种拒绝策略上的使用频率相似，但有 5 种策略的使用频率出现了显著性差异。其中，女生使用"Explanation""Gratitude"和"Pause fillers"策略的频率明显高于男生，男生使用"No""Alternative"策略的频率明显高于女生。

在拒绝请求时，不同性别的中泰缅大学生都使用了 13 种拒绝策略，他们在 6 种拒绝策略的使用频率上相似，但在 7 种策略的使用频率上存在显著性差异，具体表现为：①男生使用直接策略"No"的频率明显高于女生；②女生使用间接策略"Regret""Explanation""Attempt to dissuade interlocutor"，以及附加语策略"Positive opinion""Pause fillers""Gratitude"的频率明显高于男生。

在拒绝给予时，不同性别的中泰缅大学生都采用了 Beebe 等（1990）总结的 18 种拒绝策略中的 10 类，不同性别的两组学生使用 6 种拒绝策略的频率相似，但在 4 种拒绝策略的使用频率上出现了显著性差异，具体表现在：男生使用间接策略"Explanation"，以及附加语策略"Positive opinion""Pause fillers"和"Gratitude"的频率明显低于女生。

在拒绝建议时，不同性别的中泰缅大学生都采用了 Beebe 等（1990）总结的 18 种拒绝策略中的 10 类。两组学生在其中 5 种拒绝策略的使用频率上没有显著性差异。但是，不同性别的两组学生在另外 5 种策略的使用频率上出现了显著性差异，男生的使用频率明显低于女生。这 5 种拒绝策略是：间接策略"Explanation""Avoidance"，以及附加语策略"Positive opinion""Pause fillers"和"Gratitude"。

总的来说，不用性别的中泰缅大学生使用了 Beebe 等（1990）总结的全部 18 种拒绝策略。其中，男生使用频率低的拒绝策略有 15 种，包含两种直接策略，9 种间接策略，以及 4 种附加语策略，这 15 种拒绝策略分别是"Performative""No""Wish""Alternative""Set condition for future or past acceptance""Promise of Future acceptance""Statement of principle""Statement of philosophy""Attempt to dissuade interlocutor""Acceptance that functions as a refusal""Avoidance""Positive opinion""Empathy""Pause fillers"和"Gratitude"。男生在 2 种拒绝策略的使用频率上属于中等，它们分别是直接策略"Negative willingness/ability"和间接策略"Regret"；男生使用频率高的拒绝策略有 1 种，即间接策略"Explanation"。在 18 种拒绝策略中，女生使用频率低的有 14 种，包含 2 种直接策略、9 种间接策略、3 种附加语策略。这些策略分别是"Performative""No""Wish""Alternative"

"Set condition for future or past acceptance" "Promise of Future acceptance" "Statement of principle" "Statement of philosophy" "Attempt to dissuade interlocutor" "Acceptance that functions as a refusal" "Avoidance" "Positive opinion" "Empathy" 和 "Pause fillers"。女生使用频率处于中等的拒绝策略有 2 种，即间接策略 "Regret" 和 "Gratitude"；女生在 2 种拒绝策略的使用频率上处于高的水平，即直接策略 "Negative willingness/ability" 和间接策略 "Explanation"。此外，不同性别的中泰缅大学生在使用的 18 种拒绝策略中，有 6 种策略的使用频率出现了显著性差异。其中，男生使用直接策略 "No" 的频率明显高于女生；女生使用间接策略 "Explanation" "Alternative"，以及附加语策略 "Positive opinion" "Pause fillers" "Gratitude" 的频率明显高于男生。

二、不同性别的中泰缅大学生英语拒绝策略使用相似性讨论

从表 4.13 可见，不同性别的中泰缅大学生拒绝策略总体使用频率较低。男女学生使用频率最高的 3 组拒绝策略为 "Explanation" "Regret" 和 "Negative willingness/ability"。

"Explanation" 是两组不同性别的中泰缅大学生使用频率最高的拒绝策略。但男女学生在使用该策略时提出的理由是不同的。在拒绝邀请时，男生常常以和朋友有约在先或学校有其他安排为由，而女生则习惯以事先另有安排或陪伴家人为由。例如，在场景 1 中，有男生说 "I have to go to the hospital with my roommate"（MS13），"I have class at that time"（MS47）。在这一场景中，有女生则说 "I have already arranged some important thing to do at that time"（FS27），"I have promised my parents I will visit them that day"（FS47）。在拒绝请求时，男生也常常以和朋友有约或学校有其他安排作为解释进行拒绝，女生则以赶时间或预先有安排作为解释进行拒绝。以 Situation 4 为例，有男生说 "My friend is waiting for me..."（MS40），"I am rushing for a sports competition..."（MS59）。而在相同场景进行拒绝时，女生则常常这样拒绝 "I am in a hurry..."（FS41），"I have an appointment with my dentist, I'm going to be late..."（FS59）。在拒绝给予时，不同性别的两组学生也表现出与拒绝邀请或请求时相似的情况，即男生常常以学校有课或其他校园安排为由进行拒绝，女生则常常以预先有安排或与家人有约为由。例如，在 Situation 8 中，有男生说 "I have a regular club activity at that time..."（MS38），"I will be attending Professor A's class"（MS19）；在这一交际场景

中,有女生说到"I have promised I would visit my grandma that time…"(FS10)。

"Regret"也是不同性别的中泰缅大学生使用频率最高的拒绝策略之一。不同性别的两组中泰缅大学生常常将"Regret"策略放在话语的开头或结尾,有的学生在同一交际场景的开头和结尾都使用了该策略。在本研究中,不同性别的中泰缅大学生对该策略的使用也主要包含"Apology""Pity"和"Hoping for forgiveness"3种表达方式。

本研究发现,女生在使用"Apology"的表达方式时,其使用加强词的频率高于男生。在所有使用"Regret"拒绝策略的场景中,女生使用加强词的总频数为378次,男生使用加强词的总频数为256次。例如,在Situation 2 "The chair of the department invites his/her college student to a workshop on career planning"中,有女生在表达拒绝时说"I am really very sorry…","…I do feel sorry for that","I must express my apology to you…";"I am extremely sorry…"等。两组不同性别的中泰缅大学生也频繁地使用了"Pity"的表达方式。男生使用"Pity"表达的次数为118次,女生为175次。男女同学使用该表达方式时常用的语用套语为"What a pity""It's a pity"等。除以上2种"Regret"策略的表达方式外,本研究发现女生还使用了"Hoping for forgiveness"的表达方式。女生使用该表达方式的总频数为56次。例如,在Situation 8 "The dean of a school offers a lecture attendance chance to a college student"中,有女生在拒绝时说"I hope you won't be disappointed with me"(FS36),"Please forgive me…"(FS65)等。在访谈中,笔者了解到女生之所以采用了"Hoping for forgiveness"的表达方式是因为她们担心拒绝别人会给人带来不悦,并希望尽快了解对方被拒绝后对自己的态度。

调查发现,"Negative willingness/ability"也进入了不同性别的中泰缅大学生使用频率最高的拒绝策略之列。本研究中的男女学生使用该策略的频数都很高,分别达到了527次和639次。值得一提的是,两组不同性别的学生都频繁使用该策略是受到了本国文化的影响,中泰缅大学生普遍认为自谦是一种美德和传统习惯。许多同学在访谈中不约而同地提到了这点。此外,在本研究对"Negative willingness/ability"中,有学生在使用该策略时说"I can't accept because I have already arranged…"。在访谈中,有学生说"Take Situation 9 for example, I think to show the teacher my inability is the best way to refuse. On the one hand, it could show my modesty, on the other hand, I hope the teacher won't be angry with this since I am honest"(IS3),"Sometimes when we refuse others, we would like to show them that we are not able to do things since we have to do something else. I think it's quite common to say that in my own culture"（IS8）。

此外，不同性别的中泰缅大学生使用频率最低的 3 种拒绝策略均为直接策略"Performative"，间接策略"Wish"和附加语策略"Empathy"。男生和女生使用"Performative"策略的频率均为 2 次，对该策略使用的 4 个频次，使用者为 1 名男生和 1 名女生，均表现为"I refuse..."。笔者专门就该策略的使用采访了这 2 名同学。两名同学都表示采用"I refuse..."的方式进行拒绝是由于上课时听老师讲过西方人表达比较直接，不喜欢迂回婉转。但他们却忽略了拒绝言语行为属于面子威胁言语行为的范畴，进行直接拒绝可能会对交际对方的面子构成伤害。

"Wish"策略也是不同性别的两组学生使用频率最低的拒绝策略之一。根据牛津词典的解释，"Wish"表示"hope or express hope for another person's success or happiness or pleasure on a particular occasion"。在访谈中，使用该拒绝策略的同学表示："I use this strategy because I still want to express my hope of happiness to the speaker..."（IS17）。但大多数接受采访的学生都表示几乎不会想到使用该策略。

不同性别的两组学生使用"Empathy"策略的频率也很低。牛津词典里将"Empathy"解释为"the ability to share someone else's feelings or experiences by imagining what it would be like to be in that person's situation"。在本研究中，"Empathy"作为拒绝策略，更准确的表达应是"Showing/Expressing Empathy"。即学生在拒绝场景中表现出设身处地地对被拒绝者感受，经历等的理解。在使用该策略时，学生常用"I can really understand you...""I know your kindness..."等。本研究中的男女大学生各有 5 次使用了该策略。但遗憾的是，在随机抽样的访谈对象中，没有学生使用过该策略。有学生在访谈中说"Maybe I am not careful enough to consider how other people feel when I refuse them, so I have never used empathy as a strategy in refusal"（IS10），"Empathy, I have never thought about using such a strategy in refusal. For me, I just need to tell people why I couldn't accept"（IS17）。

三、不同性别的中泰缅大学生英语拒绝策略使用差异性讨论

不同性别的中泰缅大学生在 6 种拒绝策略使用频率上出现了显著性差异，总的来说，男生使用直接策略"No"的频率明显高于女生，女生使用间接策

略和附加语策略"Explanation""Alternative""Positive opinion""Pause fillers""Gratitude"的频率明显高于男生。究其原因,可以从以下几个方面进行解释:①社会语用能力;②感知能力;③英语语言水平。

学生的社会语用知识是导致男女学生拒绝策略使用频率不同的因素之一。早期的研究(Spolsky,1989)发现,在交际策略使用上,女生比男生更加委婉含蓄。从语义套语来看,女生通常比男生使用了更多的语义套语。这就能在一定程度上说明为什么男生使用直接策略"No"的频率明显高于女生,男生认为直接拒绝别人更能让对方理解,也更加清楚明了。在访谈中,男生说"I refuse others by saying 'No' because I think it's direct, and in Chinese we also say '不' when we refuse people"(IS3),"I think it's enough to say 'No' when I refuse people"(IS7)。女生使用"Explanation""Alternative""Positive opinion""Pause fillers"和"Gratitude"策略的频率明显高于男生。在访谈中,女生说"For me, to refuse others is a very hard thing, even if I have to do so, I hope to explain the reason clearly to make people understand"(IS9),"I think to show our gratitude to others is very necessary when we refuse other people's invitation, request, offer or suggestion"(IS12),"Sometimes when we refuse others, I am not unwilling to accept and I really want to help, so I will either show my willingness or explanation"(IS2),"In my opinion, if people invite, require, give offers or suggestions to us, whether we can accept or not, we should thank them"(IS18),"When I have to refuse people, I hope I won't make them sad. So I want to make some compensation to them and offer them some alternatives"(IS11)。根据以上访谈内容可见,女生在实施拒绝言语行为时会更多考虑交际对象的感受,她们努力将面子威胁的程度降到最低,所以更多地使用了"Explanation""Alternative""Positive opinion""Gratitude"策略。在本研究中,女生使用"Pause fillers"策略的频率也明显高于男生,女生在访谈中提到在实施拒绝言语行为时,有时需要时间思考如何组织语言,在思考的过程中,就会自然使用该策略。

不同性别学生的感知能力对他们拒绝策略的选择和使用也会产生影响。Mori 和 Gobel(2006)指出,女生对英语的感知能力较强,而男生对数学和体育的感知能力较强。也就是说,在外语学习方面,女生通常比男生表现出更加积极的态度。此外,女生在跨文化交际中会更努力地实现有效交际。男女学生对外语的不同感知能力也可以解释他们拒绝策略使用频率的不同。在本研究中,男生使用"No"策略的频率明显高于女生。在访谈中,男生说"I think it's clear and direct to refuse people by saying 'No', so I like to use this word" (IS7), "Saying 'No' is the most convenient way to refuse people" (IS14)。针对"No"策略的使用,有女生说到 "I don't like to say 'No' when I refuse people because I have never heard people say 'No' directly when they refuse people" (IS10), "It's not very polite to say 'No' directly in English communication, so I never use it to refuse others" (IS15)。由此可见,对于同一拒绝策略的使用,男生和女生由于对策略理解的差异,会直接影响他们选择或不选择使用该策略。

此外,女生使用间接策略"Explanation""Alternative"和附加语策略"Positive opinion""Pause fillers""Gratitude"的频率明显高于男生。在访谈中,笔者了解到多数女生在学习英语的过程中习得了英语语言国家的拒绝语表达习惯,在实施该言语行为时,为了减少面子威胁的程度,较常使用以上几种策略。如,在提到对"Explanation"策略的使用时,有女生说 "When I refuse people, I'd like to give people reasons and hope to get their understanding, I use this strategy because I always hear my western friends say things like that" (IS4), "My English teacher used to tell me that it's easier for people to accept my refusal if I explain to them my reason" (IS14)。提到"Alternative"策略时,有女生说 "When I refuse people, I think I should make some compensations. In my speaking class, my foreign teacher taught us that using 'Alternative' strategy is a good way" (IS15), "I think if I give some other choices when I refuse people, they would feel better" (IS18)。女生在访谈中谈到对"Positive opinion"策略的使用时说,"It seems to me that English native speakers are used to showing their interest before they refuse in the situations which people make invitations, give offers, make requests or give suggestions to them" (IS18)。提到"Gratitude"策略的使用时有女生说 "Whether people invite me or give me suggestions, I should give my thanks to them before I refuse them in order to show my politeness, and it's the way how English speakers refuse people" (IS18), "According to my English learning experience, western people like to say 'thank you' first before they refuse invitations, offers, requests or suggestions whether they would accept or not, so when I need to conduct a speech act with English, I would like to follow their habits" (IS2)。此外,女生还在访谈中提到当他们和英语母语者进行交际时,几乎没有人会直接拒绝,英语母语使用者常常会先

对邀请、请求、给予、建议表示感谢,再采用如"Explanation""Alternative""Positive opinion""Gratitude"等策略进行拒绝。因此,女生表示在使用英语实施拒绝言语行为时,也会采用和英语母语者相同的策略。基于女生对语言学习较强的感知能力和以上访谈数据,这就不难理解女生使用"Explanation""Alternative""Positive opinion""Gratitude"的频率比男生高了。

英语语言水平的差异也是导致不同性别的学生在拒绝策略使用频率上出现差异的原因之一。本研究共收集到152份有效问卷,其中男生72份,女生80份。根据本研究第三章的调查数据,笔者了解到男女生英语水平处于"lower intermediate"水平的学生分别为36名和40名。英语水平处于"upper intermediate"水平的学生分别为36名和40名。尽管在语言水平自评中,男女同学的英语水平差距不大,但不同性别的同学对自己语言水平和策略选择的思路却有所不同。例如,不少女生在访谈中表示,其英语语言水平不高是他们使用"Pause fillers"策略的主要原因,如有女生说"When I need to consider what I should say to refuse people, I would use 'Pause fillers'. I mean I would keep quiet or use the expressions as 'Urr', 'Er' and so on"(IS2),"I don't think my English is good enough to communicate flexibly, so I normally need some time to organize my expressions and maybe the pauses are like 'Pause fillers' as what you mean"(IS18)。但是,男生认为其语言水平不高是他们在表达中遇到困难时,会直接采用"No"或"Regret"策略表示拒绝。在男生使用"Regret"策略时,最常用的表达方式就是"Sorry"。在访谈中,有男生说"When I feel difficult to express my refusal to others, I'd like to select some easy ways. For example, I would say 'no' directly"(IS1),"My English is not good, and I always feel headache when I want to express myself with English, and when I am required to refuse people, what come into my mind first is 'sorry'"(IS20)。

总的来说,在校园生活场景中,不同性别的中泰缅大学生在6种拒绝策略使用频率上具有显著性差异。具体表现在男生使用直接策略"No"的频率明显高于女生。在访谈中,笔者了解到出现这一差异的主要原因是男生在交际中倾向于直截了当,他们认为这样的拒绝方式不会使交际对方产生误解,但却忽略了对交际对象的面子威胁和礼貌原则。同时,女生使用"Explanation""Alternative""Positive opinion""Gratitude"和"Pause fillers"策略的频率明显比男生高,产生这些差异的原因可以从女生的社会语用能力,对语言的感知能力较强进行解释。从采访中笔者得知,女生在交际中更能考虑交际对象的感受，她们在实施如拒绝言语行为等面子威胁言语行为时，总是希望能减轻对方的不适感，并采用合适的策略使对方不受伤害。同时，尽管从自评数据来看，男女同学的英语语言水平非常接近，女生更多地使用了"Pause fillers"策略。在访谈中，女生表示采用该策略主要是由于自己语言水平不高所致，在交际时需要时间组织语言，希望自己的表达方式得体、合理。而男生在实施拒绝言语行为时，常常为了省事，遇到自己不知如何表达时，则喜欢使用直接策略"No"或使用间接策略"Regret"。

第三节 不同英语水平的中泰缅大学生英语拒绝策略使用异同讨论

一、不同英语水平的中泰缅大学生英语拒绝策略使用异同情况

根据本研究结果，在拒绝邀请时，不同英语水平的中泰缅大学生都使用了Beebe等（1990）总结的18种拒绝策略。在其中15种拒绝策略的使用上，不同英语水平的中泰缅大学生在策略使用频率上没有显著性差异。但在2种拒绝策略的使用频率上，不同英语水平的中泰缅大学生出现了显著性差异，具体表现在：①英语水平处于"lower intermediate"的学生使用间接策略"Alternative"的频率明显高于英语水平处于"upper intermediate"的学生；②英语水平处于"upper intermediate"的学生使用间接策略"Regret"和附加语策略"Gratitude"的频率明显高于英语水平处于"lower intermediate"的学生。

在拒绝请求时，不同英语水平的中泰缅大学生都使用了Beebe等（1990）总结的13种拒绝策略。其中，2组学生在10种拒绝策略的使用频率上没有显著性差异。但是，不同英语水平的中泰缅大学生在3种拒绝策略的使用频率上出现了显著性差异，具体表现在：①英语水平处于"lower intermediate"的学生使用间接策略"Alternative"的频率明显高于英语水平处于"upper intermediate"的学生；②英语水平处于"upper intermediate"的学生使用间接策略"Regret"和附加语策略"Gratitude"的频率明显高于英语水平处于"lower intermediate"的学生。

在拒绝给予时，不同英语水平的两组中泰缅大学生都使用了Beebe等

（1990）总结的拒绝策略中的 10 种。在其中 8 种拒绝策略的使用频率上，不同英语水平的中泰缅大学生没有显著性差异。但是，在使用其中的两种拒绝策略时，不同英语水平的中泰缅大学生出现了使用频率的显著性差异，具体表现在：英语水平处于"lower intermediate"的学生使用间接策略"Regret"和附加语策略"Gratitude"的频率明显低于英语水平处于"upper intermediate"的学生。

拒绝建议时，不同英语水平的中泰缅大学生都采用了 Beebe 等（1990）总结的拒绝策略中的 10 种，不同英语水平的两组学生在所有拒绝策略使用频率上不存在显著性差异。不同英语水平的中泰缅大学生使用频率最高的策略均为间接策略"Explanation"、直接策略"Negative willingness/ability"和附加语策略"Gratitude"；使用频率最低的拒绝策略均为间接策略"Acceptance that functions as a refusal""Avoidance"和"Attempt to dissuade interlocutor"。

总的来说，根据学生英语水平的不同，其使用的拒绝策略的种类和频率也有所区别。英语水平处于"lower intermediate"的学生使用了 Beebe 等（1990）总结的 18 种拒绝策略；英语水平处于"upper intermediate"的中泰缅大学生使用了 Beebe 等（1990）总结的 17 种拒绝策略，没有使用直接策略"Performative"。在已使用的拒绝策略中，英语水平处于"lower intermediate"的中泰缅大学生使用频率低的策略共有 15 种，包括 2 种直接策略、9 种间接策略、4 种附加语策略；该组学生使用频率处于中等的拒绝策略有 2 种，即直接策略"Negative willingness/ability"和间接策略"Regret"；英语水平处于"lower intermediate"的大学生使用频率高的策略仅有 1 种，即间接策略"Explanation"。英语水平处于"upper intermediate"的中泰缅大学生使用的拒绝策略中，频率低的有 14 种，包括 2 种直接策略、9 种间接策略、3 种附加语策略；该组学生共在两种拒绝策略的使用频率上处于中等水平，即间接策略"Regret"和附加语策略"Gratitude"；英语水平处于"upper intermediate"的中泰缅大学生使用频率高的拒绝策略有 2 种，分别是直接策略"Negative willingness/ability"和间接策略"Explanation"。从总体上看，不同英语水平的 2 组学生使用 15 种拒绝策略的频率没有显著性差异，但在 3 种拒绝策略的使用频率上出现了显著性差异，分别是间接策略"Regret"和"Alternative"，以及附加语策略"Gratitude"。其差异具体表现在：①英语水平处于"lower intermediate"的学生在"Alternative"策略的使用频率上明显高于英语水平处于"upper intermediate"的学生；②英语水平处于"lower intermediate"的学生在"Regret"和"Gratitude"策略的使用频率上明显低于英语水平处于

"upper intermediate"的学生。

二、不同英语水平的中泰缅大学生英语拒绝策略使用相似性讨论

从表4.13可见，不同英语水平的中泰缅大学生拒绝策略总体使用频率较低。男女学生使用频率最高的3组拒绝策略为"Explanation""Regret"和"Negative willingness/ability"。

实际上，在本研究中，无论是不同国籍的中泰缅大学生，还是不同性别的中泰缅大学生，或是不同英语水平的中泰缅大学生，其使用频率最高的3种拒绝策略都是"Explanation""Regret"和"Negative willingness/ability"。这说明本研究的研究对象具有一定的同质性。从不同的英语水平看，英语水平处于"upper intermediate"的中泰缅大学生在以上3种拒绝策略的使用频率上都高于英语水平处于"lower intermediate"的中泰缅大学生。

"Explanation"策略是2组英语水平不同的学生使用频率最高的拒绝策略。英语水平处于"upper intermediate"的学生使用该策略的频率为803次，英语水平处于"lower intermediate"的学生使用该策略的频率为750次。就其频繁使用该策略的原因，主要也是受到本国文化的影响。大多中泰缅大学生使用该策略都是源于从交际对方的接受心理出发。他们认为在拒绝后给予适当的解释能使对方更能理解被拒绝这一交际行为。因此，在实施这一交际策略进行拒绝时，许多学生使用的语用套语为"Regret"+"Negative willing/ability"+"Explanation"。这样的语义套语结构也不难解释学生们使用以上3种拒绝策略的频率位居所有拒绝策略的榜首。以场景2"The chair of the department invites his/her college student to a workshop on career planning"为例，有学生在拒绝中说"I'm sorry, sir(Regret), I can't be there(Negative willing/ability)since I should take an examination that day(Explanation)"（HS19）。

语言能力较强的学生使用以上3种拒绝策略的频率都略高于语言能力较弱的学生这一研究结果与Prachanant（2006）和Wannaruk（2008）的研究结果不谋而合。她们认为语言能力强的学生和语言能力弱的学生在实施言语行为时，其内容表达上会有区别。换句话说，语言能力强的学生实施言语行为时，内容更加冗长，语气更加委婉；语言能力弱的学生实施言语行为时内容更短，语气更加生硬。这恰恰表明语言能力会在一定程度上影响语言学习者在实施言语行为时对策略的选择和内容。在采访中，语言能力处于"upper intermediate"和"lower intermediate"的学生都表示，语言能力对他们实施

拒绝言语行为时的策略选择有直接影响。也就是说，他们表达拒绝言语行为时或多或少都会受到语言能力的限制，也不能确定如何表达才更加合情合理、更加礼貌。正因为如此，他们常常采用"Regret"＋"Negative willing/ability"＋"Explanation"的语义套语模式。语言水平较弱的同学中有人也表示，尽管他们也想到用这样的语义套语，但是由于语言能力的限制，不知如何用英语进行表达，所以有时就尽量少用拒绝策略，用最少的话语进行拒绝。

在本研究中，两组不同英语水平的中泰缅大学生使用频率最低的3种拒绝策略为"Performative""Wish"和"Empathy"。英语水平较高的学生使用这3种策略的频数分别为6、4、0，英语水平较低的学生使用该3种策略的频数分别为4、6、4。学生们都认为在实施拒绝言语行为时，几乎不会想到用以上拒绝策略。首先，他们认为"Performative"策略过于直接，在拒绝时显得不够礼貌，他们担心这样的拒绝方式会影响和交际对象的关系。其次，在访谈中，学生提到尽管"Wish"和"Empathy"策略不会对交际对象的面子造成不好的影响，但是在本研究的交际场景中，不知为何要对交际对象表示愿望和同情，也很难合理地表示愿望和同情。

三、不同英语水平的中泰缅大学生英语拒绝策略使用差异性讨论

不同英语水平的中泰缅大学生在一些拒绝策略的使用频率上出现了显著性差异。总的来说，英语水平处于"lower intermediate"的学生使用间接策略"Alternative"的频率明显高于英语水平处于"upper intermediate"的学生；英语水平处于"upper intermediate"的学生使用附加语策略"Gratitude"的频率明显高于英语水平处于"lower intermediate"的学生。出现以上差异，可以从以下方面进行解释：

Ellis（2008）认为，二语学习者在使用二语进行交际时，其策略使用往往受到母语的影响。Eysenck（2001）也指出，人的心理认知过程包括对外部环境的认识，并在此基础上决定采取何种适宜的行为。Mclaughlin（1990）提出的信息加工模型可以很好地解释二语学习者对言语行为的理解和产出。Mclaughlin（1990）认为，二语学习者对知识的表现和对知识的处理方式密切相关。在二语交际过程中，学习者的信息处理能力和交际任务的本质密切相关。对于二语学习者来说，他们既不能完全接收语言输入的信息，也不能完全按照英语母语者的交际习惯进行沟通。但是，在跨文化交际中，不同语言水平的二语学习者的语言使用规范和母语使用者接近的程度是有所区别的。Rover

(2014) 提出，语言水平高的二语学习者比语言水平低的二语学习者的信息处理能力更强。就中介语语用策略而言，在不同语言环境下的语言使用者可能使用相同的言语行为策略。因此，二语学习者在言语行为策略使用上存在母语正迁移的可能性。当然，这种迁移更多体现在习惯性的间接表达策略方面，并对言后行为产生影响。二语水平高的学生在母语迁移的过程中能更好地调整自己的言语行为实施策略，以适应二语的语用习惯。

首先，在本研究中英语水平处于"lower intermediate"的学生使用"Alternative"策略的频率明显高于英语水平处于"upper intermediate"的学生。在访谈中，有英语水平处于"lower intermediate"的学生提到使用该拒绝策略主要还是受到了其母语文化的影响。例如，有学生说"According to the culture of my mother tongue, when we refuse others, we always show them another choice. In this way, we expect that they would feel less disappointed"（IS1），"I think we are used to giving people a make-up suggestion when we couldn't accept their invitation, offers, requests or suggestions, so I also express my ideas in this way when communicating with English"（IS11）。因此，学生在使用该策略时，常用的表达有"I can't have dinner with you today, maybe I can join you after dinner"（LS29，S3），"I am in a hurry, perhaps you can ask my friend whether he would like to help"（LS44，S4），"I have an examination at that time, and I can help for some preparation work"（LS58，S8）。由此可见，英语语言水平低的同学更易受到母语文化和母语表达习惯的影响。而语言水平高的同学则更能适应目标语文化和目标语表达习惯。

其次，在谈到"Gratitude"策略的使用时，英语水平处于"upper intermediate"的学生在访谈中更多强调了拒绝言语行为的面子威胁程度，并认为在实施面子威胁言语行为时，要尽可能缓解此类言语行为的面子威胁程度。形成对比的是，英语水平处于"lower intermediate"的学生则少有提及这点。例如，英语水平处于"upper intermediate"的学生在访谈中说"For me, showing gratitude came into my mind when I have to refuse others, because it could either show my politeness as well as release the degree of face threaten"（IS20），"Normally I would say 'thanks' before I refuse people, since it could show the willingness to accept the invitation, offer, request or suggestion, and then they may feel better"（IS15）。在跨文化交际中，英语水平处于"upper intermediate"的学生使用"Gratitude"策略的频率明显高于处于

"lower intermediate"的学生的情况，还可以从西方文化影响的角度进行解释。英语水平处于"upper intermediate"的学生同时也更多地受到了西方文化和语言习惯的影响。如，有学生说"As far as what I have learned, English native speakers love to show their appreciation first for people's invitation, offers or suggestions whether they would accept or not"(IS4)，"Normally the westerners will start a conversation in refusal by gratitude, and I just follow their habit"(IS8)。

总之，从不同英语水平的中泰缅大学生拒绝策略使用的差异来看，英语水平处于"lower intermediate"的学生受到母语干扰的程度更大。笔者从采访了解到母语负迁移正是其更多使用"Alternative"的原因。而英语水平处于"upper intermediate"的学生更频繁地使用了"Gratitude"策略，这一发现表明英语水平较高的学生更能主动缓解实施拒绝言语行为时的言后影响。Gallaher（2011）也通过观察法发现英语水平较高的学生对缓和策略的使用比英语水平较低的学生更得当和频繁。

第四节　不同情景因素下中泰缅大学生英语拒绝策略使用异同讨论

一、不同情景因素下中泰缅大学生英语拒绝策略使用异同情况

根据本研究的研究结果，中泰缅大学生在不同的社会距离、地位差距、强加程度的交际场景中，使用的拒绝策略也有所不同。在社会距离亲密和疏远的两组交际场景中，中泰缅大学生共使用了Beebe等（1990）总结的所有18种拒绝策略。但是，在关系亲密和关系疏远的交际场景中，学生对拒绝策略的选择不同。在交际双方社会距离亲密的场景中，学生使用了18种拒绝策略。然而，在交际双方关系疏远的交际场景中，学生使用了除直接策略"Performative"，间接策略"Wish"和"Statement of philosophy"外的15种拒绝策略。在所有使用的18种拒绝策略中，根据交际双方的亲疏关系不同，中泰缅大学生在3种拒绝策略的使用频率上出现了显著性差异，具体表现在：①在交际双方关系亲密的场景中，中泰缅大学生使用"Performative"策略的频率明显高于交际双方关系疏远的场景；②在交际双方关系疏远的交际场景

中,中泰缅大学生使用间接策略"Wish"和"Alternative"的频率明显高于交际双方关系亲密的场景。

在不同地位差距的交际场景中,中泰缅大学生共使用了Beebe等(1990)总结的所有18种拒绝策略。无论在交际双方地位为"高-低"的交际场景中,还是在交际双方地位平等的交际场景中,中泰缅大学生使用频率最高的拒绝策略均为直接策略"Negative willingness/ability",以及间接策略"Explanation""Regret";在不同的社会距离场景中,中泰缅大学生使用频率最低的拒绝策略均为直接策略"Performative"、间接策略"Wish",以及附加语策略"Empathy"。在地位差距为"高-低"的交际场景和交际双方地位平等的交际场景中,中泰缅大学生在5种拒绝策略的使用频率上出现了显著性差异,具体表现在:①交际场景中的地位差距为"高-低"时,中泰缅大学生使用直接策略"Negative willingness/ability"和间接策略"Regret""Pause fillers"的频率明显高于地位平等的交际情景;②在间接策略"Alternative"和"Attempt to dissuade interlocutor"的使用上,中泰缅大学生在社会地位平等的场景中的使用频率明显高于在地位差距为"高-低"的交际场景。

在不同强加程度的交际场景中,中泰缅大学生使用了Beebe等(1990)总结的所有18种拒绝策略。无论在交际对象强加程度强的交际场景中,还是在交际对象强加程度弱的交际场景中,中泰缅大学生使用频率最高的拒绝策略均为直接策略"Negative willingness/ability"和间接策略"Explanation""Regret",使用频率最低的拒绝策略均为直接策略"Performative"、间接策略"Wish",以及附加语策略"Empathy"。此外,在不同强加程度的交际场景中,中泰缅大学生在5种交际策略的使用频率上存在显著性差异,具体表现在:①在强加程度强的交际场景中,中泰缅大学生使用直接策略"Negative willingness/ability"、间接策略"Regret"以及附加语策略"Pause fillers"的频率明显高于在强加程度弱的交际场景;②在强加程度强的交际场景中,中泰缅大学生使用间接策略"Alternative""Attempt to dissuade interlocutor"的频率明显低于在强加程度弱的交际场景。

二、不同情景因素下中泰缅大学生英语拒绝策略使用差异性讨论

Brown和Levison(1987)指出交际双方的社会距离、地位差距、强加程度是在某一文化背景下实施特定言语行为时策略选择的3类主要社会影响因素。本研究正是着眼于以上3类情景因素,探讨在不同的情景因素下,中泰缅

大学生拒绝策略使用特点。首先，在不同社会距离场景下，中泰缅大学生使用直接策略"Performative"和间接策略"Wish""Alternative"的频率上都出现了显著性差异。其中，在交际双方关系亲密的场景中，学生使用"Performative"策略的频率明显高于关系疏远的场景。就其原因，在访谈中，有学生说"In the situations where we have a close relationship, I may refuse people directly because I don't think they would be angry with me"（IS10），"Since we have a close relationship, I am sure people would understand if I refuse directly"（IS12），"When the relationship between I and the listener are not close, I won't use 'Performative' strategy because it is too direct and the relationship will be broken"（IS18），"When I face people who are not close with me, I will be very careful about how to refuse. Direct refusals won't be used"（IS11）。由此可见，一些中泰缅大学生认为对关系亲密的交际对象实施拒绝言语行为时可以采用较为直接的拒绝策略。他们觉得在关系亲密的情况下，采用直接的拒绝策略不至于会伤及对方的面子，也使交流更加直截了当。而在交际双方关系疏远的场景下，学生们则更加重视拒绝策略的选择，较少使用直接策略"Performative"。究其原因，一方面是由于学生考虑到拒绝言语行为的实施本身就可能会给交际对方带来负面情绪，使用直接的拒绝策略会让交际对方感到更加不悦；另一方面是由于在本研究中，关于疏远的场景多发生在学校领导或教授和学生之间，学生认为采用直接的拒绝策略显得对领导或教授不够尊重，因此也较少使用"Performative"策略。

此外，在关系疏远的交际场景中，中泰缅大学生使用间接策略"Wish"和"Alternative"的频率明显高于交际双方关系亲密的场景。在访谈中学生们说"It's an embarrassing thing to conduct refusal speech act, especially with people who I am not familiar with, so I think to send them some good wishes after refusing may release the hurt of refusal"（IS1），"For me, I think I want to do something to make up the face-threaten feelings I give people because of refusal, and sending wishes may be a good choice"（IS3）。在提到对"Alternative"策略的使用时，学生说"Although I have to refuse others, I would normally give them another choice to show that I am not purposively doing that"（IS12），"When I refuse people who I am not familiar with, I am worried whether they would misunderstand that I don't want to accept their invitations, offers, requests or suggestions, so I would like to find some way to make up it"（IS19）。可见，学生们使用"Wish"策略和"Alternative"策

略的主要思考是为了减轻对交际对象的面子威胁程度。学生们认为实施拒绝言语行为，尤其是对关系较为疏远的交际对象实施该言语行为是一件较为尴尬甚至为难的事情，希望在交际中尽量缓解该言语行为产生的面子威胁言后行为，他们认为不论是使用"Wish"策略还是"Alternative"策略，都能够有效起到拒绝言语行为对面子伤害的弥补作用。尤其是在距离疏远的交际场景中，学生在实施拒绝言语行为时则显得更加谨慎，更希望减轻对交际对象面子威胁的程度，以保持和谐的社会关系。

在不同的地位差距情景下，中泰缅大学生也出现了拒绝策略使用频率上的差异，具体体现为中泰缅大学生在交际双方地位差距为"高-低"时，使用直接策略"Negative willingness/ability"、间接策略"Regret"和"Pause fillers"的频率明显高于交际双方地位平等的场景。在访谈中，有学生表示，在交际对象的社会地位高于自己时，尤其是在本研究中，社会地位高的交际对象往往是老师或学校领导，自己会更频繁地使用"Negative willingness/ability"策略，这是因为"When my teacher or the leader of our school asks me to do something, I am afraid I can't make them satisfied, so I would like to show them my inability to do that"（IS2），"In the communicative situations where the speaker has a higher status than me, I always think I should show my modest, so I refuse with showing my inability"（IS13），"Showing that I am not capable is a kind of politeness in my country, and I think I should do that especially in front of the people who are higher-status than me"（IS19）。从对学生的访谈结果可见，实施拒绝言语行为时，当学生的社会地位低于交际对象时，学生常常表现得较谦卑。一方面是地位差距给学生带来了交际压力，使学生在对地位高的人进行拒绝时更倾向于表达自己的不足或能力不够；另一方面是由于学生受到了其母语文化的影响，在交际过程中学生对地位比自己高的交际对象所表达的能力不足，是为了表现出谦虚的态度，学生在实施拒绝言语行为时发生了母语文化迁移。

另外，在提到对"Regret"策略的使用时，接受访谈的学生提到在进行拒绝之前首先表示抱歉是必要的礼貌行为，特别是当交际对象的社会地位高于自己时，对不能接受别人的邀请、请求、要求、建议等更应首先表示"Regret"，以表示对交际对象的尊重和礼貌。例如，在访谈中有学生说"It's better to express my regret before I refuse people, especially when they have a higher status than me. If I do that, they would think I respect them"（IS5），"In my opinion, we should show our regret when we have to refuse people who are my teachers or leaders because I think they may be angry when I refuse them, and if I show my regret at first, they may not be very angry" (IS8)。提到"Pause fillers"策略的使用时,学生认为主要是因为在面对社会地位比自己高的交际对象时,自己在拒绝时会有更多的思考,担心说错话,所以出现了更多的停顿现象(IS2,IS6,IS10,IS12,IS18)。例如,学生在拒绝社会地位高于自己的交际对象时,常用的语用套语如"I am so sorry (Regret). I afraid I can't understand the lecture (Negative willingness/ability)" (IS8)。

然而,在交际双方地位平等的场景中,中泰缅大学生使用间接策略"Alternative"和"Attempt to dissuade interlocutor"的频率明显高于交际双方地位"高-低"的场景。在交际双方地位平等时,学生表示实施拒绝言语行为时,他们的话语会更多一些,也会更完整地表达自己的想法。在提到对"Alternative"策略的使用时,学生说"When I refuse people who have the equal social status with me, sometimes I would give them give them the other choice after refusal. In this way, I hope they would feel better" (IS1); "For me, I will say less when communicate with people who have a higher social status than me. While, when I refuse people who are socially equal with me, I would like to say something to make up my refusal, such as suggesting another person to do the thing" (IS19)。此外,在交际双方社会地位平等的交际场景中,中泰缅大学生使用"Attempt to dissuade interlocutor"策略的频率也明显高于交际双方社会地位为"高-低"的场景。访谈中学生说"If the speaker invite, offer, request or suggest me to do something I don't want to accept, I might dissuade him/her, especially when we have the same social status" (IS11)。例如,学生在使用该策略时说"That's a bad idea since I won't be of any help" (S1)。

中泰缅大学生在不同强加程度的场景下实施拒绝言语行为,表现出的拒绝策略使用频率差异和不同社会差距场景下的相似,即在强加程度强的场景下,学生使用直接策略"Negative willingness/ability"、间接策略"Regret",以及附加语策略"Pause fillers"的频率明显高于强加程度弱的场景;学生在强加程度弱的场景下,使用"Alternative""Attempt to dissuade interlocutor"策略的频率明显高于强加程度强的场景。学生提到强加程度强的场景一般也是交际对象社会地位高的场景,强加程度弱的场景往往也是社会地位平等的场景。因此,学生表示在强加程度强的场景中和社会地位为"高-低"场景中的拒绝策略选择几乎一致,在强加程度弱的场景中和社会地位平等的交际场景中的拒绝策略选择大体一致。

总之，本研究发现不同的情景因素对中泰缅大学生的拒绝策略选择产生了一定影响。从访谈数据来看，学生们表示，不同的社会距离、地位差距和强加程度在一定程度上影响了他们对拒绝策略的选择。具体地说，在社会距离疏远的场景中，学生们更倾向于采取较为间接的拒绝策略，在社会距离亲密的交际场景中，学生们使用直接拒绝策略的频率更高；本研究中的地位差距和强加程度在一定程度上对学生的拒绝策略选择产生的相似的影响。本研究中地位差距大的场景也往往是强加程度大的场景，主要表现在学生和教授或学校领导之间产生对话的场景，地位差距小的场景也往往是强加程度小的场景，一般是学生和学生之间的交际场景。访谈中学生们表示，在地位差距大或强加程度大的交际场景中，他们对拒绝策略的选择更为谨慎，因此更多地使用了"Pause fillers"策略，以便给自己留出思考的时间。此外，学生们还更多使用了"Negative willingness/ability"和"Regret"策略，这说明在面对社会地位比自己高的交际对象时，学生们更愿意表现出自己的谦虚和歉意。

第六章 结 论

本章首先对本研究的研究成果进行小结,其次分析本研究结果对教学的启示,再次对本研究的研究局限进行描述,最后提出了对将来在该研究领域进行相关研究的建议。

第一节 研究结果小结

本研究着眼于调查中泰缅大学生在校园生活场景下拒绝策略使用情况。共有 180 名在校大学生参加了本次研究,收回有效问卷 152 份。数据分析结合了定量分析和定性分析的研究方法,主要回答 4 个研究问题。本研究的研究发现总结如下:

研究问题一关注中泰缅大学生拒绝策略使用情况。通过 SPSS 21.0 进行 ANOVA 数据分析后,笔者发现中泰缅大学生拒绝策略总体使用频率不高。学生们使用了 Beebe 等(1990)对于拒绝策略分类的 18 种策略。从总体上看,不同国籍的中泰缅大学生使用频率最高的 3 种策略相同。在使用频率最低的 3 种策略的使用频率上,不同国籍的中泰缅大学生在 2 种策略上的使用频率相同;在 6 种拒绝策略的使用频率上,出现了显著性差异。

研究问题二探索了不同性别的中泰缅大学生用英语实施拒绝言语行为时的策略使用情况。笔者发现男生和女生虽然都使用了 Beebe 等(1990)总结的 18 种拒绝策略。但使用情况有所不同。通过单因素方差分析,总的来说,男女学生多数拒绝策略的使用频率较低,并在 6 种拒绝策略的使用频率上存在显著性差异。简单地说,男生使用直接策略"No"的频率明显高于女生,女生使用 2 种间接策略和 3 种附加语策略的频率明显高于男生。

研究问题三探讨了不同英语水平的中泰缅大学生用英语实施拒绝言语行为

时的策略使用情况。英语水平处于"lower intermediate"的大学生使用了 Beebe 等（1990）总结的 18 种拒绝策略，英语水平处于"upper intermediate"的大学生使用了 17 种拒绝策略。不同英语水平的两组学生分别使用 15 种和 14 种拒绝策略的频率低。从总体上看，不同英语水平的中泰缅大学生在 3 种拒绝策略的使用上存在显著性差异。

研究问题四分析了在不同情景下中泰缅大学生的英语拒绝策略使用情况。本研究着眼于社会距离地位差距和强加程度 3 个情景因素。首先，在关系亲密的社会距离场景下，中泰缅大学生使用了 Beebe 等（1990）总结的 18 种拒绝策略。在关系疏远社会距离场景下，中泰缅大学生使用了 15 种拒绝策略。在不同社会距离场景下，中泰缅大学生在 3 种拒绝策略使用频率上出现了显著性差异。中泰缅大学生在不同的地位差距场景下都使用了 18 种拒绝策略。在不同的地位差距场景中，中泰缅学生使用频率最高的 3 种拒绝策略和使用频率最低的 3 种拒绝策略相同。然而，3 国大学生在不同的地位差距场景中出现了 5 种拒绝策略使用频率显著性差异。在不同强加程度的拒绝场景中，中泰缅大学生都使用了 18 种拒绝策略，并且他们使用频率最高的 3 种拒绝策略和使用频率最低的 3 种拒绝策略相同。在不同的强加程度场景中，中泰缅大学生在 5 种拒绝策略的使用频率上出现了显著性差异。

本研究以中泰缅 3 国英语学习者为例，探讨了不同国家语言文化背景下的外语学习者的拒绝言语行为策略使用情况，进一步丰富了跨文化背景下中介语语用研究的文献。基于以上研究成果，笔者提出了以下英语中介语交际能力教学启示，将在下一节进行论述。

第二节　教学启示

根据本研究结果，本研究对英语中介语交际能力教学有以下启示：

第一，英语作为一门世界通用语已被越来越多的二语学习者使用（McKay，2002；Liu，2004；Sasaki，Suzuki，Yoneda，2006）。英语非母语使用者的数量已经超过了母语使用者（Graddol，2000）。英语使用规范也不再完全按照母语使用者的规范执行（Shishavan，Sharifian，2013）。然而，英语非母语使用者由于其英语水平和交际目的的不同，在使用英语时，其语言使用合理度标准也不尽相同（McKay，2002）。因此，在英语二语教学中，教师不仅要引导学生学习大量的词汇，掌握丰富的语法知识，了解英语国家社会语言规则（Kwon，2003；Wannaruk，2008），还要帮助学生认识到虽然基础知识可以帮助他们用英语进行交流，还应对不同文化背景下的语言学习者英语使用的礼貌程度和合理程度具有广泛的包容性。要学习和接纳多元文化，并接受和包容多元文化背景下的语言使用合理度规则。

第二，不可否认的是，当今世界，英语作为世界通用语，用英语进行跨语言交际的频率日益增高（Yano，2003）。在交际过程中，英语非母语使用者或多或少都会表露出其自身的文化规范和文化价值观（Boonkongsaen，2013；Shishavan，Sharifian，2013）。然而，在一种文化背景下交际的礼貌合理性未必在另一种文化背景下就能得到认可（AL－Eryani，2007；Wannaruk，2008）。在跨文化交际中，由于不同母语的英语二语学习者的合理和礼貌标准有所差异，有可能出现交际双方不相互认可，最终导致交际失败的情况。因此，在教学中，教师不但需要向学生介绍英语母语使用者的交际原则，还应向学生引入非英语母语使用者的交际习惯和相关文化背景知识。

实际上，在课堂教学中，任何英语教师都不可能包罗万象，涵盖所有在英语二语交际中出现的文化差异现象。所以，教师在教学中可采用显性教学和隐性教学相结合的教学方法，介绍至少两种或以上文化背景下的英语二语者语言使用在语言模式，语言表达和词汇选择等方面的差异（Duan，2008）。例如，教师可使用音频视频等教学手段，向学生展示特定文化背景下如何用英语实施不同的言语行为（Kwon，2003；Wannaruk，2008）。同时，在教学中，教师还可以了解学生如何实施各种言语行为，并向学生展示其语言表达和英语母语使用者的异同（Duan，2008）。通过比较教学的方法，教师可以帮助学生更深入的了解不同国家背景下的文化差异和语用差异（Kwon，2003）。此外，教师还可以通过讨论的方式使学生进一步学习不同文化语言背景下英语使用者实施言语行为时的策略使用差异。通过以上教学方法，英语二语学习者可以更好地判断语言使用者的文化语言背景，减少在交际中出现的交际障碍和尴尬局面，有效改善和提高交际效果。

第三，本研究发现中泰缅大学生在实施拒绝言语行为时，其策略选择和策略使用频率相似之处超过不同之处。在交际能力教学中，这些差异性正是教师教学的重点。特别是对于打算从事涉外工作或海外留学的同学来说，掌握一定的跨文化语用知识则更有必要。如今，英语作为世界通用语，英语教师可以通过本研究中学生实施拒绝言语行为的语义套语习惯，在一定程度上了解中泰缅3国大学生语用行为的母语迁移情况，了解其文化特点和语言使用习惯。中泰缅3国的英语学习者也可以借鉴本研究结果，进一步了解不同国家间的文化差异，加强跨文化交际效果。

第四，本研究发现中泰缅大学生在拒绝策略使用频率上存在性别差异。男女学生在语言学习上存在学习兴趣和学习动机的不同。女生通常在语言学习方面表现得更加合作。在学习外语的过程中，女生也常常更容易接受目标语规则和形式。在实施拒绝言语行为时，女生使用的语义套语常常多余男生，且内容表达更为丰富和冗长。教师在教学中可针对男女学生语用策略使用的不同发现其差异性，突出共性，找到平衡点，促进不同性别间学生交际能力发展，最终提高有效交际的比例。

第五，本研究还发现不同语言水平的学生在一些拒绝策略使用频率上存在显著性差异。在访谈中，语言能力较弱的学生表示英语水平不高是限制其实施拒绝言语行为的主要原因。有限的英语词汇量和语法知识使他们在表达时只能用较为简短的话语进行拒绝，但内心的真实想法不能完全表达出来。因此，对于这些学生而言，提高语言水平则是帮助他们更好实施言语行为和提高交际能力的根本。在教学中，教师则要加强这部分学生的语言基本功训练，从语言基本技能和语法知识入手，帮助学生扩大词汇量，引导学生加强口头交际能力，训练语言表达能力，丰富跨文化知识，最终提高跨文化交际能力。

第六，本研究统计了在不同社会场景下学生拒绝策略的使用情况，并发现在不同社会距离，不同地位差距以及不同强加程度场景下，学生在一些拒绝策略的使用频率上都有所不同。在教学中，教师可以就不同社会场景为专题进行教学，帮助学生在跨文化学习中，了解不同社会场景下语用策略使用的细小差异，灵活掌握和运用二语，成功实现跨文化交际。

尽管本研究为中泰缅大学生的英语语用策略研究做出了一定的努力，但从研究工具设计、研究对象选择、数据收集方法和数据分析方法等方面开看，都存在一些不足之处，这些研究不足都需要在今后的研究中加以改善。下一节笔者将对本研究的不足之处进行分析。

第三节　本研究的研究局限

尽管笔者精心设计了本研究总体框架和各个步骤，但任何研究都不可能面面俱到，本研究的仍在以下几个方面存在不足，接下来将就 WDCT 设计、研究对象选择、研究工具,以及拒绝策略统计的不足之处进行逐一分析。

第一,在设计本研究的 WDCT 时,首先考虑的一点是所有语境能否反映出真实的语言使用情况。也就是说,这些语境是否在学生的现实生活中发生,是否能够引出学生自然交际中的实施拒绝言语行为时的策略使用情况。在本研究设计 WDCT 时,笔者对 21 名中泰缅大学生进行了半结构化访谈,了解预设情景是否可能在其现实交际中发生,并根据访谈结果对场景描述进行了调整,以更好地适应交际需求。尽管如此,本研究的场景设计并没有在现实生活中对学生的实际交际进行观察,并从中大量收集语料,找出出现频率最高的情景,以保证多数参与调查的学生对预设场景较为熟悉,从而使他们自然流露出日常生活中常用的拒绝策略。此外,本研究只涉及了 4 类拒绝场景,即邀请、请求、给予和建议,但现实生活中可能出现的拒绝场景远远不止 4 类。因此,本研究在跨文化交际研究领域只能起到抛砖引玉的作用。

第二,在选择研究对象时,笔者采用了随机抽样原则和方便原则,从中泰缅 3 国共选取了 180 名大学生进行调查研究,收回有效问卷 152 份。但是,由于实际条件的限制,这些学生都来自每个国家的同一所大学。所以本研究的研究结果并不能完全代表中泰缅 3 国大学生的拒绝策略使用情况,本研究结果具有一定的片面性。

第三,从研究工具看,本研究仅采用了书面表达 DCT 和半结构化访谈作为研究工具,在本研究的研究过程中,没有设计口头表达和角色扮演的数据收集工具。在跨文化交际研究中,采用课堂观察法收集口头表达数据更能全面了解学生的拒绝策略使用情况。本研究由于实际情况的限制,几乎不可能将不同国家和不同专业的学生召集起来,同时培训教师进行课堂观察,因此很难通过课堂观察法收集到口头交际数据和肢体语言、面部表情等数据。

第四,在统计学生所使用的拒绝策略时,笔者以 Beebe 等(1990)总结的拒绝策略分类为主要参考。即使该分类是笔者目前能找到的最全面的也是适用范围最广的拒绝策略分类,但也不能囊括所有在实际交际中可能出现的拒绝策略。因此,本研究对学生拒绝策略的分类还有不全面之处。

基于以上研究局限,笔者从 WDCT 设计、研究对象选择、研究工具、拒绝策略统计,以及研究方法几个方面提出了对今后在该研究领域的研究建议,并在下一节进行描述。

第六章 结 论

第四节 对将来研究的建议

本研究探索了中泰缅大学生拒绝策略使用情况，交际场景均为校园生活。研究对象为 180 名中泰缅大学生，收回有效数据 152 份，数据收集工具为 WDCT 和半结构化访谈，数据统计借用了 Beebe 等（1990）的拒绝策略分类，定量数据分析使用了 SPSS 21.0 的描述性统计方法、单因素方差分析法，定性数据分析采用了内容分析法。

首先需要指出的是，任何一项研究都不可能覆盖其研究领域的全部范围，也不可能将所有相关变量纳入考虑。在数据收集方面，言语行为研究主要有 6 种数据收集工具，本研究选用了其中 2 种。基于以上考虑，笔者提出了在跨文化言语行为研究领域对将来研究的几点建议。

第一，对跨文化言语行为研究而言，交际场景的真实性尤为重要。在将来的研究中，可以通过观察法搜集学生在日常生活中出现的交际场景，以获得更加真实的语料。此外，本研究仅设计了 4 种不同情形下的 12 个拒绝言语行为交际场景。在今后的研究中，可以设计更多情形下的交际场景。除了拒绝言语行为以外，还可探讨如感谢、赞扬、道歉等其他言语行为的跨文化使用情况。交际情景除了校园生活，还可涉及其他领域，如交友、购物、运动等。

第二，在本研究中，由于实际条件的限制，笔者在中泰缅 3 国都根据方便原则各抽取了一所学校的大学生作为研究对象。在今后的研究中，可选取不同学校、不同专业、不同英语学习年限的学生作为研究对象，并以更多变量假设为其言语行为策略使用的影响因素，探索在不同变量下的英语二语学习者的策略使用异同。此外，在将来的研究中，还可选取英语母语使用者和英语非母语使用者作为研究对象，比较其交际策略的使用情况。

第三，在研究工具选择上，除了书面表达 DCT 外，还可采用多项选择DCT、口头表达 DCT、课堂观察，以及角色扮演等多种数据收集方法，以获得更加丰富真实的语料。通过口头表达 DCT 和角色扮演等数据收集方法，不仅可以收集到学生在实施言语行为时的策略使用情况，还能了解学生在实施言语行为时的面部表情、肢体动作等，从而更好地了解不同学生在实施言语行为时的策略使用共性和区别。

第四，在进行策略统计时，可借用多个学者的策略分类方法，并根据实际情况进行整理，也可自行对拒绝策略进行分类，以便更好地对语言学习者的策略使用情况进行统计。在研究过程中，语言学习者还可能使用在已有策略分类中没有出现的言语行为实施策略，研究者可将这些策略补充到已有策略分类中，建立适合研究对象的策略分类体系。

第五，除了比较不同母语使用者外语使用的言语行为策略以外，研究者还可以比较同一组研究对象的母语和外语言语行为实施策略异同，以了解语言学习者在使用母语和外语进行交际时是否使用了相似或不同的交际策略。同时，通过对母语和外语的言语行为实施策略进行比较，研究者还可以了解外语学习者使用外语时的母语迁移情况。

本章小结

本章为本研究的结论部分。本研究以国籍、性别、英语水平、情景因素为变量，以定量定性数据为依据，以对数据的客观描述为出发点，系统分析了中泰缅大学生英语拒绝策略使用情况。本章首先对本研究的研究结果进行了总结，其次阐释了本研究的研究结果对教学的启示，再次分析了本研究的局限，最后在研究局限的基础上提出了对将来研究的建议。

本研究对英语中介语语用学提供了文献参考，也为研究多国外语学习者的语用行为开辟了思路。本研究将中泰缅3国英语学习者的拒绝言语行为策略使用进行对比研究，并发现其相似性和差异性，这一研究结果可为3国间的跨文化交流提供借鉴。本研究还发现了性别、英语水平和情景因素对学生的拒绝策略选择存在一定影响，并在此基础上提出了对跨文化交际教学中一些建议。希望本研究结果能提高中泰缅3国英语学习者的跨文化交际效果，增进不同文化背景下英语学习者的交流和沟通。

参考文献

Abdul Sattar H Q, Che Lah S, Raja Suleiman R R. Refusal strategies in English by Malay university students [J]. Journal of language studies, 2011, 11 (3): 69-81.

Al-Eryani A A. Refusal strategies by Yemeni EFL learners [J]. The Asian EFL journal, 2007, 9 (2): 19-34.

Al-Kahtani S. Refusals realizations in three different cultures: A speech act theoretically-based cross-cultural study [J]. Journal of King Saud University, 2005 (18): 35-57.

Allami H, Naeimi A. A cross-linguistic study of refusals: an analysis of pragmatic competence development in Iranian EFL learners [J]. Journal of pragmatics, 2011 (43): 385-406.

Al-Shboul Y, Maros M, Yasin M S. An intercultural study of refusal strategies in English between Jordanian EFL and Malay ESL postgraduatestudents [J]. The southeast asian journal of English language studies, 2012, 18 (3): 29-39.

Amarien N. Interlanguage pragmatics: A study of the refusal strategies of Indonesian speakers speaking English [J]. TRFLIN journal, 1997, 8 (1): 22-39.

Austin J L. How to do things with words [M]. Oxford: Clarendon Press, 1962.

Azarmi A, Behnam B. The pragmatic knowledge of Iranian EFL learners in using face keeping strategies in reaction to complaints at two different levels [J]. English language teaching, 2012, 5 (2): 78-92.

Bacelar Da Silva A J. The effects of instruction on pragmatic development: teaching polite refusals in English [J]. Second language studies, 2003, 22

(1): 55-106.

Bachman L F. Fundamental considerations in language testing [M]. New York: Oxford University Press, 1990.

Bachman L F, Palmer A S. Language testing in practice [M]. New York: Oxford University Press, 1996.

Barron A. Acquisition in interlanguage pragmatics: Learning how to do things with words in a study abroad context [M]. Amsterdam: John Benjamins, 2003.

Beebe L M, Takahashi T, Uliss-Weltz R. Pragmatic transfer in ESL refusals [M] //Scarcella R C, Anderson E S, Krashen S D. Developing communicative competence in a second language. New York: Newbury House, 1990: 55-73.

Beebe L M, Cummings M C. Natural speech act data versus written questionnaire data: How data collection methods affects speech act performance [M] //Gass S, Neu J. Speech acts across cultures. Berlin: Mouton, 1996: 64-86.

Billmyer K, Varghese M. Investigating instrument-based pragmatic variability: effects of enhancing discourse completion tests [J]. Applied linguistics, 2000 (4): 517-552.

Blum-Kulka S. Learning how to say what you mean in a second language: A study of speech act performance of learners of Hebrew as a second language [J]. Applied linguistics, 1982 (3): 29-59.

Blum-Kulka S. The metapragmatic of politeness in Israeli society [M] // Watts R, Ide S, Ehlich K. Politeness in language: studies in its history, theory and practice. New York: Mouton de Gruyter, 1992: 255-280.

Blum-Kulka S, House J, Kasper G. Investigating cross-cultural pragmatics: an introduction [M] //Blum-Kulka S, House J, Kasper G. Cross-cultural pragmatics: Requests and apologies. Norwood, NJ: Ablex Publishing Corporation, 1989: 1-36.

Blum-Kulka S, Olshtain E. Requests and apologies: a cross-cultural study of speech act realization patterns [J]. Applied linguistics, 1984, 5 (3): 196-213.

Bonikowska M P. The choice of opting out [J]. Applied linguistics, 1988, 9

(2): 169-181.

Boonkongsaen N. Filipinos and Thais saying "no" in English [J]. Manusya journal of humanities, 2013, 16 (1): 23-40.

Boxer D. Complaining and commiserating: a speech act view of solidarity in spoken American English [M]. New York: Peter Lang, 1993.

Brown P, Levinson S C. Politeness: some universals in language usage [M]. Cambridge: Cambridge University Press, 1987.

Canale M. From communicative competence language pedagogy [M] // Richards J D, Schmidt R W. Language and communication. London: Longman, 1983: 2-29.

Canale M, Swain M. Theoretical bases of communicative approaches to second language teaching and testing [J]. Applied linguistics, 1980, 1 (1): 1-47.

Cap P, Nijakowska J. Current trends in pragmatics [M]. Newcastle Upon Tyne: Cambridge Scholars Publishing, 2007.

Celce-Murcia M, Dörnyei Z, Thurrell S. Communicative competence: a pedagogically motivated model with content specifications [J]. Issues in applied linguistics, 1995, 6 (2): 5-35.

Chaidaroon S S. When shyness is not incompetence: A case of Thai communication competence [J]. Intercultural communication studies, 2003, 12 (4): 294-307.

Chang Y F. Interlanguage pragmatic development: the relation between pragmalinguistic competence and sociopragmatic competence [J]. Language sciences, 2011 (33): 786-798.

Chapman S. Philosophy for linguists: an introduction [M]. London: Routledge, 2000.

Chen J, Boonkongsaen N. Compliment response strategies by Thai and Chinese EFL teachers: a contrastive study [J]. Theory and practice in language studies, 2012, 2 (9): 1860-1867.

Chuenpraphannusorn T. Thai Studies [M]. Bangkok: Rajabhat Institute Suan Dusit Book Center, 2002.

Clyne M, Sharifian F. English as an international language: Challenges and possibilities [J]. Australian review of applied linguistics, 2008, 31 (3): 1

—28.

Cohen A D. Developing the ability to perform speech acts [J]. Studies in second language acquisition, 1996, 18 (2): 253—267.

Cook V. Going beyond the native speaker in language teaching [J]. TESOL quarterly, 1999, 33 (2): 185—209.

Cruse D A. Meaning in language: an introduction to semantics and pragmatics [M]. New York: Oxford University Press, 2000.

Cutting J. Pragmatics and discourse: a resource book for students [M]. London: Routledge, 2002.

DeCapua A. An analysis of pragmatic transfer in the speech act of complaints as produced by native speakers of German in English [D]. New York: Columbia University, 1989.

Duan L. The effects of explicit and implicit instruction on appropriacy of English refusal by Chinese EFL students [D]. Nakhonratchasima: Suranaree University of Technology, 2008.

Eelen G. A critique of politeness theories [M]. Manchester: St. Jerome Publishing, 2001.

Ellis R. The study of second language acquisition [M]. New York: Oxford University Press, 2008.

Eslami Z R. Refusals: How to develop appropriate refusal strategies [M] // Martínez-Flo A, Usó-Juan E. Speech act performance: theoretical, empirical and methodological issues. Amsterdam: John Benjamins, 2010: 217—236.

Fahey M P. Speech acts as intercultural danger zones: A cross-cultural comparison of the speech act of apologizing in Irish and Chilean soap operas [J/OL]. Journal of intercultural communication, 2005 (8): 25—41 [2019-3-25]. http://www.immi.se/intercultural/nr8/palma.htm.

Farnia M, Abdul Sattar H Q. Intercultural communication: Malay and Thai university students' refusals to request [J]. Journal of Belgrade English language and literature studies, 2010 (2): 113—132.

Farnia M, Wu X. An intercultural communication study of Chinese and Malaysian university students' refusal to invitation [J]. International journal of English linguistics, 2012, 2 (1): 162—176.

Felix-Brasdefer J C. Interlanguage refusals: Linguistic politeness and length of residence in the target community [J]. Language learning, 2004, 54 (4): 587-653.

Felix-Brasdefer J C. Perceptions of refusals to invitations: exploring the minds of foreign language learners [J]. Language awareness, 2008, 17 (3): 195-211.

Félix-Brasdefer J C. (2010). Data collection methods in speech act performance: DCTs, role plays, and verbal reports [M]//Martínez-Flor A, Usó-Juan E. Speech act performance: theoretical, empirical and methodological issues. Amsterdam: John Benjamins, 2010: 41-56.

Ferrara A. Pragmatics [M]//Van D. Teun A. Handbook of discourse analysis, Volume 2. Dimension of discourse, 1985: 137-158.

Fraser B. On apologizing [M]//Coulmas F. Conversational routine. Mouton: Hague, 1981: 259-271.

Gallaher B M. The speech act of complaint in English and Russian and its emergence in the pragmatic competence of adult American learners of Russian [D]. Pennsylvania: Bryn Mawr College, 2011.

Gass S M, Houck N. Interlanguage refusals: A cross-cultural study of Japanese-English [M]. New York: Mouton de Gruyter, 1999.

Geyang Z. A pilot study on refusal to suggestions in English by Japanese and Chinese EFL learners [C]. Bull. Grad. School Educ. Hiroshima University, 2007 (56): 155-163.

Gidden D A. An analysis of the discourse and syntax of oral complaints in Spanish [D]. Los Angeles: University of California, 1981.

Goffman E. Interaction ritual: essays on face to face behavior [M]. London: Doubleday, 1967.

Golato A. Studying compliment responses: a comparison of DCTs and recordings of naturally occurring talk [J]. Applied Linguistics, 2003 (1): 90-121.

Graddol D. The future of English: a guide to forecasting the popularity of the English language in the 21st Century [M]. London: The British Council, 2000.

Gumperz J J. Foreword [M]//Brown P, Levinson S T. Some politeness:

Some universals in language usage. Cambridge: Cambridge University Press,1987:xiii—xiv.

Guo Y. Chinese and American refusal strategy: A cross-cultural approach [J]. Applied Linguistics,2012 (5):121—162.

Grice H P. Logic and conversation [M]//Hutchby I. Sage benchmarks in social research methods: methods in language and social interaction. London:SAGE Publications Ltd,2008 (1):24—40.

Han D. On the classification of speech act refusals in Chinese: evidence and motivating factors [J]. CELEA journal,2006,29 (3):64—71.

Hassani R,Mardani M,Dastjerdi H V. A comparative study of refusals: gender distinction and social status in focus [J]. The international journal: language society and culture,2011 (32):37—46.

Hinkel E. Appropriateness of advice: DCT and multiple choice data [J]. Applied linguistics,1997,18 (1):1—26.

Hong W. Refusals in Chinese: how do L1 and L2 differ? [J]. Foreign language annals,2011,44 (1):122—136.

Hymes D H. On communicative competence [M]//Pride J B,Holmes J. Sociolinguistics. Harmondsworth:Penguin Books,1972:269—293.

Kachru B. World Englishes: approaches,issues,and resources [J]. Language teaching,1992,25 (1):1—14.

Kasper G. Pragmatic transfer [J]. Second language research,1992,8 (3):201—231.

Kasper G,Dahl M. Research methods in interlanguage pragmatics [J]. Studies in second language acquisition,1991,13 (2):215—247.

Kasper G,Rose K R. Pragmatic development in a second language [M]. Malden,MA:Blackwell Publishing,2002.

Kasper G,Schmidt R. Developmental issues in interlanguage pragmatics [J]. Studies in second language acquisition,1996,18 (2):149—169.

Kittisiriprasert T. English refusal strategies used by Silpakorn university postgraduate students [D/OL]. Bangkok:Silpakorn University,2011 [2018-11-2]. http://www.thapra.lib.su.ac.th/thesis/showthesis_th.asp?id=0000006895.

Knapp A. Using English as a lingua franca for (mis-) managing conflict in an international university context: an example from a course in engineering [J]. Journal of pragmatics, 2011 (43): 978-990.

Korsko P. The narrative shape of two-party complaints in Portuguese: a discourse analytic study [D]. Columbia: Columbia University, 2004.

Knutson T J. Comparison of Thai and U. S. American cultural values: "Mai pen rai" versus "just do it" [J/OL]. ABAC journal, 1994 (14): 1-38 [2018-1-22]. http: //www. library. au. edu/ABAC-Journal/v14-n3-1. pdf.

Kraft B, Geluykens R. Complaining in French L1 and L2: A cross-linguistic investigation [M]//Foster-Cohen S H, Ruthenberg T, Poschen M L. EUROSLA Yearbook. Amsterdam: John Benjamins Publishing Company, 2002: 227-242.

Kubota M. Teach ability of conversational implicature to Japanese EFL learners [J]. IRLT bulletin, 1995 (9): 35-67.

Kuchuk A. Politeness in intercultural communication: some insights into the pragmatics of English as an international language [D/OL]. Arizona: University of Arizona, 2012 [2017-3-15]. http: //arizona. openrepository. com/arizona/bitstream/10150/238633/1/azu _ etd _ 12262 _ sip1 _ m. pdf.

Kuriscak L M. The effect of individual-level variables on speech act performance [M]//Martínez-Flor A, Usó-Juan E. Speech act performance: theoretical, empirical and methodological issues. Amsterdam: John Benjamins Publishing Company, 2010: 23-59.

Kwon J. Pragmatic transfer and proficiency in refusals of Korean EFL learners [D]. Boston: Boston University, 2003.

Lakoff G. Hedges: a study in meaning criteria and the logic of fuzzy concepts. New York: Springer Netherlands, 1975.

Leech G. Principles of pragmatics [M]. London: Longman, 1983.

Li P, Zheng S, Yang W. Factors that influence the severity of Chinese and American University Students [J]. Foreign language teaching and research, 2006, 38 (1): 56-60.

Lin M. An interlanguage pragmatic study on Chinese EFL learners' refusal: perception and performance [J]. Journal of language teaching and research,

2014, 5 (3): 642-653.

Liu J D. Measuring interlanguage pragmatic knowledge of Chinese EFL learners [D]. Hongkong: City University of Hong Kong, 2004.

Liu J, Xie L. Examining rater effects in a WDCT pragmatics test [J]. Iranian journal of language testing, 2014, 4 (1): 50-65.

LoCastro V. (1996). English language education in Japan [M] //Coleman H. Society and classroom. Cambridge: Cambridge University Press: 40-58.

LoCastro V. An introduction to pragmatics: social action for language teachers [M]. Ann Arbor: University of Michigan Press, 2003.

MacKey A, Gass S M. Second language research: methodology and design [M]. New Jersey: Lawrence Erlbaum Associates, 2005.

McKay S L. Teaching English as an international language [M]. Oxford: Oxford University Press, 2002.

McKay S L. Toward an appropriate EIL pedagogy: Re-examining common ELT assumptions [J]. International journal of applied linguistics, 2003, 13 (1): 1-22.

McLaughlin B. Restructuring [J]. Applied linguistics, 1990, 11 (2): 113-128.

Mihalicek V, Wilson C. Language files: Materials for an introduction to language and linguistics [M]. 11th ed. Columbus: Ohio State University Press, 2011.

Misso V, Maadad N. The English language and cultural appropriateness [J]. Sosiohumanika, 2011, 4 (1): 111-128.

Nelson G L, Al Batal M, El Bakary W. Directness and indirectness: Egyptian Arabic and US English communication style [J]. International journal of international Relations, 2002 (26): 39-57.

Nemati M, Rezaee A A, Mahdi H M. Assessing pragmatics through MDCTs: a case of Iranian EFL learners [J]. Iranian journal of applied language studies, 2014, 6 (2): 43-66.

Nguyen T M P. Cross-cultural pragmatics: refusals of requests by Australian native speakers of English and Vietnamese learners of English [D]. Queensland: University of Queensland, 2006.

Niezgoda K, Röver C. Pragmatic and grammatical awareness [M] //Rose K R, Kasper G. Pragmatics in language teaching. Stuttgart: Ernst Klett Sprachen, 2001: 63—79.

Nurani L M. Methodological issue in pragmatic research: is discourse completion test a reliable data collection instrument? [J]. Jurnal sosioteknologu edisi, 2009, 17 (8): 667—678.

Odlin T. Language transfer: Cross-linguistic influence in language learning [M]. Cambridge: Cambridge University Press, 1989.

O'Keeffe A, Clancy B, Adolphs S. Introducing pragmatics in use [M]. London: Routledge, 2011.

Olshtain E, Cohen A D. Speech act behaviour across languages [M] //Dechert H W, et al. Transfer in production. Norwood: Ablex Publishing, 1989: 53—68.

Olshtain E, Weinbach, L. Interlanguage features of the speech act of complaining [M] //Kasper G, Blum-Kulka S. Interlanguage pragmatics. Oxford: Oxford University Press, 1993: 108—122.

Panichkul S. An acoustic study of Thai pause fillers in relation to their syntactic positions in monologues [D]. Bangkok: Chulalongkorn University, 2003.

Pearson L. Preface [M] //Martínez-Flor A, Usó-Juan E. Speech act performance: Theoretical, empirical and methodological issues. Amsterdam: John Benjamins, 2010: xiii—xiv.

Peccei J S. Pragmatics [M]. London: Routledge, 1999.

Prachanant N. Pragmatic transfer in responses to complaints by Thai EFL learners in Thai hotel business [D]. Nakhonratchasima: Suranaree University of Technology, 2006.

Quirk R. The English language in a global context [M] //Quirk R, Widdowson H G. English in the world: Teaching and learning the language and literature. Cambridge: Cambridge University Press, 1985: 1—6.

Röver C. Validation of a web-based test of ESL pragmalinguistics [J]. Language testing, 2006, 23 (2): 229—256.

Röver C. Testing ESL pragmatics [M]. New York: Peter Lang, 2014.

Sadock J. Speech acts [M] //Horn L R, Ward G. The handbook of pragmatics. Oxford: Blackwell, 2006: 53—73.

Safont M P. Instructional effects on the use of request acts modification devices by EFL learner [M]//Martinez-Flor A, Uso E, Ferandez A. Pragmatic competence and foreign language teaching. Castellon: Servei de Publications de la Universitat Jaume I, 2003: 211-231.

Sasaki M, Suzuki T, Yoneda M. English as an international language in non-native settings in an era of globalization [J]. Comparative sociology, 2006 (5): 381-404.

Sairhun T. English refusal strategies in Thai learners of English as a foreign language: a study of pragmatic transfer [D]. Bangkok: Chulalongkorn University, 1999.

Schauer G A. Interlanguage pragmatic development: the study abroad context [M]. London: Continuum, 2009.

Schauer G A, Adolphs S. Expressions of gratitude in corpus and DCT data: vocabulary, formulaic sequences, and pedagogy [J]. System, 2006 (34): 119-134.

Schneider E W. English around the world: an introduction [M]. Cambridge: Cambridge University Press, 2011.

Searle J R. Speech acts [M]. Cambrdge: Cambridge University Press, 1969.

Searle J R. The classification of illocutionary acts [J]. Language in society, 1976 (5): 1-24.

Searle J. What is a speech act? [M]//Hutchby I. Sage benchmarks in social research methods: methods in language and social interaction. London: Sage Publications Ltd., 2008 (1): 8-23.

Seidlhofer B. A concept of international English and related issues: From "real English" to "realistic English"? [M/OL]. Strasbourg: Council of Europe, 2003 [2018-2-22]. http://www.coe.int/T/DG4/Linguistic/Source/SeidlhoferEN.pdf.

Seidlhofer B. English as a lingua franca [J]. ELT journal, 2005, 59 (4): 339-341.

Shishavan H B, Sharifian F. Refusal strategies in L1 and L2: a study of Persian-speaking learners of English [M]. Multilingua, 2013, 32 (6): 801-836.

Sinthukiow S, Modehiran P. The use of refusals among Thai bank employees:

an implication for workplace English training programs [J/OL]. Journal of education, 2013, 8 (1): 2740-2750 [2018-1-31]. http://www.edu.chula.ac.th/ojed/doc/V81/v81d0212.pdf.

Spolsky B. Communicative competence, language proficiency, and beyond [J]. Applied linguistics, 1989, 10 (2): 138-156.

Tabatabaei S, Farnia M. Learner's English proficiency and their pragmatic competence of refusal speech acts [J]. Beyond words, 2015, 3 (1): 53-77.

Takahashi T, Beebe L. The development of pragmatic competence by Japanese learners of English [J]. JALT journal, 1987 (8): 131-155.

Tanck S. Speech act sets of refusal and complaint: A comparison of native and non-native English speakers' production [J/OL]. TESOL working papers, 2004, 4 (2): 1-22. [2018-2-22]. http://aladinrc.wrlc.org/handle/1961/5233.

Thomas J. Cross-cultural pragmatic failure [M] //Bolton K, Kachru B B. World Englishes: critical concepts in linguistics, Volume 4. London and New York: Routledge, 2006: 22-48.

Tian X. Investigating L2 refusals: A case study of Chinese native speakers' L2 pragmatic competence [J]. Theory and practice in language studies, 2014, 4 (1): 212-216.

Trosborg A. Interlanguage pragmatics: requests, complaints and apologies [M]. Berlin: Mouton de Gruyter, 1995.

Van Dijk T A. Text and context explorations in the semantics and pragmatics of discourse [M]. London: Longman, 1977.

Verschueren J. Understanding pragmatics [M]. New York: Oxford University Press, 1999.

Watts R J. Politeness [M]. Cambridge: Cambridge University Press, 2003.

Wannaruk A. Say "No": A cross cultural comparison of Thais and Americans refusals [C]. English language studies forum, Volume 1, 2004: 1-22.

Wannaruk A. Pragmatic transfer in Thai EFL refusals [R]. Paper presented at the 13th Annual KOTESOL International Conference. Seoul: Sookmyung Women's University, 2005.

Wannaruk A. Pragmatic transfer in Thai EFL refusals [J]. RELC journal,

2008, 39 (3): 318-337.

Wen Q. Language learning strategies [M]. Shanghai: Shanghai Foreign Language Education Press, 2000.

Wildner-Bassert M. Intercultural pragmatics and proficiency: "polite" noises for cultural appropriateness [J]. IRAL XXXII, 1994 (1): 3-17.

Wolfson N. An empirically based analysis of complimenting in American English [M] //Wolfson N, Judd E. Sociolinguistics and language acquisition. Rowley: Newbury House, 1983: 82-95.

Yaghoobi B. A cross-linguistic study of requestive speech acts in email communication [D/OL]. Leeds: University of Leeds, 2002. [2018-2-20]. http://etheses.whiterose.ac.uk/833/.

Yano Y. Communicative competence and English as an international language [J]. Intercultural communication studies, 2003, 12 (3): 75-83.

Yano Y. Cross-cultural Communication and English as an international language [J]. Intercultural communication studies, 2006, 15 (3): 22-31.

Yuan Y. An inquiry into empirical pragmatics data-gathering methods: written DCTs, oral DCTs, filed notes, and natural conversations [J]. Journal of pragmatics, 2001 (33): 271-292.

Yule G. Pragmatics [M]. Oxford: Oxford University Press, 1996.

Zhang T. Face: the art of face on the Chinese social stage [M]. Beijing: Earthquake, 2006.

附　录

附录一　Self-assessment of Spoken English Proficiency

Instructions: Read the descriptions of the Spoken English Proficiency, and then check (√) in the right column where the standards match your level.

Description of your spoken English	Yours
Level 1: Use of isolated words and phrases • Be able to communicate short messages on highly predictable, everyday topics that affect you directly (e.g., where you live, people you know, and things you have).	
Level 2: Use of sentence-level language • Be able to create with the language when talking about familiar topics related to your daily life; • Be able to recombine learned material in order to express personal meaning; • Be able to ask simple questions and can handle a straightforward survival situation.	
Level 3: Use of paragraphs • Be able to engage in conversation in a clearly participatory manner in order to communicate information on autobiographical topics (e.g., topics relevant to one's own life), as well as topics of community, national, or international interest; • Be able to deal with a social situation with an unexpected complication.	

Description of your spoken English	Yours
Level 4: Use of extended discourse without unnaturally lengthy hesitation • Be able to communicate with accuracy and fluency in order to participate fully and effectively in conversations on a variety of topics in formal and informal settings from both concrete and abstract perspectives (e.g., your interests and special fields of competence, social and political issues); • Be able to construct and develop hypotheses to explore alternative possibilities.	
Level 5: Use of highly sophisticated and tightly organized extended discourse as well as cultural and historical references • Be able to use language skilfully, and with accuracy, efficiency, and effectiveness; • Be able to reflect on a wide range of global issues and highly abstract concepts in a culturally appropriate manner; • Be able to use persuasive and hypothetical discourse • for representational purposes, allowing you to advocate a point of view that is not necessarily your own; • Be able to tailor language to a variety of audiences by adapting your speech and register in ways that are culturally authentic.	

附录二　Discourse Completion Task Questionnaire

Directions: The following are twelve short dialogues, in each dialogue, a situation will be given. You are required to write down how you ***refuse*** people to make the dialogue complete.

Situation 1
A college student invites another student, to whom he/she has met several times before, to his/her graduate thesis defense.

How strong do you think the degree of imposition in this situation is?
☐ not strong at all
☐ somewhat strong
☐ strong
☐ very strong
☐ extremely strong

A: Hi, Jack, I am going to have my graduate thesis defense on next Friday, could you come?

B: _____

_____

A: Alright, that's ok.

Situation 2
The chair of the department invites his/her college student to a workshop on career planning.

How strong do you think the degree of imposition in this situation is?
☐ not strong at all
☐ somewhat strong
☐ strong

187

☐very strong

☐extremely strong

A: Good morning, chair.

B: Good morning. There is a workshop about career planning on this Saturday morning, would you like to come?

A: _____

_____

_____

B: Oh, that's OK, don't worry about it.

Situation 3
A college teacher invites a college student to have dinner with other students.

How strong do you think the degree of imposition in this situation is?
☐not strong at all
☐somewhat strong
☐strong
☐very strong
☐extremely strong

A: Hello, Rose, how are things going?

B: Good afternoon, Mr. Robinson, everything goes well, thank you.

A: We are planning to have dinner together, would you like to join us?

B: _____

_____

_____

A: OK.

Situation 4
A college student requests another college student, whom he/she meets for the first time, to complete an interview for about 10 minutes.

How strong do you think the degree of imposition in this situation is?
☐not strong at all

☐somewhat strong

☐strong

☐very strong

☐extremely strong

A: Excuse me, may I take you a few minutes?

B: Yeah?

A: I am doing a small project on online-shopping, may I have an interview with you for about 10 minutes?

B: _____

_____

_____

A: That's alright, sorry to bother you.

Situation 5
A tablemate requests his/her tablemate to check his/her homework.

How strong do you think the degree of imposition in this situation is?

☐not strong at all

☐somewhat strong

☐strong

☐very strong

☐extremely strong

A: Hi, Betty, are you busy now?

B: What?

A: I have done a lot of homework today, could you help me to check my answers?

B: _____

_____

_____

A: Oh, OK.

Situation 6
A professor requests a college student to attend an orientation for the new students.

How strong do you think the degree of imposition in this situation is?

☐ not strong at all

☐ somewhat strong

☐ strong

☐ very strong

☐ extremely strong

A: Good morning, Mr. Brown.

B: Good morning, Charles. I ask you to come to my office because there is an orientation for the new students in the afternoon, and I hope you can give them some suggestions.

A: _____

_____

B: That's OK.

Situation 7
A classmate offers help to his/her classmate in an assignment.

How strong do you think the degree of imposition in this situation is?

☐ not strong at all

☐ somewhat strong

☐ strong

☐ very strong

☐ extremely strong

A: This task is so difficult.

B: Let me have a look. Oh, I did that kind of exercise before.

A: Really?

B: Yes, I can tell you how to do it.

A: _____

B: OK, up to you.

Situation 8
The dean of a school offers a lecture attendance chance to a college student.

How strong do you think the degree of imposition in this situation is?

☐ not strong at all

☐ somewhat strong

☐ strong

☐ very strong

☐ extremely strong

A: Good afternoon, Mr. Black.

B: Oh, you are coming, Christina. Here is a chance for the students to attend a lecture. I want to give this chance to you.

A: Thank you, Mr. Black. May I know the topic, the time and the place?

B: Sure, I will show you the material.

A: _____

_____

B: What a pity!

Situation 9
A college teacher offers a part-time teaching job to a college student.

How strong do you think the degree of imposition in this situation is?

☐ not strong at all

☐ somewhat strong

☐ strong

☐ very strong

☐ extremely strong

A: Hi, Jenny, how are things going?

B: Fine, Miss Carter.

A: I heard you like to play with children, is that right?

B: Yes.

A: Here is a part time teaching job for children, are you interested in it?

B: _____

_____

A: Fine.

Situation 10
A new college student suggests another new college student to join in a school activity.

How strong do you think the degree of imposition in this situation is?

☐ not strong at all

☐ somewhat strong

☐ strong

☐ very strong

☐ extremely strong

A: Hi, guy, join us?

B: Nice to meet you, my name is Frank.

A: Nice to meet you, I am Jason, a freshman here. Why not join us to play basketball?

B: _____

_____

A: Alright.

Situation 11
An old friend suggests his/her old friend to take the entrance examination for a master degree.

How strong do you think the degree of imposition in this situation is?

☐ not strong at all

☐ somewhat strong

☐strong

☐very strong

☐extremely strong

A: I really worry about my future. I don't know what I can do after graduation.

B: Take it easy, dear. There are many jobs offers, then.

A: Yes, but you know my major, archaeology, and looking for a satisfied job might not be easy for me.

B: Then, why not try to take the entrance examination for a master degree. With a higher degree, maybe things will be easier.

A: _____

_____

_____

B: Yes, maybe you are right.

Situation 12
A professor suggests a college student to present research in a conference.

How strong do you think the degree of imposition in this situation is?

☐not strong at all

☐somewhat strong

☐strong

☐very strong

☐extremely strong

A: Hi, George, I am so happy you will attend the conference.

B: Prof. Smith, thank you so much for give me this chance to be anaudience.

A: As a matter of fact, you can be a speaker to present your research, do you want to have a try?

B: _____

_____

_____

A: OK, I can understand.

附录三 半结构化访谈问题

No.	Interview questions
1	What did you notice when you responded in these situations?
2	Did the status of interlocutors in the situations have effect on your responses? If yes, in which aspect did it affect you?
3	Did the relationship between you and the interlocutors affect your responses? If yes, in which aspect did it affect you?
4	Did the degree of imposition of the speakers have effect on your responses? If yes, in which aspect did it affect you?
5	Did you have difficulties in finishing the WDCT, if yes, what are they?
6	What kind of response do you use the most frequently in refusing invitations, why?
7	What kind of response do you use the least frequently in refusing invitations, why?
8	What kind of response do you use the most frequently in refusing requests, why?
9	What kind of response do you use the least frequently in refusing requests, why?
10	What kind of response do you use the most frequently in refusing offers, why?
11	What kind of response do you use the least frequently in refusing offers, why?
12	What kind of response do you use the most frequently in refusing suggestions, why?
13	What kind of response do you use the least frequently in refusing suggestions, why?
14	What factors do you take in consideration when you refuse people?
15	How do you release the degree of face threatening when you refuse people?

附录四　Classifications of Refusal Strategies For Assessing the Performances of Written DCT

Ⅰ. Direct

1. Performative (e.g., "I refuse.")
2. Nonperformative statement
   1) "No"
   2) Negative willingness/ability ("I can't.", "I won't.", "I don't think so.")

Ⅱ. Indirect

1. Statement of regret (e.g., "I'm sorry..."; "I feel terrible...")
2. Wish (e.g. "I wish I could help you...")
3. Excuse, reason, explanation (e.g., "My children will be home that night."; "I have a headache.")
4. Statement of alternative
   1) I can do X instead of Y (e.g., "I'd rather..." "I'd prefer...")
   2) Why don't you do X instead of Y (e.g., "Why don't you ask someone else?")
5. Set condition for future or past acceptance (e.g., "If you had asked me earlier, I would have...")
6. Promise of future acceptance (e.g., "I'll do it next time"; "I promise I'll..." or "Next time I'll...", using "will" of promise or "promise")
7. Statement of principle (e.g., "I never do business with friends.")
8. Statement of philosophy (e.g., "One can't be too careful.")
9. Attempt to dissuade interlocutor
   1) Threat or statement of negative consequences to the requester (e.g., "I won't be any fun tonight.")
   2) Guilt trip (e.g., waitress to customers who want to sit a while: "I can't make a living off people who just order coffee.")

3) Criticize the request/requester, etc. (statement of negative feeling or opinion); insult/attack (e.g., "Who do you think you are?"; "That's a terrible idea!")

  4) Request for help, empathy, and assistance by dropping or holding the request

  5) Let interlocutor off the hook (e.g., "Don't worry about it."; "That's okay")

  6) Self-defense (e.g. "I'm trying my best." "I'm doing all I can do.")

10. Acceptance that functions as a refusal

  1) Unspecific or indefinite reply

  2) Lack of enthusiasm

11. Avoidance

  1) Nonverbal

   a. Silence

   b. Hesitation

   c. Do nothing

   d. Physical departure

  2) Verbal

   a. Topic switch

   b. Joke

   c. Repetition of part of request, etc. (e.g., "Monday?")

   d. Postponement (e.g., "I'll think about it.")

   e. Hedging (e.g., "Gee, I don't know." "I'm not sure.")

Adjuncts to Refusals

  1. Statement of positive opinion/feeling of agreement ("That's a good idea..."; "I'd love to...")

  2. Statement of empathy (e.g., "I realize you are in a difficult situation.")

  3. Pause fillers ((e.g., "uhh"; "well"; "oh"; "uhm")

  4. Gratitude/appreciation

(Cited in Beebe, Takahashi, Uliss-Weltz, 1990: 72-73)